NAVIGATING an IOU SCHOOL CULTURE

DR. JOE FAMULARO

PH2E VENTURES
NEW YORK

Copyright © 2025 by Dr. Joe Famularo

Published by:

PH2E VENTURES
New York
www.PH2Eventures.com

This book is the proprietary work of Dr. Joe Famularo. Many terms and illustrations in this book, including the 12 Essential Life Anchors, 12 Essential School Anchors, PH2E®, IOU Living®, IOU Life Leadership® and the Strategic School Map (SSM), are trademarks of Dr. Joe Famularo.

All rights reserved. No part of this publication may be reproduced, stored in a retrieval system, or transmitted in any form or by any means, mechanical, electronic, photocopying, recording, or otherwise, without written permission from the publisher. The only exceptions are brief quotations in printed or online reviews, academic citations, and educational discussions with proper attribution.

For permissions, consulting, or speaking engagements, contact us at:
Email: iou@iouliving.com
Website: www.iouliving.com

Library of Congress Control Number: 2025906243

ISBNs:
978-1-963175-02-8 (Paperback)
978-1-963175-03-5 (Hardcover)
978-1-963175-04-2 (eBook)

First Edition
Printed in the United States of America

Dedication

To all the educators who illuminate the path of knowledge and wisdom, guiding our future leaders with dedication and passion. Your commitment to fostering growth, curiosity, and leadership in every student is the beacon leading us towards a brighter, more enlightened world.

May you continue to "Inspire to Aspire," nurturing minds and hearts with hope that all students receive Peacefulness, Happiness, Healthiness, and Excellence (PH2E) throughout their lives.

By embodying the IOU principles, you are integral to cultivating a dynamic and positive school culture. This book is a testament to your tireless efforts and boundless inspiration, and a tribute to your indispensable part in shaping the future of our world.

NAVIGATING an IOU SCHOOL CULTURE

DR. JOE FAMULARO

PH2E VENTURES
NEW YORK

Table of Contents

Endorsement Stephen M. R. Covey xi

Praise for Navigating an IOU School Culture xiii

Introduction xxiii

School Leadership Manual Overview xxvii

How to Use This School Leadership Manual
for Personal Reflection and Growth xxxv

Part I: Internalizing the IOU Principle:
Inspire to Aspire 1

Chapter 1: What is an IOU School Culture? 5

Chapter 2: Inside-Out Living and Leading 17

Chapter 3: The IOU 12 Essential School Anchors 27

Part II: Developing Your IOU Strategic School Map:
A Framework for Inside-Out Alignment 37

Chapter 4: The IOU 6 Inward School Anchors:
Anchoring the Inward Journey 43

    1. School Selfculture 47
    2. School Vision 65
    3. Daily School Mission 81
    4. School Leadership Principles 99
    5. School Core Values 119
    6. School Goals 137

Chapter 5: Developing Your Inward School Map (ISM):
Mapping the School's Foundational Identity 179

Chapter 6: The IOU 6 Outward School Anchors:
Launching the Outward Journey 199

       1. Inspire IOU Trust 207
       2. Practice Positive Communication 225
       3. Create Common Language 255
       4. Construct a Cohesive Environment 273
       5. Establish Everlasting Traditions 291
       6. Model a Mindset of Propelling PH2E 305

Chapter 7: Developing Your Outward School Map (OSM):
Navigating Actions and Relationships 321

Chapter 8: Synergizing Your Inward & Outward School Maps
into a Comprehensive Strategic School Map:
Full Steam Ahead 337

Part III: Reaching Your IOU Destination 385

Chapter 9: The Lighthouse Guide:
The Path to Upward Living 389

Part IV: Navigating Your IOU Strategic School Map
(SSM) 405

Chapter 10: Propelling Your ISM and OSM to Your Destination:
Putting Your Strategic School Map into Action 407

Conclusion: Navigating an IOU School Culture 421

References 427

Appendix A: IOU School Culture Continuum Reflection Tool 429

Appendix B: The Strategic School Map (SSM) Template 431

       • ISM: Inward School Map
       • OSM: Outward School Map

Appendix C: REBEL Goals Framework:
Strategic Goal-Setting Template 437

Appendix D: IOU School Culture Assessment 439

- Instructions 439
- Assessment (The 12 Essential School Anchors)
  - Inward School Anchors (ISM) 440
  - Outward School Anchors (OSM) 443
- Scoring & Interpretation Guide 445
- Reflection & Action Planning 446

Appendix E: IOU Framework Presentation Guide 447

About the Author 449

Acknowledgments 451

Endorsement
Stephen M. R. Covey

As someone deeply committed to the principles of trust and principle-centered leadership, I am inspired by Dr. Joe Famularo's latest work, *Navigating an IOU School Culture*. Building on the foundational concepts in his bestselling book *IOU Life Leadership*, this new book offers a comprehensive and transformative framework specifically designed for educational leaders.

Through the IOU (Inward, Outward, Upward) Principle, Dr. Joe provides a clear and actionable guide for schools to develop a Strategic School Map (SSM). This map is much more than a planning tool—it serves as a pathway to align a school's internal identity (Inward Anchors) with its external relationships (Outward Anchors), fostering a thriving, positive, and upward dynamic school culture. These 12 Essential School Anchors—6 Inward and 6 Outward—serve as the foundation for creating an environment of trust, collaboration, and excellence, which will propel school communities toward their aspirational goal of Upward Living.

Dr. Joe's insights deeply resonate with my belief that leadership is most effective when it begins from the "inside out." As I have written in *The Speed of Trust* and *Trust & Inspire*, trust is the currency of high-performing cultures, and this book demonstrates how trust can be created and extended within schools. By integrating IOU principles into daily practice, education leaders can intentionally build high-trust relationships and become empowered to inspire staff and students to achieve their highest aspirations, enabling them to elevate their school community to its greatest potential.

Navigating an IOU School Culture is both visionary and practical. It equips educational leaders with the tools they need to create a culture where every stakeholder—educators, students, and families—feels valued and empowered to contribute. This book is a must-read for those looking to transform their schools into dynamic, high-performing communities of trust, collaboration, innovation, and upward growth.

—**STEPHEN M. R. COVEY,** *The New York Times* and #1 *Wall Street Journal* bestselling author of *The Speed of Trust* and *Trust & Inspire*

Praise for Navigating an IOU School Culture

"With decades of experience leading education systems, including serving as Commissioner of Education for New York State, I understand the critical importance of intentional leadership and a clear plan for success. Overseeing 700 school districts and working with millions of students, educators, and stakeholders taught me that a unified vision is essential to thriving school cultures. Dr. Joe Famularo's *Navigating an IOU School Culture* provides a powerful framework for school leaders to unite their communities around a shared vision of excellence.

The foundation of any thriving school system is a well-defined plan—or, as Dr. Joe describes it, a "Map." This Leadership Manual empowers leaders to align the IOU 12 School Anchors with their current practices, offering a clear process to identify gaps in both the Inward and Outward aspects of their school culture. Where gaps exist, the IOU anchors provide actionable strategies to develop a Strategic School Map that engages all stakeholders and charts a clear path forward. For those already excelling, these anchors foster continuous improvement and innovation.

Dr. Joe's insights on leadership offer a practical approach for school leaders to build unified, high-performing cultures. *Navigating an IOU School Culture* is an invaluable guide for addressing gaps, fostering collaboration, and creating a clear vision that drives lasting success."

    —**MARYELLEN ELIA,** Former New York State Commissioner of Education

"As the Executive Director of the New York State Council of School Superintendents, I recognize the critical role that governance and strategic planning play in ensuring the success of school districts. Dr. Joe Famularo's *Navigating an IOU School Culture* provides a clear framework for district leaders to develop a strategic school plan—what Dr. Joe aptly calls a "Strategic School Map."

This book is an invaluable resource for superintendents and district leaders who work closely with school boards, staff, and the wider school community to align vision, mission, and goals with daily actions. The 12 Essential School Anchors outlined in this work offer a comprehensive guide for fostering clarity, collaboration, and excellence across all levels of leadership.

Dr. Joe's insights resonate deeply with the commitment to advancing educational leadership and ensuring the success of public education. *Navigating an IOU School Culture* is a must-read for leaders dedicated to building strong, dynamic school districts that inspire meaningful change and long-term success."

> **—CHARLES DEDRICK,** Executive Director for the New York State Council of School Superintendents

"Effective governance is the foundation of a thriving school system. School boards play a critical role in shaping the policies, vision, and leadership that drive student success. In *Navigating an IOU School Culture*, Dr. Joe Famularo provides a powerful framework that empowers school leaders and governance teams to align purpose with action, fostering a culture of collaboration, excellence, and continuous improvement.

The IOU Framework—Inward (self-awareness), Outward (action), and Upward (results)—closely aligns with the core values of NSBA, emphasizing intentional leadership, innovation, and engagement. Dr. Famularo's concept of the *Strategic School Map* ensures that school boards and education leaders can connect their vision to daily practices, creating an environment where students, educators, and communities can thrive.

School boards serve as the bridge between policy and practice, and this book is an invaluable resource for any board member, superintendent, or school leader committed to effective governance and transformational leadership. *Navigating an IOU School Culture* is a must-read for those dedicated to empowering school communities and ensuring that every student has access to a high-quality, student-centered education."

> **—VERJEANA MCCOTTER-JACOBS,** Esq, Executive Director & CEO, National School Boards Association (NSBA)

"*Navigating an IOU School Culture* brings leadership back to its core mission: serving people. Dr. Joe Famularo understands how to inspire trust, foster collaboration, and drive results—not through lofty concepts, but by aligning principles, purpose, and action.

As a former Naval Officer who served on nuclear submarines during the Cold War, I've seen firsthand how leadership and culture determine success, especially in high-pressure environments. Dr. Famularo's use of nautical terms and symbols throughout this book brilliantly illustrates the importance of intentional leadership and clear direction. Whether you're leading sailors on a submarine or guiding a school community, the principles are the same: clarity of mission, intentional leadership, and fostering a sense of belonging and shared responsibility.

Through his IOU Framework (Inward, Outward, Upward) and the 12 Essential School Anchors, Dr. Famularo provides leaders with a practical and inspiring compass to navigate challenges, build trust, and create environments where people feel valued and empowered to excel. Each anchor serves as a foundational guide, keeping schools steady and aligned with their mission, even amidst waves of change.

This is more than a book about education—it's a leadership playbook that transcends industries, offering timeless principles for creating cultures of excellence. If you're serious about building a team that thrives on shared purpose and trust, *Navigating an IOU School Culture* will steer you in the right direction. Dr. Famularo reminds us that great leadership isn't just about strategy; it's about heart, intention, and the daily decisions that shape a legacy."

> —**JON S. RENNIE,** Former Naval Officer (Nuclear Submarines), CEO of Peak Demand Inc., and Leadership Advocate, Author of *I Have the Watch* and *All in the Same Boat*

"Having spent a decade leading the operations at The Walt Disney World® Resort, I've learned that the key to any successful organization lies in its culture—a culture where every individual understands their purpose, role, and impact. Dr. Joe Famularo's *Navigating an IOU School Culture* applies this principle to education, offering school leaders a framework to create environments where every stakeholder—from students to staff—feels empowered to contribute meaningfully to a shared vision that inspires individuals to aspire, unlock their potential, and achieve enduring success.

At Disney, success is built on creating an environment where every team member is aligned with a shared vision of excellence and empowered to contribute meaningfully to the mission. Similarly, Dr. Joe's IOU Framework (Inward, Outward, Upward) and the 12 Essential School Anchors provide actionable strategies for connecting purpose with performance, ensuring that schools operate with clarity, collaboration, and a relentless commitment to excellence.

Dr. Joe's concept of the Strategic School Map mirrors the tools we used at Disney to bridge vision with action. Made up of an Inward School Map and an Outward School Map, this framework connects "who you are" with "what you do," ensuring alignment between internal principles and external practices. This approach fosters collaboration, drives innovation, and creates a culture where individuals feel motivated and inspired to achieve their highest potential—a philosophy similar to the one I advanced at Disney to align our teams and deliver exceptional results.

Navigating an IOU School Culture is a masterclass in leadership and culture-building, equipping leaders with the tools to make lasting, impactful positive change in their organizations. Dr. Joe's work is an invaluable manual for any leader seeking to inspire meaningful change and create a legacy of success. Educators create magic one student at a time!"

—**LEE COCKERELL,** Former Executive Vice President of Operations, Walt Disney World® Resort

"Dr. Joe Famularo's *Navigating an IOU School Culture* is a masterful blueprint for creating schools where each individual can thrive. By weaving together powerful principles like Inside-Out leadership with his 12 Essential Anchors, this book provides a clear and practical pathway for cultivating trust, collaboration, and excellence within our schools. Dr. Famularo inspires educators to reflect deeply, lead intentionally, and build vibrant cultures rooted in positivity and purpose. A must-read for leaders committed to transforming their schools into dynamic, high-performing communities where both people and possibilities flourish."

—**THOMAS C. MURRAY,** Director of Innovation for Future Ready Schools, Best-Selling Author of *Learning Transformed: 8 Keys to Designing Tomorrow's Schools*

"I highly recommend to anyone involved in school leadership or "aspiring" to be a leader to read *Navigating an IOU School Culture*. Dr. Famularo has followed up on his book *IOU Life Leadership* and built on those principles to give educational leaders a map to creating highly effective school systems.

The call to action of "Inspire to Aspire" is the perfect mindset to move any organization in an upward and positive direction. The nautical symbolisms and metaphors are perfectly aligned with school district leadership and governance.

Learning and incorporating the 12 School Anchors and making it a part of the daily school culture will help every school system achieve the ultimate outcome of PH2E. Thank you Dr. Famularo, for reminding us to live *with intention* and not *by default*."

> —**ROBERT VECCHIO,** Executive Director, Nassau-Suffolk School Boards Association

"*Navigating an IOU School Culture* by Dr. Joe Famularo is a transformative guide that empowers educational leaders to build intentional, values-driven school environments. Grounded in the innovative IOU Framework and enriched by actionable tools and the 12 Essential School Anchors, this book offers a clear roadmap for cultivating a thriving culture of clarity, trust, and excellence."

> —**DR. DONNA DESIATO,** Superintendent of Schools, East Syracuse Minoa Central School District; President New York State Council of School Superintendents; 2022 New York State Superintendent of the Year

"Dr. Joe Famularo's *Navigating an IOU School Culture* offers a comprehensive guide for school leaders aiming to create thriving school environments. Drawing on nearly five decades as a superintendent, I've witnessed how intentional leadership and strategic planning can transform school cultures. This book delivers a step-by-step framework, built around the 12 Essential School Anchors, to align a school's Inward identity, Outward actions, and Upward results.

The 12 Essential School Anchors provide a practical roadmap—referred to by Dr. Joe as a "Map"—for developing a Strategic School Plan. Grounded in the IOU Framework, this manual equips leaders with tools to foster collaboration, inspire innovation, and build a culture of excellence. It's a valuable resource for driving meaningful change and achieving long-term success.

For leaders committed to continuous improvement, this book is a must-read. It offers actionable strategies and a visionary approach to creating schools where leadership, strategic planning, and collaboration empower every member of the community to thrive."

> —**HANK GRISHMAN,** Educational Leader, Superintendent of Schools - Jericho School District, Past President of NYSCOSS, NYS Superintendent of the Year

"It is with great pleasure that I endorse *Navigating an IOU School Culture*. I am a believer that establishing and maintaining a positive school culture is most important for moving a school towards higher achievement. This text is a practical guide for school and district leaders (current and future) to embrace and implement a plan for "maximizing leadership, collaboration and excellence" so that students may achieve their utmost! Navigating the change process using the 12 Essential School Anchors gives direction to school leaders to pursue excellence with their teachers and students.

As an author and Associate Director of the Stony Brook Educational Leadership Program, I see a clear pathway for school leaders to develop and support each and every student to achieve at their highest levels. I clearly see a roadmap for leaders to adopt and implement in their respective environments that can bring constituents together to focus on change in culture while concomitantly enhancing student achievement.

Joe hit a homerun by embracing a strong theoretical underpinning and aligning it with practical application."

> —**DR. KENNETH FORMAN,** Associate Director, Educational Leadership Program, Stony Brook University; Co-Author, *Diving into Leadership*

"As the Executive Director of SCOPE Education Services, which supports New York State school districts through professional development and leadership programs, I am deeply inspired by innovative strategies such as Dr. Joe Famularo's *Navigating an IOU School Culture*. This leadership manual is a significant contribution to advancing educational leadership and fostering excellence.

Dr. Joe's transformative framework aligns perfectly with our mission to empower educators and leaders. By highlighting the IOU principles of Inward, Outward, and Upward leadership, he provides a clear and actionable roadmap for cultivating school cultures built on trust, collaboration, and continuous improvement.

His insights address the real challenges and opportunities faced by today's educational leaders. The emphasis on the Strategic School Map and the 12 Essential School Anchors equips schools with practical tools to establish environments where students, educators, and communities thrive.

Navigating an IOU School Culture is a visionary yet practical guide, essential for anyone committed to enhancing the success and well-being of school districts. It stands as an invaluable resource for leaders aiming to create dynamic, high-performing educational environments."

>—**GEORGE DUFFY III**, Executive Director/CEO, SCOPE Educational Services

"Dr. Joe Famularo's *Navigating an IOU School Culture* is an invaluable guide for educational leaders seeking to foster vibrant, intentional, and dynamic school environments. Grounded in Inward, Outward, and Upward (IOU) leadership principles, this book offers a transformative framework that aligns leadership vision with actionable strategies to cultivate a culture of Peacefulness, Happiness, Healthiness, and Excellence.

As an experienced superintendent and author of *Setting the Atmosphere: Beliefs, Practices, and Protocols for Faith-Filled Educational Leaders*, I deeply resonate with Dr. Famularo's emphasis on the power of aligning internal principles with external actions. His use of the 12 Essential School Anchors provides a timeless and adaptable roadmap for school leaders to navigate challenges, inspire collaboration, and achieve sustainable success.

Dr. Famularo's work is both thought-provoking and practical, weaving together powerful visual metaphors, actionable tools, and reflective exercises that guide leaders in creating a positive and thriving school culture. This book is an essential resource for anyone committed to advancing educational excellence and nurturing meaningful growth in their schools.

With heartfelt appreciation for Dr. Famularo's contributions to leadership development, I wholeheartedly endorse *Navigating an IOU School Culture* as a must-read for educators seeking to transform their school communities."

>—**DR. DEBORAH L. WORTHAM,** AASA 2024 Woman Superintendent in Leadership, Retired Superintendent and Author of *Setting the Atmosphere: Beliefs, Practices, and Protocols for Faith-Filled Educational Leaders*

"*Navigating an IOU School Culture* is an inspirational and aspirational book. The IOU (Inward, Outward and Upward) Principle is more than a manual for educational leaders; it is a thorough and thought-provoking book that enables the reader to be more reflective, introspective, and collaborative in creating a nurturing education environment. This is not a cookbook approach to leadership, rather it enables educational leaders to go deep into their own beliefs, attitudes, and philosophy so that they can ensure that the community of learners they serve will reach their potential in a safe, kind, and caring and productive environment.

The book is divided into four parts that provide a wealth of information on reaching your goals and aspirations as a school leader. Dr. Famularo provides prompts and examples on how to develop their own IOU School Culture, strategies, and monitoring progress. I believe that education leaders will find the Strategic Thinking Questions, Mindset Questions, and Guiding Questions found throughout the book, an excellent springboard for discussion and professional development for all stake holders. The engaging visuals enhance the content, and the critical message of the underlying philosophy of trust, respect and collaboration will be transformative to all who read this book.

Dr. Famularo guides the reader through a journey with a wealth of information, practical recommendations and specific questions that prompt higher level thinking, introspection, and reflection. The format also allows the reader to review key components and will be used as a resource and reference for all educational leaders. I strongly believe that this book will change you and enable you to be an introspective leader, who treats all parties with dignity and respect and appreciates the need to create a learning environment where all will flourish.

This is not merely a checklist of things leaders need to do, checking off the box and move on, rather it is a process that reinforces the commitment to lifelong learning.

Finally, the principles espoused in *Navigating an IOU School Culture* have wide ranging applications beyond the school environment. It can enable everyone to be more intentional, more reflective, more thoughtful, and more collaborative in their daily lives."

>   —**BARRY EDWARDS MCNAMARA, Ed.D.,** Professor of Education
>   Touro University, Author

"Leadership is a journey, not a destination. Along the way, the road we choose determines not only our own growth but the culture we create for those we serve. Dr. Joe Famularo's *Navigating an IOU School Culture* is the ultimate guide for leaders who are ready to take that journey with purpose, intentionality, and a commitment to elevating their school communities.

Much like my Road to Awesome philosophy, Dr. Joe's IOU Framework (Inward, Outward, Upward) challenges leaders to look beyond daily challenges and build a school culture where positivity, vision, and empowerment are the driving forces. His Strategic School Map serves as a field guide for leaders at every level, ensuring that their actions align with who they are and what they aspire to achieve.

If you are a school leader ready to take the leap and elevate your school culture, *Navigating an IOU School Culture* will give you the mindset, strategies, and tools to make it happen. This book is a must-read for those who are ready to choose the road to excellence and never look back."

—**DR. DARRIN PEPPARD,** Author of *Road to Awesome*, Speaker, Leadership Coach

Introduction

What if your school culture could be mapped, like a captain charting a course through open waters? Imagine a school where every leader, teacher, and student move with purpose, steering toward excellence instead of drifting by default. Some schools thrive with a clear direction, while others struggle in the tides of daily challenges.

The difference? Leadership that is intentional, trust-driven, and guided by a shared vision.

In this uplifting Leadership Manual, we introduce the **IOU Framework**, a structured approach to intentionally shaping school culture rather than letting it form by chance. An **IOU School Culture** is about empowering every member of the school community to embrace leadership from within and create an environment where everyone is inspired to aspire.

The journey begins on the inside, with personal growth and self-awareness **(Inward – "I")**. It then moves outward, strengthening relationships and interactions **(Outward – "O")**, and ultimately lifts the entire school community toward a positive, upward trajectory **(Upward – "U")**.

This upward journey is not just an aspiration; it is a strategic framework, a purposeful course set toward achieving **Peacefulness, Happiness, Healthiness, and Excellence: PH2E®**.

Just as a ship must navigate with purpose, a school must have a clear roadmap for its vison. Without intentional leadership, schools risk drifting into a stagnant or even toxic culture. But with the **IOU Framework as your guide,** you can chart a course toward a thriving, dynamic, and positive school community.

Leaders This Book Serves

This Leadership Manual is designed for all educational leaders who seek to build a thriving, intentional school culture. Whether you are a:

- **Superintendent** shaping a district-wide vision
- **Principal or school administrator** developing a positive leadership culture
- **Board of Education member** aligning policy and vision
- **Teacher or staff member** fostering leadership in students
- **District leadership team member supporting** principals and school improvement efforts

Navigating an IOU School Culture provides a strategic framework to align vision, leadership, and daily actions to create an Upward Dynamic Positive School Culture. This book will serve as your map, your compass, and your guiding light, helping you navigate with confidence toward an **Upward Dynamic Positive School Culture.**

Consider this manual your trusted companion—always within reach. It is not a one-time read but an essential resource to revisit frequently, allowing you to quickly access specific sections relevant to your immediate needs, whether aligning your vision and goals, refining leadership principles, enhancing communication, or addressing daily challenges. Keep it close, refer back to it often, and let it consistently support your journey toward intentional leadership and sustained personal and professional growth and success.

School Leadership Manual Overview

The **IOU School Culture Leadership Manual** is built around the theme of *Inspire to Aspire*, inviting schools to embark on a **strategic mapping journey** to create a nurturing and thriving educational environment. This journey unfolds across four parts, each symbolized by a distinct navigational instrument that guides the reader through:

- **Internalizing the IOU Principle** – Establishing a foundation of purpose, belief, and direction through SelfCulture and the 12 Essential School Anchors
- **Developing a Strategic School Map (SSM)** – Aligning Inward identity with Outward actions to build a culture of clarity, consistency, and trust
- **Reaching Upward Living** – Defining and receiving the schoolwide results of alignment: Peacefulness, Happiness, Healthiness, and Excellence (PH2E®)
- **Navigating with Intention** – Sustaining alignment through continuous reflection, refinement, and intentional leadership

Each step leads toward the ultimate goal of an **Upward Dynamic Positive School Culture**.

Throughout this book, we use the term *school* to represent the environment where these principles are applied. However, the **IOU School Culture Framework is universal**. These principles can be applied at any level within a school district, department, leadership team, classroom, or even for personal growth.

Wherever you are on your leadership journey, you can adapt these strategies to fit your unique needs. Simply substitute the word *school* with the context that applies to you, ensuring that you fully benefit from the renewing power of the **IOU Framework**.

Part II – Developing Your IOU Strategic School Map: A Framework for Inside-Out Alignment

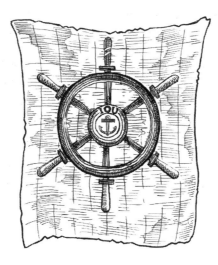

The 12 Essential School Anchors

We now transition to the visual of a captain's wheel on a map, each of its six handles representing one of the 12 Essential School Anchors. The anchor introduced in Part I now moves to the center of the wheel, symbolizing leadership, direction, and commitment. Just as a captain must skillfully navigate a ship, school leaders must guide their communities with clarity and intention.

This section focuses on developing a school's Strategic School Map (SSM) using the 12 Essential School Anchors: 6 Inward and 6 Outward. These anchors help leaders build a culture that is principled, consistent, and purpose-driven.

This section focuses on:

- Creating an **Inward School Map (ISM)** and **Outward School Map (OSM)**
- Establishing a **strategic framework** to guide the school's **journey toward Upward excellence**
- Aligning **internal principles** with **external actions** through a **comprehensive Strategic School Map (SSM)**

A well-developed Strategic School Map ensures a unified and cohesive approach to decision-making, communication, and growth, anchoring your school's identity while propelling it toward Upward excellence.

Part III – Reaching Your IOU Destination

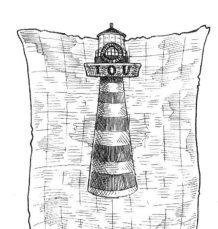

We now approach the **lighthouse on a map**, a beacon of guidance and success as schools near their IOU destination. Just as a lighthouse provides **clarity and direction**, this stage represents the culmination of strategic efforts, leading toward an **Upward Dynamic Positive School Culture**.

This section explores:

- **Upward Living**, the peak of the IOU journey, where **Inward (I) intentions and Outward (O) actions** align to create **Upward (U) positive results**
- The essential role of **Peacefulness, Happiness, Healthiness, and Excellence (PH2E®)** in shaping a thriving school culture
- The importance of envisioning and defining your **Upward (U) Desired Outcomes**

To support this journey, two reflection tools are introduced to ensure momentum is sustained:

- The **PH2E Self-Assessment**, available at www.PH2E.com, helps individuals and schools reflect on their current balance across the four PH2E dimensions using the visual metaphor of the Life Propeller.
- The **IOU School Culture Assessment**, found in **Appendix D**, enables leadership teams to evaluate alignment across all 12 IOU School Anchors. It serves as a powerful tool for identifying strengths, clarifying priorities, and generating high-level conversations when completed individually and reviewed collaboratively.

Upward Living isn't a one-time destination; it's an ongoing rhythm you sustain. It is not something you control directly, but a **byproduct of intentional Inward clarity**, **aligned Outward action**, and a schoolwide commitment to continuous reflection and improvement. This section challenges schools to **define what success truly looks like**, **align daily actions with that vision**, and **foster a culture that sustains momentum** through **purposeful growth** and **collective alignment**.

Part IV – Navigating Your IOU Strategic School Map (SSM)

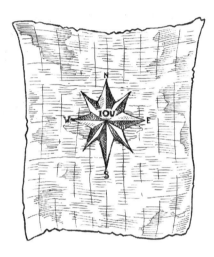

In the final part of our journey, we turn to the **compass** on a map as a symbol of **navigation, alignment, and continuous improvement**. Just as a compass helps travelers stay on course, the **Strategic School Map (SSM)** serves as a **living guide**, ensuring that the **Inward School Map (ISM) and Outward School Map (OSM)** remain aligned with **IOU Leadership principles**.

This section emphasizes the **SSM as an active tool**, driving:

- **Continuous improvement** through reflection and refinement
- **Integration of leadership principles** into daily school life
- **Inside-Out alignment**, ensuring that actions reflect the school's vision and aspirations

Key strategies include **embedding IOU principles into the school community**, utilizing the **IOU School Guiding Handle of SelfCulture and Trust**, and implementing the **SSM with intention**, allowing schools to **proactively shape their culture and maintain an Upward trajectory**.

Committing to Upward Living and Schoolwide Alignment

Throughout this Leadership Manual, we have invited readers to embark on an **intentional journey**, using *Inspire to Aspire* as their guiding light. This book serves as both a **strategic framework** and a **practical Leadership Manual**, offering a **clear framework for educators, administrators, school board members, and all stakeholders** committed to building and sustaining a thriving school culture.

By internalizing, developing, reaching, and navigating the IOU principles, schools can chart a course toward becoming beacons of **Peacefulness, Happiness, Healthiness, and Excellence (PH2E®)**, fully embodying an **Upward Dynamic Positive School Culture**.

How to Use This School Leadership Manual for Personal Reflection and Growth

This manual is designed to be **interactive**, providing space for you to reflect, take notes, and engage deeply with the material. We encourage you to **mark it up**, personalize your journey, and actively interact with the **IOU Principles**.

- This book is intended to serve as an active tool for fostering ongoing growth for you and your school.
- You don't need to complete every section before beginning to implement. Focus on the anchors and strategies most relevant to your school's immediate needs.
- Keep returning to this book for strategic planning, alignment, and the ongoing development of a thriving, purpose-driven school environment.

By actively applying these principles, you can ensure that **IOU Leadership becomes embedded in your school's culture**, not just as a concept, but a lived reality.

How to Use This Leadership Manual With Your Team

Whether you're a superintendent, principal, or part of a leadership team, this Leadership Manual is designed to be a practical, interactive tool, not just a book to read, but a guide to live by.

Use it to lead conversations, shape culture, and align your school or district around shared vision, principles, and action.

Ways to Engage Your Team:

- **Strategic Planning Meetings:**
  Use each anchor section as a reflective guide during leadership retreats or school improvement sessions.

- **Anchor-by-Anchor PD:**
  Break the content into short sessions or faculty meetings focused on one Inward or Outward Anchor at a time.

- **Leadership Book Club:**
  Read together in parts. Use the mindset and strategic thinking questions to drive meaningful dialogue.

- **Team Reflections:**
  Use the **Anchor Models** and reflection prompts to guide your leadership or instructional teams in aligning practices with your school's vision and values.

- **Goal Setting and Culture Walks:**
  Use the Strategic School Map (SSM) to review school displays, language, and practices, ensuring visible alignment with your school's core identity.

- **Cabinet or District Leadership Team Meetings:**
  Use this manual to anchor monthly cabinet meetings or leadership team sessions. Select a section to review and discuss as a "booster talk" to refocus on vision, culture, and alignment.

- **Board of Education Engagement:**
  Share relevant sections with Board of Education members to align with district school community initiatives, vision, and leadership philosophy. Use it as a foundation for retreats, presentations, or onboarding new trustees.

Remember:
You don't need to finish the entire manual before implementing.
Start where it matters most for your school, and build from there.
This manual is your leadership guide, not your checklist.

Visual Aids

Throughout this book, **original visual symbols** are used to illustrate key concepts and school anchors, reinforcing the **IOU Framework** in an **engaging and memorable way**.

IOU Inward and Outward School Anchors

 The **Captain's Wheel** is the central visual symbol, representing leadership, direction, and guidance. At the center of the wheel is an anchor, symbolizing the stability and foundational principles that ground a strong school culture.

- Each handle on the captain's wheel represents a **School Anchor**, which a school leader actively grasps to steer the culture forward.
- **Inward School Anchors (I):** Arrows point toward the center anchor, symbolizing **self-awareness and internal principles**, the foundation of leadership.
- **Outward School Anchors (O):** Arrows point outward to the handle, indicating the **focus on external actions and interactions**.

This visual reinforces the balance between Inward and Outward leadership, emphasizing that school leaders must actively take hold of the **Captain's Wheel**, steering their school culture with **purpose** and **direction** while staying anchored to the **vision** and **principles of the school**.

School Anchor Mindset Questions

To illustrate mindset questions for each school anchor in the book, we use two visual symbols that highlight the difference between **operating on autopilot** and **leading with intentionality**. These images serve as powerful reminders of the importance of proactive leadership in fostering a thriving school culture.

Default Thinking: Operating on Autopilot

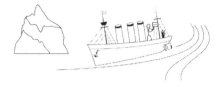

The visual depicts a captain on a boat, unaware of their surroundings, casually distracted, looking away as the boat drifts toward danger. This symbolizes what happens when leadership becomes **routine, reactive, and unexamined**, relying on habit rather than intentional course-setting.

- It represents leadership that is **well-intended but passive**, navigating based on past routines instead of responding to present realities.
- Without conscious navigation, schools may **drift off course before realizing it.**
- **Key reflection:** *Are we truly steering our school's culture, or are we coasting on what's familiar, without asking if it still serves our purpose?*

Intentional Thinking: Leading with Intentionality

In contrast, the intentional thinking visual shows a ship with the sun shining and a captain firmly gripping the wheel, looking ahead with confidence and clarity.

- It represents leadership that is **focused, principle-driven, and adaptable**, continuously aligning decisions with the school's vision.
- School leaders must **actively take the wheel**, making thoughtful decisions that drive a culture of trust, growth, and excellence.
- **Leadership reflection:** *What would it look like if we paused, evaluated, and intentionally shaped our school's culture, every single day?*

School Anchor Strategic Thinking Questions

For each anchor, we use a **visual of a person with their hand on their chin**, representing deep thought and reflection. Above the figure, an **anchor with question marks** symbolizes the process of inquiry, analysis, and refinement: critical components of **strategic thinking**.

This image serves as a reminder that **effective leadership requires ongoing reflection and thoughtful decision-making**. By continuously questioning and refining their approaches, school leaders ensure that their **actions align with their vision, mission, principles, and core values**.

These strategic thinking visuals are included to:

- **Encourage deliberate planning** rather than reactive decision-making.
- **Reinforce a mindset of continuous improvement** in leadership and school culture.
- **Prompt reflection** on how each anchor applies to daily practices within the school community.

By embracing strategic thinking, school leaders create an environment that is **dynamic, forward-focused, and intentionally designed for success**.

Guiding Questions

At the end of each School Anchor section, you'll find a visual of a **spyglass**, an old-time navigational tool used by captains to scan the horizon and fix their sights on a distant point. This symbol represents the **Guiding Question**, a singular, powerful reflection prompt designed to help school leaders **pause, refocus,** and **align their next steps with deeper purpose**.

Just as a spyglass helps a navigator look beyond the immediate surroundings to gain clarity on direction, the Guiding Question invites school teams to **zoom out, regain perspective**, and ensure that decisions remain **aligned with the school's vision, mission, and values**.

This visual reinforces that effective leadership requires not just action, but **reflection**. At key points in the book, the spyglass serves as a moment to:

- **Reflect** on how the anchor connects to your school's identity and purpose
- **Sharpen your school's focus** before moving forward
- Encourage **meaningful dialogue** that elevates daily practices

Used consistently, the Guiding Questions become a **habit of clarity**, helping school leaders lead with **insight, intention, and alignment**.

Anchor Statements and Practical Examples

Throughout this book, you will see a **lifebuoy with an anchor in the middle of it**, symbolizing the **practical application of the anchor principles**. Just as a lifebuoy serves as a **lifeline in open water**, these visuals represent **real-world examples** that can be used to strengthen and sustain a positive school culture.

At the end of each anchor section, these visuals will highlight:

- **Actionable steps** that translate IOU principles into daily school practices.
- **Successful examples** that illustrate how schools can effectively implement these strategies.
- **Guidance for applying leadership principles** in real-life situations within your school environment.

By incorporating these **lifebuoy examples**, this book ensures that the **IOU School Culture framework is not just theoretical but practical, adaptable, and ready for implementation**. These tools will help guide and support your journey toward creating a **dynamic and thriving school culture**.

School Anchor Models

At the end of each **School Anchor discussion**, you will see a **visual of a sextant**. This symbol indicates that you are in the **School Anchor Model** section, which serves as both a **summary** and a **strategic tool** to stimulate thinking and discussion with your team.

The **sextant** represents:

- **Precision and careful measurement**, essential for navigating toward school goals.
- **Strategic planning and reflection**, ensuring that leadership decisions are intentional.
- **Continuous alignment with vision and values**, reinforcing the importance of staying on course.

These models succinctly summarize each anchor's core definitions, explanations, and key points previously explored in detail, providing a clear and concise restatement. This structure allows educational leaders to easily reproduce and distribute these summaries as handouts for team meetings, professional development sessions, or leadership retreats. By using these focused summaries, leaders can confidently facilitate meaningful discussions, ensuring each anchor is not only understood but effectively applied with accuracy, clarity, and intentionality.

Leadership Snapshots

The Captain's Wheelhouse represents strategic leadership in action. This symbol includes essential nautical tools: a captain's wheel, compass, marine telegraph, and map, each reinforcing the idea that effective leadership requires clarity, coordination, and direction.

Leadership Snapshots appear throughout the book to highlight real-world moments where school leaders navigate challenges or make critical decisions. This image reminds readers that just like a ship's captain, leaders must know their tools, understand their environment, and steer with confidence.

- **The wheel** symbolizes hands-on leadership and direction.
- **The compass** represents foundational principles and alignment.
- **The marine telegraph** stands for clear, timely communication.
- **The map** reflects strategic planning and long-term vision.

Together, these elements reinforce that strong leadership is intentional, well-equipped, and guided by purpose.

IOU Island Map: A Symbol of an Intentional School Culture

At the center of the **IOU Strategic School Map (SSM)** lies **IOU Island**, symbolizing the foundation of an **intentional school culture**. The **SSM is the heart of this book**, providing a clear structure for **developing and sustaining a thriving school environment**.

IOU Island represents the three essential elements that shape school culture:

- **Inward (I)** – Self-awareness and foundational values that ground leadership.
- **Outward (O)** – Actions and interactions that build relationships and trust.
- **Upward (U)** – The desired results of **Peacefulness, Happiness, Healthiness, and Excellence (PH2E®)**.

As the focal point of the **SSM**, IOU Island reminds leaders that **successful school culture is intentional**: it must be **mapped, developed, and navigated** with purpose. It reinforces that **schools must align their vision, mission, leadership principles, core values, and goals with intentional daily actions** to create a truly **Upward Dynamic Positive School Culture**.

Why IOU Island Matters:

IOU Island is more than a symbol: it serves as the **foundational centerpiece** of the **IOU Strategic School Map (SSM)**, representing the **intentional culture-building process** that drives a school toward **sustained success**. At the center of the SSM, it serves as a constant **reminder of the interconnectedness of leadership, strategy, and daily actions**.

- **Anchored in Intention:** IOU Island anchors the **SSM framework**, reinforcing that school culture must be **built with intention, not left to chance**.
- **Guidance:** It serves as a **fixed point of reference**, ensuring that all decisions align with the school's **vision, mission, leadership principles, and core values**.
- **Practical Connection:** Appearing consistently throughout the book are **templates**, **planning tools**, and **practical examples**. IOU Island ensures that schools can **apply the framework in real-world scenarios**.

By keeping **IOU Island at the center**, school leaders ensure that their **SSM remains a living, adaptable guide**, leading their community toward **Peacefulness, Happiness, Healthiness, and Excellence (PH2E®)**.

Part I

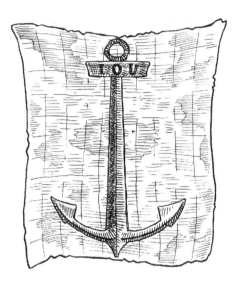

Internalizing the IOU Principle:
Inspire to Aspire

The anchor on the map represents the starting point of your school's **IOU journey**: a journey rooted in principles, purpose, and direction. Just as an anchor provides stability before a voyage begins, schools must first establish a strong foundation by internalizing the **IOU Principle**. This means embracing an **Inside-Out approach**, where leadership begins with self-awareness and shared responsibility, which then expands outward into meaningful relationships and purposeful actions.

The theme **Inspire to Aspire** is central to **Part I**. It calls on schools to inspire from within, to connect deeply with their vision, mission, leadership principles, and core values, and to aspire toward a culture grounded in **Peacefulness, Happiness, Healthiness, and Excellence (PH2E®)**.

But it also means something more. To **Inspire to Aspire** is not only to pursue your own growth, but to **inspire others to reach their aspirations as well**. It is about creating a culture where students, staff, and the entire school community are uplifted, encouraged, and empowered to pursue their highest potential. When schools live this message, inspiration becomes contagious, and aspirations become shared.

Schools that internalize these principles aren't just reacting to challenges, they are **navigating with intention, clarity, and a shared sense of purpose**. Part I sets the course for a school culture that is **led by principle, driven by vision, and united by a collective aspiration** to become an **Upward IOU School Culture**.

Part I Chapters Overview

Chapter 1: What is an IOU School Culture?

This chapter defines the **IOU Framework — Inward, Outward, and Upward** — and sets the foundation for an inspiring school culture. It introduces the anchor as a symbol of stability, emphasizing the importance of grounding leadership in timeless principles. Here, schools are invited to reflect on what they truly stand for and to begin aligning their culture with those ideals. The message: before you can motivate others to aspire, you must be inspired by your core.

Chapter 2: Inside-Out Living and Leading

Leadership that lasts begins from within. This chapter focuses on the **power of Inside-Out leadership**, where individuals model what they believe, and where self-awareness and intentionality guide every action. By living and leading from the inside out, schools create a ripple effect of trust, authenticity, and purpose. This approach inspires all members of the community to contribute to a shared aspiration.

Chapter 3: The IOU 12 Essential School Anchors

This chapter introduces the **12 Essential School Anchors**, which serve as the **foundational elements** for developing a school's **Strategic School Map (SSM)**. Each anchor is grounded in **timeless, universal principles** found in the best of leadership theory and practice, making them not just aspirational ideas, but **practical guides for purposeful action**.

These anchors represent the foundational **principles and practices** needed to build a **strong, cohesive, and principle-centered school community**. Together, they establish a shared language and framework for how schools define who they are

(Inward), how they act and relate to others (Outward), and the results they hope to achieve (Upward).

The 12 School Anchors serve as **beacons that inspire schools to aspire higher**, helping teams align their decisions and behaviors with their vision of excellence. They symbolize the strategic steps schools take to navigate confidently toward a **vibrant, thriving, and positive culture**.

By grounding every action and decision in these **universal and principle-based anchors**, schools build a sustainable pathway to Peacefulness, Happiness, Healthiness, and Excellence (PH2E®), and begin to **live their Strategic School Map with clarity and intention**.

Chapter 1

What is an IOU School Culture?

When you walk into a school, you immediately feel something. The tone in the hallways, the way staff greet students, the energy in classrooms and offices—it all tells a story. That feeling? That's **culture**. Some schools radiate optimism, unity, and purpose. Others feel tense, disconnected, or simply stuck in routine. The difference is rarely about resources or programs: **it's about leadership rooted in intentional, principle-centered culture-building**.

An **IOU School Culture** is a dynamic, nurturing, and uplifting environment where a school leads with intention and operates with clarity. It is built around three interconnected components:

- **"I" – Inward:** The foundational principles, vision, mission, leadership principles, and core values that define the school's identity and guide its direction.
- **"O" – Outward:** The systems, actions, and relationships that express those inward principles through schoolwide practices, communication, trust-building, and community interactions.
- **"U" – Upward:** The aspirational byproduct of alignment between inward beliefs and outward actions. It's a school culture that thrives with Peacefulness, Happiness, Healthiness, and Excellence (PH2E®).

A school's greatest strength is its people: students, teachers, staff, families, administrators, and board members. How those people interact, lead, and learn together is shaped by the **structures, priorities, and principles established by leadership**. School culture is never static. It evolves daily through intentional decisions or lack of them.

An IOU School Culture embraces a mindset of **continuous improvement**, where the school itself becomes a living model of its mission and values. The phrase **Inspire to Aspire** is central. When a school inspires through purpose, clarity, and action, it creates an environment where everyone is encouraged to aspire by growing, contributing, and reaching for excellence.

The IOU Framework is grounded in the **Inside-Out principle of leadership**; a school's internal clarity must come before external change. When a school clearly defines who it is and what it stands for, it can better align actions with intentions, fostering trust, coherence, and long-term impact.

An **IOU School Culture is built on timeless universal principles**, guided by purpose, and propelled by design. It is a place where vision and values are not just words on a wall, but deeply embedded in how the school operates—day in and day out.

In the chapters ahead, you'll explore the concepts of the **IOU Continuum**, and the **12 Essential School Anchors**: practical tools that help your school develop and live its **Strategic School Map (SSM)**. These tools will support your team in cultivating a culture where excellence is intentional, and **PH2E®** becomes the natural outcome of a well-led, well-aligned school community.

Inspire to Aspire

The Latin root of the word *inspire* is *inspirare*, which means "to breathe life into." This simple but powerful phrase captures the essence of what inspiration truly is: infusing others with energy, vision, and purpose. When a school inspires, it breathes life into its people, encouraging them to aspire to be their best and to pursue something greater than themselves.

In the IOU Framework, **Inspire to Aspire** is more than a motto: it's a leadership mindset and schoolwide design principle. It is about designing a school environment that lifts people up, fuels motivation, and aligns everyone around meaningful purpose. It transforms the ordinary into the extraordinary by aligning people with mission-driven purpose.

The lighthouse stands as a powerful symbol of this work. A lighthouse doesn't move—it stands firm, radiating light. In schools, this light symbolizes guidance, hope, and clarity. Like a lighthouse guiding ships through storms and toward safe harbor, schools that inspire serve as beacons, providing vision, direction, and reassurance through all conditions.

Inspiration in schools takes many forms:

- A **teacher** igniting a student's passion for learning
- A **principal** modeling clarity and positivity in the face of change
- An **administrator** celebrating growth and nurturing staff potential
- **Colleagues** supporting one another with encouragement and trust

Each of these moments is a breath of fresh air and a chance to elevate not just performance, but spirit. When people feel inspired, they are more likely to **aspire**: to take risks, grow, contribute, and strive for excellence.

As you move deeper into the IOU Principle and the journey of **Inside-Out alignment**, remember **inspiration is the catalyst for aspiration**. It is the spark that fuels momentum. By cultivating a culture that consistently breathes life into its people, schools create an environment where **Upward Living** becomes possible, where every member feels empowered to grow, connect, and lead.

Through the strategic implementation of the **12 Essential School Anchors**, schools don't just talk about aspirations: they build the systems and structures to achieve them. The result is a thriving, principle-driven educational culture anchored in clarity, aligned in action, and propelled by purpose.

Only two sailors, in my experience, never ran aground.
One never left port, and the other was an atrocious liar.
—Don Bamford

IOU School Continuum

Every school has a culture. The question is: **In what direction is it moving?**

Culture is not static. It is constantly forming and reforming based on the priorities, decisions, and daily interactions within the school community. Some schools thrive with alignment and clarity. Others operate on autopilot, drifting without direction. And some face declining trust, morale, or performance: signs of a downward trend.

The **IOU School Continuum** helps leaders assess and understand where their culture stands, providing a reflective tool to evaluate the present and align for the future. Grounded in the IOU Framework, this continuum connects your school's **Inward clarity** (vision, mission, leadership principles, core values, and goals) with its **Outward actions** (relationships, systems, and communication). When both are intentionally aligned, the school community experiences an **Upward byproduct**: Peacefulness, Happiness, Healthiness, and Excellence (PH2E®).

Think of three schools:

One is vibrant and focused: staff collaborate with energy, students are known and celebrated, and every initiative connects back to a shared purpose. That's an **Upward Leading** school **(IOU)**.

Another operates with good intentions, but lacks clarity. Some days feel smooth; others, scattered. There's no real harm, but also no momentum. That's a **Wayward Drifting** school **(IOW)**.

The third feels heavy. Morale is low, communication is strained, and staff feel stuck. Even well-meaning efforts often fall flat. That's a **Downward Draining** school **(IOD)**.

These three examples reflect a powerful truth: school culture always has a direction. The **IOU School Culture Continuum** helps you name it, and start navigating it with intention.

The chart below summarizes the key differences among the three culture types. Use it to reflect on your current state, identify areas for growth, and guide strategic planning moving forward.

IOU SCHOOL CULTURE CONTINUUM

School Culture	IOU	IOW	IOD
Trajectory:	Upward Leading	Wayward Drifting	Downward Draining
Impact:	Dynamic & Positive	Static & Neutral	Toxic & Negative
Performance:	Effective	Mediocre	Ineffective
Outcomes:	**School Gifts:** Peacefulness Happiness Healthiness Excellence (PH2E)	**School Impassivities:** Apathy Indifference Unfitness Mediocrity	**School Drains:** Anxiety Unhappiness Unhealthiness Ineffectiveness

Breakdown of the Continuum Components

To understand the full spectrum of school culture, from thriving to declining, it's important to examine the core dimensions that shape every school environment. Each category below highlights a different lens through which to assess your school's alignment, health, and performance. Together, they form a continuum of school culture: **IOU (Upward Leading), IOW (Wayward Drifting), and IOD (Downward Draining)**.

School Culture Trajectory

Trajectory refers to the path your school is on. It reflects the long-term direction of your growth, improvement efforts, and sense of momentum. Understanding trajectory helps leaders recognize whether the school is progressing with purpose, coasting without focus, or heading toward disengagement.

1. **Upward Leading:** Moving toward growth, alignment, and positive outcomes.
2. **Wayward Drifting:** Lacking direction, resulting in a static or neutral state.
3. **Downward Draining:** Declining toward dysfunction and school culture erosion.

School Culture Impact

Impact describes the emotional and relational tone of your school environment. It's what people feel when they walk through the halls, attend meetings, or engage with one another. A school's impact can uplift and energize, or deflate and disconnect. It's the heart of school culture in action.

- **Dynamic & Positive:** Energized, unified, and values-driven.
- **Static & Neutral:** Unchanging, disengaged, and unintentional.
- **Toxic & Negative:** Tense, disjointed, and damaging to well-being.

School Culture Performance

Performance addresses how effectively your systems, strategies, and daily actions align with your vision and goals. Strong performance reflects intentional effort and sustained progress, while poor performance reveals misalignment, inconsistency, or stagnation.

- **Effective:** Consistently aligned with goals and producing growth.
- **Mediocre:** Average performance without meaningful momentum.
- **Ineffective:** Failing to meet expectations or drive improvement.

School Culture Outcomes

Outcomes are the lived results of your school culture, the byproducts of your school's inward and outward alignment (or misalignment). What your community experiences over time, whether positive, passive, or draining, reflects the health and trajectory of your school at its core.

IOU School Culture – School Gifts (PH2E®)

When a school is intentionally aligned inwardly and outwardly, it naturally receives these school gifts:

- **Peacefulness:** A calm and centered environment built on clarity and connection.
- **Happiness:** A sense of purpose, joy, and belonging.
- **Healthiness:** Physical, emotional, and organizational well-being.
- **Excellence:** The pursuit and achievement of high standards and impact.

Chapter 1: What is an IOU School Culture?   11

IOW School Culture – School Impassivities

When schools drift, they unintentionally foster conditions that result in:

- **Apathy:** Lack of energy, ownership, or motivation.
- **Indifference:** Emotional distance and disconnection from purpose.
- **Unfitness:** Diminished well-being and readiness to perform.
- **Mediocrity:** Settling for "good enough" without pushing toward excellence.

IOD School Culture – School Drains

In cultures that are off course or in decline, these negative byproducts emerge:

- **Anxiety:** High levels of stress and reactivity.
- **Unhappiness:** Widespread discontent and lack of joy.
- **Unhealthiness:** Poor morale and burnout.
- **Ineffectiveness:** Systems and actions that undermine success.

Understanding Each Level on the Continuum

To make these categories more tangible, the following three school culture types illustrate how trajectory, impact, performance, and outcomes work together. Use them as reference points to help you assess where your school stands and where you want it to go.

1. IOU School Culture – Upward Leading

- **Trajectory:** Clear, principle-driven progress.
- **Impact:** Dynamic, inspiring, and mission-aligned.
- **Performance:** Effective strategies leading to meaningful results.
- **Outcomes:** The community experiences **PH2E®**—*Peacefulness, Happiness, Healthiness, and Excellence.*

2. IOW School Culture – Wayward Drifting

- **Trajectory:** Directionless or reactive; growth is inconsistent and lacks focus.
- **Impact:** Passive or neutral; neither toxic nor uplifting.
- **Performance:** Occasional progress with limited cohesion or sustainability.
- **Outcomes:** The school functions in a state of **Impassivities**—*Apathy, Indifference, Unfitness, and Mediocrity.*

3. IOD School Culture – Downward Draining

- **Trajectory:** Regressive, leading to disengagement or dysfunction.
- **Impact:** Toxic, divisive, and disempowering.
- **Performance:** Systems and interactions are misaligned, resulting in poor outcomes.
- **Outcomes:** The community suffers from **School Drains**—*Anxiety, Unhappiness, Unhealthiness, and Ineffectiveness.*

Reflecting on Your School's Current State

Before moving into application, take time to reflect on your school's current culture using the **IOU Continuum Reflection Tool** on the next page. This tool allows leadership teams to assess their school's **trajectory, impact, performance, and outcomes** across the three culture types: IOU, IOW, and IOD.

Use the **reflection prompts** to guide conversation, surface honest insights, and identify early opportunities for alignment. This activity is not about judgment—it's about clarity. The goal is to create a shared understanding of where your school is today so you can begin designing the path forward with purpose.

Note:

*You will also find this reflection tool available in **Appendix A** for continued use with leadership teams, staff planning sessions, and ongoing culture work.*

School Culture Continuum Reflection Tool

Use this tool to assess your school's current position across four key dimensions of school culture. Begin with the reflection question in each row to guide your thinking, then consider where your school currently aligns across the continuum.

Category	Reflection Prompt	IOU – Upward Leading	IOW – Wayward Drifting	IOD – Downward Draining
School Culture Trajectory	Where is our school currently headed? What evidence supports this?	Clear, principle-driven progress	Directionless or reactive; inconsistent growth	Regressive; disengagement or dysfunction
School Culture Impact	What is the emotional tone in our school? How do people feel here?	Dynamic, inspiring, and mission-aligned	Passive or neutral; not toxic but not uplifting	Toxic, divisive, and disempowering
School Culture Performance	Are our actions aligned with our goals? What's working, what's not?	Effective strategies leading to meaningful results	Occasional progress with limited cohesion	Misaligned systems resulting in poor outcomes
School Culture Outcomes	What are students and staff truly experiencing each day?	PH2E – Peacefulness, Happiness, Healthiness, Excellence	Impassivities – Apathy, Indifference, Unfitness, Mediocrity	School Drains – Anxiety, Unhappiness, Unhealthiness, Ineffectiveness

Applying the IOU Continuum in Your Schools

When your school's **Inward clarity** and **Outward actions** are positive and effective, the natural result is an **Upward Leading Culture**, or **IOU**. In this state, leadership is intentional, relationships are strong, and actions are aligned with a shared vision and purpose. This level of school culture is uplifting. It unlocks the full potential of your staff, energizes your students, and creates the conditions for the entire school community to experience the **School Gifts** of Peacefulness, Happiness, Healthiness, and Excellence (PH2E®). This state of alignment and momentum is what we call **IOU School Leadership.**

In contrast, schools that fall into the middle zone experience what we refer to as **IOW**—a **Wayward Drifting Culture**. These schools are not toxic, but they are not thriving either. Instead, they often feel stuck in neutral. Leadership tends to be reactive rather than proactive, systems are inconsistent, and energy may be low or scattered. The result is a culture that lacks clarity and cohesion. These schools often face what we call **School Impassivities**: Apathy, Indifference, Unfitness, and Mediocrity. IOW School Drifting is the byproduct of unintentional leadership and a lack of consistent alignment between inward beliefs and outward actions.

At the lowest point of the continuum lies **IOD**, a **Downward Draining Culture** where the school ship is slowly sinking. In these environments, inward clarity is often ignored or absent, and outward actions may be harmful, divisive, or misaligned. The results can be damaging and far-reaching: trust erodes, morale suffers, and learning environments become unstable. These schools tend to experience the **School Drains**: Anxiety, Unhappiness, Unhealthiness, and Ineffectiveness. Without intervention, IOD cultures compromise the wellbeing of both staff and students, and stall meaningful growth.

Understanding the IOU Continuum is a powerful tool for reflection and decision-making. It offers:

- A clear framework to **assess the current state** of your school's culture
- A language to **discuss strengths and challenges**
- A reference point to **guide intentional planning and alignment**

By identifying where your school currently falls on the continuum, leadership teams can make informed, strategic decisions to shift their culture upward. It promotes clarity, encourages shared ownership, and supports setting goals that are anchored in principles, not just programs.

It's also important to recognize that culture is **fluid**. Schools can move in and out of these levels over time, even within a single year. The continuum helps teams monitor this movement and continuously strive to **grow within the IOU School Culture range**, pushing toward greater alignment, consistency, and impact.

Use the **IOU Continuum** as a strategic tool: to frame leadership conversations, reflect on your school's current **alignment and environment**, and shape a plan for improvement.

Chapter 2

Inside-Out Living and Leading

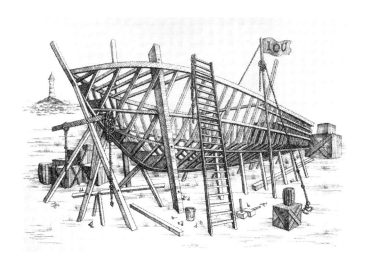

*The highest reward for a person's toil is not what they get for it,
but what they become by it.*
—John Ruskin

Leadership Snapshot: A Tale of Two School Cultures

In neighboring communities, two districts served similar student populations. Each had experienced educators, caring leaders, and community support. But spending time inside their buildings (whether the high school, middle school, or elementary), you could immediately sense the difference.

In one district, everything just clicked. The atmosphere was warm yet focused. Hallways felt calm and inviting. Interactions between staff and students showed respect, consistency, and purpose. You could tell this wasn't just a well-managed building—it was a well-led culture.

Staff understood and could articulate the school's foundational anchors. There was clarity around their shared vision, mission, leadership principles, core values, and *goals. There was trust. You could hear a common language being used: words and phrases that meant something in that community. The environment, both physical and relational, felt intentionally designed. There were traditions that united people, and a clear mindset of growth and continuous improvement. This was a school living with intention, aligned inwardly and outwardly, charting a course toward what we call an* **Upward Dynamic Positive Culture**.

In the second school, things looked organized on the surface, hallway posters displayed the school's mission, and inspirational words adorned bulletin boards. At first glance, everything seemed in order. But beneath the surface, the culture felt disconnected and unanchored. The vision and values weren't actively guiding decisions or conversations. Meetings focused on logistics rather than leadership. There was no shared language that tied people together: just isolated efforts driven by individual commitment rather than collective clarity and alignment.

This was a school filled with well-intentioned people doing their best, but operating on **default**. *Without consistent reference to the school's Inward identity or Outward actions, momentum drifted. There was no sense of alignment between the deeper "why" and the daily "what." What began as passion had settled into routine. Without realizing it, this school had entered a* **Wayward Drifting Culture**: *neutral, static, and susceptible to the pull of whatever was most urgent that day.*

Both schools had talent, commitment, and potential. The difference wasn't programs, funding, or staffing: it was **Inside-Out alignment**. *One school lived with intention, grounding its culture in shared principles and purposeful action. The other operated on default, with no clear map to guide their decisions.*

Culture doesn't just happen. It's built intentionally and maintained. *The question is: will yours be designed by intention or shaped by default?*

Living with Intention: The Key to Inside-Out Alignment

The difference between these two schools wasn't surface-level. It was a matter of intentional alignment: living and leading from the inside out.

Inside-Out Living and Leading is s a mindset. It begins with **Inside-Out alignment**: clarity of purpose, vision, and principles that drive outward leadership and daily actions. This approach emphasizes that true school improvement starts from within, by intentionally aligning a school's internal beliefs, leadership principles, and identity foundation with its outward actions and decisions.

When a school is grounded in its Inward Anchors, such as vision, mission, leadership principles, core values, and goals, it becomes stronger, more resilient, and better prepared to influence and navigate its external environment. This kind of intentional alignment builds momentum from the inside out, ensuring that what the school stands for is reflected in everything it does.

This chapter invites you to reflect on how your school should be built, from the inside out. Just as a ship must first be carefully constructed below the surface before it can safely navigate the sea, schools must develop a strong internal foundation before they can effectively lead, adapt, and grow. When that foundation is clear, consistent, and shared by all, the school becomes capable of steering confidently through both calm and stormy waters.

Ship-building Symbol: Inside-Out Leadership

The process of building a ship serves as a powerful metaphor for Inside-Out leadership. A well-constructed vessel doesn't begin with its sails or surface. It starts by creating an intentional, structured foundation.

At the beginning of this chapter, you saw an image of a wooden boat under construction, a ladder leaning on its side, and a flag marked **IOU** rising from the shell. This visual served as a symbolic start to our exploration of Inside-Out leadership. Now, as we revisit that image, its deeper meaning becomes clear: **leadership is built, not installed**. The unfinished frame reminds us that true strength begins beneath the surface, and that no vessel becomes seaworthy without a carefully constructed internal foundation.

Just as we saw in the Leadership Snapshot, the strength of a school lies not in what's immediately visible, but in how deeply its beliefs, principles, and values are embedded. The same is true for sustainable culture.

A thriving school must be built from the inside out, anchored in a **clear vision, strong principles, and aligned leadership**. Without that solid internal structure, a school may appear successful on the surface, but remain fragile when real challenges arise.

This ship-building image reminds us that **Inside-Out alignment isn't a phase. It's the foundation.** Leadership, culture, and long-term impact begin with intentional design and continual care.

*A ship doesn't sink because of the water around it.
It sinks because of the water that gets in it.*
—Unknown

The Framework of Strength
In shipbuilding, the internal frame is constructed first. This strong foundation provides the **strength and stability needed for the ship to withstand the pressures of the sea**. Similarly, a school must begin with a clearly defined **Inward School Map (ISM)**: its vision, mission, leadership principles, core values, and goals. These internal anchors create alignment, build resilience, and consistently guide decision-making through both calm waters and challenging storms.

Crafting with Precision
Every plank, beam, and bolt in a ship must be placed with care and intention. The structure depends on precision. In the same way, schools must thoughtfully design their internal systems, relationships, and community expectations. The small, daily practices, routines, rituals, shared language, and norms, are what give the organization its strength and coherence.

The finer the details, the stronger the structure: but even the most carefully built framework must be sealed tightly with integrity. Without it, outside forces find their way in.

Ensuring Integrity
A ship's hull must be tightly sealed to prevent taking on water. In schools, this represents the alignment between inward principles and outward actions. When a school's culture is built on a shared vision, core values, and leadership principles, it becomes more resilient to external pressures.

When internal clarity is strong, external challenges don't define the school's direction. But even the smallest leak, misalignment, confusion, or inconsistency, can cause drift. Sealing the hull is about keeping your internal foundation intact and guiding your school confidently forward.

Adding the Essentials
Once the structure is in place, a ship receives its engine, navigation tools, and living quarters. These represent the **systems and practices** that bring a school's vision to life: professional development, strategic planning, student supports, and instructional leadership. Each must be integrated with care, so they function cohesively.

Launching with Confidence

After intentional preparation, the ship is launched. The school, too, moves from planning to practice, ready to face external pressures with focus and clarity. A school with a well-developed Inward School Map is equipped to move with purpose, adjusting its course without losing sight of its destination.

Continuous Maintenance

Even the best-built ship needs regular maintenance to stay seaworthy. Likewise, a school culture requires continuous reflection and refinement. Leadership must revisit foundational principles often, asking:

Are we still aligned?
Do our actions reflect who we are and where we're going?

Final Thought

Building from the inside out is not a one-time event. It's a **mindset of ongoing Inside-Out alignment**. When schools strengthen their internal foundation and align their daily practices, they create the conditions for long-term success. Strong foundations don't just keep the ship afloat, They carry it forward. But even the strongest vessel must be sealed with integrity. **Alignment, sealing the hull, is what protects the culture and propels the school confidently through both calm waters and storms.**

> *"What's not aligned within will drift without."*
> —Dr. Joe Famularo

Living by Default vs. Living with Intention

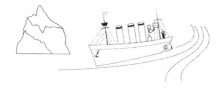

Living by default means drifting: reacting instead of leading, repeating routines instead of renewing purpose. When schools operate on autopilot, they may stay afloat, but they aren't steering, and they don't know where they are going. Default thinking creates a slow drift that can lead to missed opportunities, misalignment, or unforeseen obstacles.

In contrast, living with intention means leading proactively, not reactively. It's about consciously choosing your thoughts, actions, and decisions: rather than simply responding to what happens around you. Schools that live with intention take ownership of their direction and make deliberate choices that reflect their vision, values, and goals.

This kind of leadership is like a captain at the helm: aware of the conditions, steady on the wheel, and navigating toward a well-charted destination. The sun is shining, the course is clear, and the ship is moving with purpose.

In **Part II** of this book, **each school anchor includes a reflection question designed to assess your school's current approach**: Are you operating with intentional thinking or default thinking? This reflective process helps identify where your school may be drifting, and where intentional alignment can steer you toward a clearer, purpose-driven destination.

Intention in the School Environment

Inside-Out living with intention means leading with clarity, purpose, and alignment. In a school environment, this begins with school leaders and extends through every layer of the community. It's about making deliberate choices that reflect your school's vision, mission, leadership principles, and values, not just reacting to external pressures or routines.

When schools lead with intention, they cultivate a dynamic and positive culture where learning thrives, relationships grow, and goals are pursued with shared commitment. This kind of culture doesn't happen by chance. It's designed, reinforced, and actively lived daily.

While Inside-Out living can be applied across all areas of life, this manual focuses on the **strategic application of intention in schools**. Whether at the organizational level, within departments or teams, or through individual leadership, the principle remains the same: **strong internal alignment creates meaningful external impact**.

In the next section, we'll look at how this principle shows up in different areas of school life, and how it can guide you to build a culture grounded in purpose and propelled by action.

Improving Organizational School Culture

Inside-Out leadership begins with clarity, and culture grows from the inside out. When a school's internal principles are clearly defined and actively lived, the entire organization becomes stronger, more focused, and more resilient.

Here's how intention can shape your school's organizational culture:

- **Lead from Within**: Establish a mindset that **everyone is a leader, of themselves and with others.** Model emotional intelligence, trust, and authenticity at every level.
- **Clarify and Live the Principles**: Ensure your school's mission, vision, leadership principles, and core values **guide all actions and decisions**. These aren't just posters. They are the anchors for culture.
- **Build Trust and Collaboration**: Foster a culture where respect is practiced, **voice is honored, and collaboration is the norm**. When trust is high, alignment becomes easier.
- **Recognize and Reinforce**: Celebrate behaviors that reflect the school's values. Recognize staff not only for results, but also for how those results were achieved, through principle-centered actions.

By leading with intention, your school culture becomes more than a collection of routines, It becomes a living system of purpose, growth, and excellence.

Improving Department Effectiveness

Departments are the engines of a school. When they operate with shared intention and alignment, they strengthen the school's culture and drive student success.

Here's how to apply Inside-Out leadership at the department level:

- **Clarify the Collective Purpose**: Regularly reaffirm how the department's goals clearly connect to the school's overall mission and vision.
- **Foster Intentional Communication**: Encourage open, honest, and purposeful dialogue. Ensure meetings, feedback, and collaboration are rooted in trust and respect.
- **Align Systems and Roles**: Make sure routines, responsibilities, and expectations reflect the school's values. When structure aligns with culture, teams function more effectively.
- **Support Growth and Celebrate Progress**: Provide professional learning opportunities that align with both schoolwide goals and team interests. Acknowledge and celebrate progress regularly. Consistent recognition builds momentum and motivates continued growth.

When departments lead from the inside out, they create consistent experiences across classrooms, build cohesion, and contribute meaningfully to a school's upward trajectory.

> *"Default drifts. Intention steers."*
> —Dr. Joe Famularo

The Path Forward: From Intention to Action

While the IOU Framework applies to self, family, team and organizational, leadership, this book focuses on its application within schools. Specifically, we'll guide you through the development of an **IOU School Culture**, using the **12 Essential School Anchors**—6 Inward, 6 Outward—as the foundation for your Strategic School Map (SSM).

These anchors are principled action steps that drive **Inside-Out alignment**: connecting internal clarity with external consistency. When applied intentionally, they help transform culture, deepen relationships, and foster growth across the school community.

For leaders interested in applying the IOU model beyond the school context, we recommend the companion #1 bestselling book, ***IOU Life Leadership: You Owe It to Yourself and Others***—a resource for living and leading with intention across every part of life.

Next, we'll explore the **12 Essential School Anchors**, the framework that brings the **IOU School Culture to life.**

Chapter 3

The IOU 12 Essential School Anchors

Schools don't drift into excellence; they anchor themselves to it. The **IOU 12 Essential School Anchors** provide that foundation. They serve as **guiding principles** that secure your school's direction and **propel your culture upward**. These 12 School Anchors—**6 Inward** and **6 Outward**—form the backbone of an **intentional, dynamic, and principle-centered** school community.

In the journey toward building an IOU School Culture, these anchors help define **who you are, how you lead, and where you're going**. The **6 Inward Anchors** shape the school's **identity, clarity, and internal strength**. The **6 Outward Anchors** ensure that your **relationships, environment, and systems** reflect those internal principles. Together, they create a **living structure of Inside-Out alignment** that guide your school community toward **Peacefulness, Happiness, Healthiness, and Excellence (PH2E®).**

These anchors come to life in the **IOU School Living Wheel**, a visual framework introduced later in this chapter that illustrates the **balance between inward identity and outward action**.

The Importance of Essential Anchors

The term **"essential"** is used intentionally. These **anchor principles** have been carefully distilled from decades of leadership research and effective school practices. They represent the foundational, high-impact elements necessary to build and sustain a positive, purposeful, and thriving school culture. While countless strategies and initiatives come and go, the IOU 12 Essential School Anchors are not fleeting programs. They are **principles that endure**.

At the center of the Inward Anchors is **SelfCulture**: the lived identity of the school in action. It's not just a belief system; it's how those beliefs show up every day in interactions, decisions, and priorities. SelfCulture sets the tone for every other Inward Anchor, serving as the internal guide for alignment.

At the center of the Outward Anchors is **Trust**: the foundation of all healthy relationships and the thread that connects people, teams, and communities. Without trust, even the strongest inward principles struggle to take root in daily school life.

By focusing on these anchor principles, schools create a culture that doesn't just survive. It thrives. They ensure that every member of the school community: students, teachers, staff, families, administrators, and board members feels connected, empowered, and inspired to contribute. These anchors ground your school in clarity, shape your direction, and **propel your actions with intention**.

THE 6 ESSENTIAL INWARD SCHOOL ANCHORS

The 6 Inward School Anchors focus on defining the school's identity and fostering a culture of self-awareness and intentionality. The 6 Inward Anchors make up the **Inward School Map (ISM)**. These anchors include:

1. **SelfCulture:** The collective beliefs, behaviors, and attitudes that define the school's unique identity and character. SelfCulture is nurtured by embracing the other anchors, establishing a foundation for a dynamic and positive school environment.
2. **School Vision:** A future-oriented statement that inspires and directs the school's aspirations and activities. It serves as a beacon, motivating all members to aspire towards a common purpose and excellence in education.
3. **Daily School Mission:** The specific objectives and strategies that drive the school's daily operations, aligned with the vision. The mission statement instills a sense of purpose and daily direction, guiding the actions of students, teachers, staff, and administrators.
4. **School Leadership Principles:** These are the fundamental beliefs that guide the school's culture, emphasizing a commitment to principles of excellence in education. They serve as the guiding force that shapes decision-making and behavior within the school community.

5. **School Core Values:** The internal beliefs and priorities that inform decision-making and behavior within the school. School Core Values such as trust, respect, and collaboration create a positive and supportive culture that foster academic success and personal growth.
6. **School Goals:** These are the measurable targets and milestones that track progress toward the vision. By setting clear and achievable goals, the school community is motivated to strive for continuous improvement and excellence in all aspects of school life.

THE 6 ESSENTIAL

OUTWARD SCHOOL ANCHORS

The 6 Outward School Anchors focus on defining the school's relationships, interactions, and trust, forming the **Outward School Map (OSM).**

1. **Inspire IOU Trust**: This anchor is achieved when individuals inspire and influence each other, aligning their School Anchor Principles for mutual benefit and growth, building a foundation of trust.
2. **Practice Positive Communication:** Emphasizes empathic listening and creating a safe environment for open, honest, and respectful communication within the school community.
3. **Create Common Language:** This anchor focuses on intentionally developing shared language across the school community to reinforce identity, clarify expectations, and strengthen alignment across school culture.
4. **Construct a Cohesive Environment:** Focuses on creating physical and relational environments that align with the school's vision and mission, promoting collaboration, teamwork, and a sense of safety, happiness, and learning.
5. **Establish Everlasting Traditions:** Building traditions that celebrate achievements, promote team building, and connect to the school's history fosters a sense of pride and belonging among all members.

6. **Model a Mindset of Propelling PH2E:** Encourages individuals to continuously improve their Peacefulness, Happiness, Healthiness, and Excellence (PH2E) by living according to The IOU 12 Essential School Anchors, propelling the school toward its highest potential.

By aligning decisions and actions with The **IOU 12 Essential School Anchors**, schools can create a comprehensive roadmap for developing a **Strategic School Map (SSM)**. This alignment fosters a **dynamic and positive culture**. One that doesn't just respond to change but leads it with clarity and purpose.

The anchors are the **secret sauce** behind intentional school culture. They turn vague aspirations into focused leadership, surface-level practices into deeply rooted principles, and everyday decisions into culture-shaping actions.

> *"When schools anchor themselves to these principles,*
> *they don't drift—they lead.*
> *And when those anchors are lived with consistency,*
> *the school begins to rise."*
> —Dr. Joe Famularo

Leadership Snapshot: From Good Intentions to Clear Direction

"We always said the right things, like 'students first,' 'relationships matter,' but it wasn't until we defined our anchors that we began to lead with clarity. Our vision came alive when it connected to real actions. Staff stopped asking, 'What are we doing?' and started saying, 'This is who we are.'"

—Principal reflection during a leadership team session

Chapter 3: The IOU 12 Essential School Anchors   33

IOU SCHOOL LIVING WHEEL

The School Living Wheel is a powerful tool that captures the Inside-Out principle, representing the **synergy of the 12 Essential School Anchors**. This wheel guides your school and its members towards a dynamic and positive culture, embodying positive and effective intentional living and leading. Just as a captain uses a wheel to navigate a ship, the School Living Wheel helps steer your school towards its goals. At the center is the anchor symbolizing your school and its members, with **6 Inward Anchors pointing inward** to represent the school's identity and Inward Principles, and **6 Outward Anchors pointing outward** to the wheel's handles, signifying your Outward Actions and interactions of the school community.

The Inward Anchors include **SelfCulture, School Vision, Daily School Mission, School Leadership Principles, School Core Values, and School Goals**. They are your foundation, guiding your internal decisions and actions. Much like the carefully crafted framework of a ship, these anchors ensure that your **"School Ship"** is resilient and ready to navigate the complexities of the educational journey. By providing stability and direction, these anchors root your school's culture in strong, well-defined principles, allowing you to chart a purposeful and steady course toward upward success.

The Outward Anchors focus on your interactions and relationships within the school community. These include **Inspire IOU Trust, Practice Positive Communication,**

Create Common Language, Construct a Cohesive Environment, Establish Everlasting Traditions, and Model a Mindset of Propelling PH2E (Peacefulness, Happiness, Healthiness, and Excellence). These anchors guide how you implement your school's principles and values in everyday actions, fostering a collaborative and supportive environment.

The School Living Wheel is more than a theoretical concept; **it's a practical framework for intentional, effective living and leading for all school stakeholders.** It emphasizes effectiveness over efficiency, ensuring that your school stays on the right course towards its aspirations. By embracing both the Inward and Outward Anchors, schools can create a balanced, thriving culture that nurtures success and well-being for all community members.

Navigating the Stages of the IOU School Living Wheel

The stages of the **IOU School Living Wheel** represent a journey of growth and development within a school community, **emphasizing the progression from individual awareness to collective synergy**, ultimately leading to the desired outcome of a dynamic and positive culture.

I – You: This initial stage focuses on the individual, encouraging self-awareness, introspection, and personal growth. It is about understanding oneself, one's strengths, weaknesses, principles, and goals. Additionally, the "I" in this stage encompasses the identity of the school, including its school vision, mission, principles, core values, and goals. It is about aligning individual aspirations with the broader goals and principles of the school community, inspiring each member to aspire to contribute meaningfully.

This is where you *Know your "I"*—the foundation of intentional leadership.

O – We: In the second stage, the focus shifts from the individual to the group. It emphasizes the importance of trust, collaboration, teamwork, and community building. This stage is about recognizing that we are all interconnected and that our actions impact others. It involves building strong relationships, fostering trust, and working together towards common goals, inspiring each other to aspire towards collective excellence.

This is where you *Own your "O"*—living out your principles through positive relationships.

U – Desired Results of I and O: The final stage represents the desired outcome of the I and O stages coming together. It is about creating an **Upward Culture** that is the result of individuals who are self-aware and engaged in positive relationships with others, while also aligned with the vision, mission, principles, values, and goals of the school. This stage reflects a sense of cohesiveness, shared purpose, and a commitment to continuous improvement. It is about creating an environment where everyone feels valued, supported, and inspired to be their best selves, inspiring and aspiring towards a culture of excellence.

This is where you *Receive the "U"*—the byproduct of alignment: Peacefulness, Happiness, Healthiness, and Excellence (PH2E).

In conclusion, an **IOU School Culture** is a dynamic and impactful approach that centers on the interconnectedness of individuals within the school community. By navigating the stages of the IOU School Living Wheel through a focus on individual self-awareness, collaborative relationships, and shared outcomes, schools can cultivate an environment of trust, continuous improvement, and collective excellence.

Align your Inward identity with your Outward actions to receive the *Upward* school environment, community, and leadership outcomes you strive for.

Part II: Developing Your IOU Strategic School Map: A Framework for Inside-Out Alignment

With the foundation of the IOU Framework established in Part I, we now shift from understanding to building. Part II guides you through the development of your **Strategic School Map (SSM)**: a living framework that transforms school culture through intentional, principle-centered leadership.

In the chapters ahead, we'll explore each of the **12 Essential School Anchors** in depth, beginning with the **6 Inward Anchors** that define your school's inward identity, followed by the **6 Outward Anchors** that shape how that identity is lived and experienced.

By constructing both your **Inward School Map (ISM)** and **Outward School Map (OSM)**, you begin to bring your culture to life from the inside out. These maps serve not just as guides, but as commitments: aligning beliefs with behaviors, and purpose with practice. Together, they help your school **Inspire to Aspire**, cultivating an **Upward culture** of Peacefulness, Happiness, Healthiness, and Excellence.

Chapters 4 through 8 provide **practical steps, reflection tools, and visual models** to help you develop your SSM with clarity and intention. More than a compass, your Strategic School Map becomes the steering wheel that directs your daily actions, long-term goals, and the collective energy of your entire school community.

Now anchored in vision and ready for action, your school is prepared to build forward: developing each anchor into a dynamic roadmap for a thriving, united, and purpose-driven school culture.

Part II

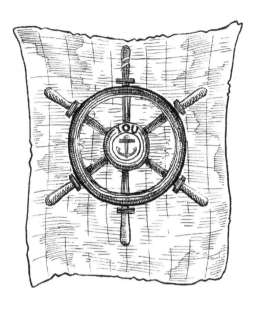

**Developing Your IOU Strategic School Map:
A Framework for Inside-Out Alignment**

Part II focuses on refining your school's strategic direction through the development of two essential frameworks: the **Inward School Map (ISM)** and the **Outward School Map (OSM)**. These maps form the foundation of your **Strategic School Map (SSM)**, aligning your school's internal beliefs with outward actions.

Chapter 4 introduces the **6 Inward School Anchors**, helping your leadership team clarify the principles, purpose, and vision that define your school's identity. **Chapter 5** walks you through the process of building and refining your **Inward School Map (ISM)**, integrating the 6 Inward Anchors into a cohesive, purpose-driven framework.

Chapter 6 shifts the focus outward, introducing the **6 Outward School Anchors**: practices and behaviors that bring your school's inward commitments to life through action and relationship. **Chapter 7** helps you translate the 6 Outward Anchors into the **Outward School Map (OSM)**, the living guide for how your school builds trust, communicates with purpose, and fosters a connected, caring culture.

Chapter 8 then guides you in unifying and aligning both the Inward and Outward Maps into the **Strategic School Map (SSM)**, a comprehensive tool that harmonizes inward clarity with outward consistency.

Your Strategic School Map (SSM) will become a powerful and comprehensive tool. As a leader, you can confidently present it to your Board of Education, staff, families, and the broader school community. It tells the story of your school's vision and values through a structured, intentional framework. Importantly, remember that it does not need to be perfect or complete before sharing it. The strength of the SSM lies in its ability to grow with your leadership. Continue building it as you lead. Let it evolve with your team. Use it as a compass for conversations, alignment, and action.

This alignment ensures that every element of the school's environment and activity is grounded in intention, purpose, and shared vision. The SSM becomes a living framework, directing all decisions and actions toward an **Upward, Dynamic Positive IOU School Culture.**

ISM + OSM = SSM

Inward School Map + Outward School Map = Strategic School Map

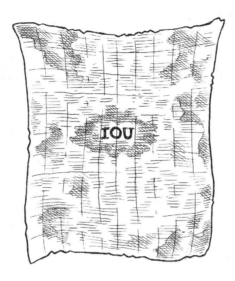

Before we begin the journey through the 12 Essential School Anchors, it's important to understand the power of paradigms and maps. These internal and external tools shape how we see our schools, how we respond to challenges, and how we design meaningful, positive change in school culture.

Navigating Change: The Power of Paradigms and Maps in Strategic School Planning

To lead schools effectively through change, we need clear mental models and strategic direction. In education, two powerful tools help us do this: **maps and paradigms**.

Maps do more than help us get from point A to point B. They help us **make the unknown known**, turning abstract goals into concrete steps. A school map does the same. It brings clarity to where your school is now, where it wants to go, and how to get there.

Paradigms are our internal maps: our beliefs, assumptions, and ways of seeing the world. They shape how we lead, how we make decisions, and how we interact with others in our school community. Just like physical maps, paradigms determine the route we take, the obstacles we anticipate, and the outcomes we pursue.

Understanding that **paradigms are mental maps** reminds us how important it is to align our thinking with our purpose. Without intentional reflection, we may default to outdated or unclear beliefs that slow progress. When our internal maps are aligned with our school's vision, mission, principles, and values, however, we can lead with focus, consistency, and confidence.

Just like a captain uses a map to stay on course, especially in stormy waters, school leaders need clear paradigms to steer their school through both steady growth and turbulent change. When these mental maps are aligned with a school's goals, they:

- Help visualize progress
- Anticipate challenges
- Strengthen the connection between where you are and where you want to go

If our paradigms are unclear or, even more concerning, misaligned, they can cause drift, confusion, or conflicting priorities.

That's why **intentional thinking** is so important. Every step we take toward school improvement starts with how we think. When our thinking is grounded in shared values and purpose, we're more likely to make decisions that move us forward together.

By checking and realigning our mental maps, we lay the groundwork for a strategic plan that is not only ambitious, but also achievable, sustainable, and focused on what matters most.

Understanding this connection between maps and paradigms is especially important when navigating change. Whether it's a new initiative, a shift in leadership, or organizational alignment, meaningful change doesn't happen by accident. It requires clarity, consistency, and shared understanding.

When your leadership team holds aligned mental maps: shared beliefs, clear vision, and strategic direction, it becomes much easier to:

- Stay focused during uncertainty
- Respond to challenges with confidence
- Make decisions that reflect your principles and values
- Keep the entire community moving in the same direction

Without this shared alignment, change efforts often stall, become reactive, or fall short of their potential.

The key takeaway? **You don't just need a plan—you need a mindset that supports the plan.** When your thinking is aligned with your destination, your actions will follow with clarity and purpose

Leadership Snapshot: A New Paradigm, A New Map

Let's step into the shoes of one teacher to see how a shift in thinking reshaped not just her role, but her classroom and her students.

I used to think school culture was something the principal created, something discussed in staff meetings or written into our handbook. I stayed in my lane, focused on my students, and assumed the rest would take care of itself. But once we started building our Inward and Outward Maps together, something shifted.

I realized I wasn't just following a plan. I was shaping it. Every greeting at the door, every hallway conversation, every decision I made in my classroom was part of the map. And once I saw that, my perspective changed. It wasn't just about doing things differently. It was about thinking differently.

That new mindset, my paradigm shift, brought new clarity to my role. I stopped asking, 'What's expected of me?' and started asking, 'What kind of culture are we creating together?' That question didn't just reframe my leadership. It reshaped my classroom.

My students noticed the difference. With shared language, clearer expectations, and stronger alignment across the school, they started stepping up. They held each other accountable. They celebrated each other's growth. They started to lead not because I told them to, but because they felt ownership.

It all started with a shift in how we think. When you change your paradigm, you change your map. And when the map changes, everyone can move forward together in the same direction with clarity, confidence, and purpose.

The Next Step: Building the Inward School Map

The Leadership Snapshot you just read highlights a powerful truth: school culture doesn't shift through programs alone. It transforms through people, and it starts with a mindset shift.

Now, with a deeper understanding of how maps and paradigms work together, you're ready to begin developing your **Inward School Map (ISM)**. This map is built from six foundational elements: your **Inward School Anchors: School SelfCulture, School Vision, Daily School Mission, School Leadership Principles, School Core Values, and School Goals**.

These 6 Inward Anchors form your school's internal compass, guiding beliefs, daily intentions, and long-term aspirations. In the chapters ahead, each anchor will be explored in depth, helping you clarify identity, align purpose, and create a culture that is consciously designed rather than passively inherited.

Chapter 4 begins this journey by examining each Inward Anchor individually, allowing your leadership team to assess strengths, uncover opportunities, and establish shared priorities. Collectively, these six Inward Anchors form your **Inward School Map (ISM)**: a comprehensive representation of your school's core identity. This is the first and most vital step in living and leading from the inside out, anchoring your school's culture with clarity, intentionality, and purpose.

Chapter 4

The
IOU 6 Inward School Anchors

Anchoring the Inward Journey

Developing your **Inward School Map (ISM)** is the first essential step in creating your IOU Strategic School Map. This inward journey involves intentionally anchoring your school community in six foundational elements: **School SelfCulture, School Vision, Daily School Mission, School Leadership Principles, School Core Values, and School Goals.** These Inward Anchors establish a principled and unified foundation from which your school's actions and culture will grow.

When clearly defined and collaboratively developed, these anchors act as a stabilizing force: a framework that aligns beliefs with behaviors and creates purpose-driven clarity for all. This is strategic **anchoring**, ensuring that everything your school does outwardly is rooted in what it stands for inwardly.

This is the essence of **Inside-Out Alignment**: cultivating an educational environment that reflects your school's principles, elevates its daily purpose, and inspires collective excellence.

As you explore each anchor, you'll find questions, models, and tools designed to bring clarity, foster collaboration, and support your work in building a cohesive, principle-centered school culture.

A Reminder: Using Anchor Models to Guide Strategy and Dialogue

As noted earlier in the book, each Inward and Outward Anchor section concludes with a corresponding Anchor Model, marked by the sextant symbol. It's worth repeating here because this is where the models truly come to life.

These models are not just visual summaries: they are strategic tools designed to prompt reflection, clarify thinking, and spark meaningful dialogue among your leadership team. Like a sextant guiding navigators by the stars, these Anchor Models help keep your school's culture work focused, aligned, and purpose-driven.

Use them intentionally:

- **To facilitate collaborative planning**
- **To deepen shared understanding**
- **To connect each anchor to actionable outcomes**

These tools are meant to be used—not just read. Feel free to reproduce the Anchor Models and use them as handouts, posters, team discussion prompts, or visual reference points in faculty meetings, planning retreats, or leadership workshops. Whether printed or displayed digitally, they are designed to anchor your conversations and support strategic alignment throughout the school year.

As you move forward, let these models serve as check-in points for your team: opportunities to stay on course, reinforce alignment, and propel your school toward your aspirational vision.

Transition to Anchor 1: School SelfCulture

With your sextant in hand and the journey mapped, it's time to begin building your Inward School Map: starting with the foundational Inward Anchor: **School SelfCulture**.

This anchor is the core of your school's identity, the internal compass that guides everything else. When SelfCulture is clearly defined, every other part of your school's strategy gains clarity and cohesion.

In the next section, we'll explore how a strong SelfCulture answers the question: *Who are we as a school community, and what do we stand for?* You'll reflect on the beliefs, principles, and shared language that make your culture unique, and begin crafting a vision that inspires action and alignment at every level.

Inward School Anchor 1

SCHOOL SELFCULTURE

The Principle of Self-Identity

At the center of your being, you have the answer: you know who you are, and you know what you want.
—Lao Tzu

School SelfCulture: Embracing the Principle of Self-Identity Through Inspiration and Aspiration

Central to every school's journey is a fundamental question: **Who are we?** This question is answered through your **School SelfCulture**: the embodiment of your school's internal identity, guided by the **Principle of Self-Identity** and fueled by the spirit to *Inspire to Aspire*.

SelfCulture is a composite of your school's **foundational identity**, including the other five Inward Anchors: **School Vision, Daily School Mission, School Leadership Principles, School Core Values, and School Goals**. It also includes the visible elements of your school's brand: mascot, colors, logos, and symbols. All of which must align with and reinforce your deeper mission and vision.

When developed with intention, SelfCulture becomes the anchor of the **Inward School Map (ISM)**: a strategic reflection of who you are and what you stand for. The ISM provides a framework for building a learning environment that is both effective and uplifting, uniting your community around shared principles and purpose.

Through the lens of **Self-Identity**, your culture shifts from something that haphazardly happens to something you actively create. A strong SelfCulture fosters a shared language, a sense of belonging, and a positive momentum toward your school's highest aspirations. It's the foundation of an **Upward Dynamic Positive IOU School Culture**, where every student, educator, and stakeholder is aligned, inspired, and empowered.

Defining Features of an IOU School's SelfCulture

A strong SelfCulture is the result of deliberate alignment across key elements of school life. Below are key components that help shape and sustain an IOU School Culture grounded in clarity, consistency, and aspiration:

- **Defined Vision and Mission**: A clear articulation of your school's purpose and direction, guiding decision-making and setting the tone for everything you do.
- **Articulated Guiding Leadership Principles**: Principle-centered beliefs that shape leadership decisions, behaviors, and expectations at every level of the organization.
- **Established Core Values**: The foundational principles that define the character of the school and influence how people interact, learn, and lead.

- **Strategic School Goals**: Ambitious yet attainable goals that translate the school's vision into focused, measurable progress.
- **Cultivated Trust and Respect**: Intentional efforts to build meaningful relationships rooted in mutual respect and psychological safety.
- **Open and Effective Communication**: Transparent, consistent, and welcoming communication practices that connect and empower all stakeholders.
- **Vibrant and Positive Atmosphere**: A culture that is energized, joyful, and supportive, where positivity is felt and shared daily.
- **Welcoming and Safe Environment**: A school climate where every person feels seen, valued, and secure, regardless of background or identity.
- **Recognition of Achievements**: Systems and traditions that regularly celebrate progress, effort, and excellence—big and small.
- **Empowered Leadership**: Providing opportunities for students, staff, and families to lead in ways that reflect the school's vision and values.
- **Commitment to Growth**: A culture of continuous improvement that embraces feedback, learning, and forward movement at every level.

Shaping Success: From Default to Intentional Thinking in School SelfCulture

At the beginning of this Leadership Manual, we introduced a powerful concept that will frame your entire Strategic School Map journey: **Default Thinking vs. Intentional Thinking**.

This is the first of twelve anchor explorations (six Inward, six Outward), and each one will include a **Mindset Question** rooted in this thinking framework. This section is the only time we'll walk through the full explanation. After this, the reflection questions will stand on their own.

Let's revisit the guiding principle:

Default Thinking is passive. It's like **operating on auto-pilot**, relying on inherited norms, surface-level routines, and unexamined assumptions. In this mindset, school culture becomes something that happens to you, rather than something you intentionally shape. Instead of leading your culture, you react to it.

And here's the key point:

When you live in default thinking, outside forces define its culture. Whether it's shifting student behavior, staff burnout, conflicting personalities, or community pressure: your SelfCulture, vision, mission, principles, core values, and goals will be shaped by whatever is loudest, most urgent, or most convenient in the moment.

The result?
A school culture that is **random, inconsistent, and directionless.**

It sounds like:

- "This is just the way things are."
- "We'll handle problems when they come up."
- "There's no need to change what's working, for now."

In contrast, **Intentional Thinking** is proactive, purpose-driven, and principle-centered. It's about **leading with intentionality**: choosing each action and decision with alignment, clarity, and care. This mindset invites every member of the school community to align their thinking and actions with clearly defined beliefs and aspirations. With intentional thinking, culture becomes something you **design on purpose**. It is not something you inherit by default.

This mindset asks:

- "What kind of culture are we choosing to build together?"
- "Are our beliefs, words, and actions aligned with our guiding principles?"
- "What do we want to be known for: and how are we reinforcing that every day?"

This shift from **operating on auto-pilot to leading with intentionality** is not a one-time decision. It's a **daily practice**. It's foundational to building your Inward and Outward Maps, and ultimately, your Strategic School Map (SSM).

When schools embrace intentional thinking:

- Foundational principles are clearly defined and shared
- Culture is cohesive, focused, and purpose-driven
- Change is led from the **Inside-Out**—not dictated by external pressure
- Everyone knows the "why" behind their work

As you begin mapping your school's SelfCulture, pause and reflect:

Are we letting outside forces define who we are, or are we choosing our direction with purpose?

School SelfCulture Mindset Question

Which type of thinking does your school use – Default or Intentional?

- **Default Thinking:**

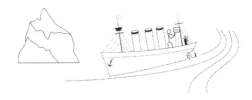

"Our school culture is fine, and when we see it's slipping, we address it."

This mindset is reactive. It may maintain the status quo, but it often leads to missed opportunities and delayed responses. The culture becomes something that's adjusted only when problems arise, rather than something that is intentionally shaped every day. In many schools, this thinking doesn't feel "wrong"; it feels normal. That's the trap. Without realizing it, the school starts slipping into a culture shaped by habit instead of intention.

- **Intentional Thinking:**

"Our school culture is a top priority, and we have the will and tools to continually move toward a school culture that is positive and effective, propelling Peacefulness, Happiness, Healthiness, and Excellence (PH2E)."

This proactive stance centers culture as a daily strategic priority. It reflects a shared commitment to improvement, clarity, and alignment, where actions and decisions are grounded in principles, not just policies or programs.

Why This Matters

Most school teams don't choose default thinking. It often starts subtly. One small decision. One tough week. One missed opportunity to reset. Then another. And slowly, **the school begins slipping into default mode**, where culture is left to form on its own.

When that happens, **outside forces begin to define who you are**, and not always in ways that align with your mission. Over time, this creates an identity that is reactive, scattered, and disconnected from the school's highest aspirations.

When a school embraces intentional thinking, the SelfCulture becomes clear and aligned. Strategic decisions reflect shared purpose. Language is consistent. Energy is focused. The community begins to see the difference—and feel it.

As you review each anchor, the mindset questions are designed to spark honest reflection and guide your school from default habits to intentional alignment. They help uncover where thinking may be reactive or unclear, so that strategic action can follow. If your school resonates, even slightly, with the default thinking side, **you are not alone**. That is why this book exists: to offer practical guidance for each anchor, helping you move from scattered to aligned and from intention to impact.

Your school's culture is already forming—every day. The real question is: Are you letting it slip into default and operating on autopilot, or are you leading it with intention?

Guided Reflections: Navigating Each Anchor with Intention

As you draft and refine your Strategic School Map, anchored by both the Inward and Outward School Maps, self-reflection becomes an essential part of the process. That's why each anchor in this Leadership Manual includes a series of strategic thinking questions.

These questions are designed to help you slow down, look inward, and think deeply about how your current practices align with your school's identity, purpose, and aspirations.

We begin with SelfCulture because it is the foundation for everything else. The questions that follow will guide you in uncovering the strengths and gaps in your current culture and help you begin to articulate the identity your school community truly wants to live by.

By making space for reflective dialogue, both individually and as a team, you strengthen the intentionality behind your map. This reflection ensures that your school culture is not left to chance. It is actively shaped with clarity, alignment, and purpose.

Let's begin with the strategic thinking questions for **Inward Anchor 1: School SelfCulture**.

Strategic Thinking Questions for Inward School Anchor 1: School SelfCulture

Vision and Identity Reflection:

1. *What words or phrases currently describe our school's identity?*

___

2. *How does the identity we envision align (or misalign) with our current practices and environment?*

___

3. *What principles and beliefs most clearly define our school culture?*

___

Aspirations and Perceptions:

1. *What are our school's highest aspirations in terms of culture, achievement, and community impact?*

   _____
   _____
   _____
   _____
   _____
   _____

2. *How do we want our school to be perceived by students, families, staff, and the wider community?*

   _____
   _____
   _____
   _____
   _____
   _____

3. *In what ways can we foster a deeper sense of belonging, pride, and positivity for everyone who enters our school?*

   _____
   _____
   _____
   _____
   _____
   _____

Experience and Environment:

1. *How do we want students, staff, and visitors to feel when they walk into our school?*

_____
_____
_____
_____
_____
_____

2. *What intentional actions can we take to ensure our environment reflects our shared principles and aspirations?*

_____
_____
_____
_____
_____
_____

Leadership and Relationships:

1. *How can leadership at all levels (students, staff, admin) shape and support the culture we want to create?*

_____
_____
_____
_____
_____
_____

2. *What strategies can we implement to build high trust, respectful and supportive relationships within our school community?*

___

3. *How do we currently celebrate achievements, and who is involved in this process?*

___

Continuous Improvement:

1. *What structures or routines promote a culture of continuous improvement across all levels of the school?*

___

2. *How do we intentionally build habits of reflection and growth into our daily practices as individuals and teams?*

_____
_____
_____
_____
_____
_____
_____

Brand and Symbols:

1. *How well do our school's visual elements, such as logos, mascots, colors, and traditions, align with our mission and vision?*

_____
_____
_____
_____
_____
_____

2. *Are there symbols or traditions that need to evolve to better represent who we are and where we're going?*

_____
_____
_____
_____
_____
_____

Establishing the Foundation:
Initial Drafts of Your SelfCulture Statement

Now that you've reflected on the identity, beliefs, and aspirations that shape your school's culture, it's time to begin drafting your SelfCulture Statement: a clear and inspiring reflection of who you are and what you stand for as a school community.

This initial draft is not meant to be final. **Don't overthink it.** Let your thoughts flow naturally, capturing your instinctive reflections on your school's current culture and your highest hopes for where it can grow. This is a starting point: an early articulation of your identity that will evolve over time.

As you continue working through the remaining Inward Anchors: **School Vision, Daily School Mission, School Leadership Principles, School Core Values, and School Goals**, you'll gain new insights and clarity. After completing all 6 Inward Anchors, you'll return to this SelfCulture Statement and refine it, ensuring it reflects a fully developed and integrated school identity.

> **Anchor Note**: Your **SelfCulture Statement** is intended primarily for **internal use** by leadership teams and guiding coalitions. It provides the foundational compass for shaping policies, practices, and internal decision-making. While your **School Vision, Mission, Leadership Principles, and Core Values** are meant to be shared broadly and communicated across the school community, your SelfCulture Statement offers internal alignment and coherence.
>
> **School Goals** may include both internal strategic targets and public-facing objectives, depending on their focus and intended audience.

This SelfCulture Statement will serve as the foundation of your Inward School Map. Let it evolve alongside your strategic work, and revisit it regularly as your school continues to grow with intention and purpose.

Initial Thoughts for Your School SelfCulture Statement:

___
___
___
___
___
___
___
___
___
___
___
___
___
___
___
___
___
___
___

SelfCulture Statement Examples:

The following are examples of SelfCulture Statements, each beginning with a memorable motto:

1. Empowering Unity and Excellence:

"In our school, every hallway whispers stories of unity, respect, and mutual support, creating a tapestry of shared principles and values that uplifts everyone. Here, academic excellence is pursued with passion, and personal growth is nurtured with compassion. Our culture thrives on the aspiration to foster an environment where students, staff, and parents are empowered to achieve their fullest potential, contribute to a dynamic community, and embark on continuous journeys of learning and improvement. We are committed to cultivating a school identity that thrives on the power of belonging, the strength of character, and the pursuit of excellence."

2. Cultivating Compassionate Leaders:

"Our school is a training ground for developing compassionate leaders who are ready to face the challenges of tomorrow with integrity and innovation. We are dedicated to building a culture that values empathy, encourages ethical leadership, and inspires every individual to act with kindness and responsibility. Through a shared commitment to our core values and goals, we strive to create a welcoming and supportive environment that prepares students not only for academic success but for meaningful contributions to society. Our aspirational culture is one where leadership is cultivated in every classroom and integrity guides every decision."

3. Fostering a Culture of Belonging and Achievement:

"At the heart of our school lies a deeply rooted belief in the power of belonging: a culture where every student, teacher, and staff member feels valued, understood, and connected. We will aspire to weave a fabric of belonging and achievement, where unique talents are celebrated, and academic excellence is achieved together. We envision a school where the joy of learning is ubiquitous, and the pursuit of personal and collective goals drives us forward. Our commitment is to an educational journey that uplifts, inspires, and propels everyone toward their highest aspirations in a safe, dynamic, and positive environment."

4. Inspiring Innovation and Creativity:

"Our school stands as a beacon of innovation and creativity, where boundaries are expanded, and ideas flourish. We aspire to cultivate a culture that embraces change, encourages risk-taking, and nurtures the inventive spirits of our students and staff. By fostering an environment that supports critical thinking and creative problem-solving, we aim to prepare our community for a future where they not only thrive but lead with vision and resilience. Our culture statement reflects our dedication to inspiring each member of our school to dream big, explore uncharted territories, and achieve groundbreaking success."

5. Building a Legacy of Responsibility and Respect:

"Within the walls of our school, we are crafting a legacy of responsibility and respect: a culture where every action is taken with consideration for others and the world around us. Our aspiration is to instill a deep sense of social responsibility in our students, encouraging them to lead with respect, empathy, and a commitment to positive change. By aligning our school's goals, values, and principles towards this mission, we strive to develop not just scholars but conscientious citizens who are prepared to make ethical, impactful contributions to their communities and beyond. Our culture is one of proactive engagement, mindful leadership, and a relentless pursuit of excellence, defined by the respect and responsibility we hold for ourselves and each other."

6. Centering the Whole Child, Every Day

"We are committed to nurturing the whole child: intellectually, socially, emotionally, and physically. Our SelfCulture prioritizes relationships, wellness, and joy in learning, knowing these are essential for long-term success. By centering the needs and gifts of every student, we build a culture of healthiness, peacefulness, and academic achievement that lasts well beyond the classroom."

The SelfCulture Anchor Model

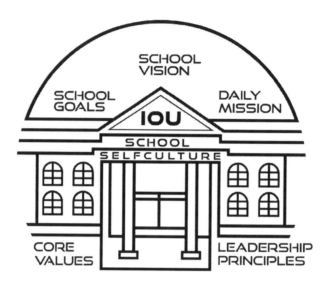

SelfCulture: Rooted in the Principle of Self-Identity

The Principle of Self-Identity is about knowing who you are at your core—your beliefs, values, and purpose. *Self-Identity* means living and leading from that internal clarity rather than reacting to external pressures. It is about being grounded in your "I" before influencing others through action. This principle reminds us that schools, like people, have a cultural identity that either forms by default or by design. For the SelfCulture anchor, Self-Identity ensures that a school's internal beliefs and guiding principles are consistently reflected in daily experiences, interactions, and decisions. It's what transforms abstract ideals into a living, breathing culture.

Where Identity Lives and Leadership Begins

At the center of every IOU School is its **SelfCulture**: the central anchor that reflects and drives the school's unique identity, purpose, and daily experiences. This model is a visual representation of how the IOU 6 Inward School Anchors work together, with SelfCulture as the unifying force that shapes all other components.

Imagine the front of your school. Above the doorway are the words: **"IOU School SelfCulture"**

The structure is built as follows:

- **The Foundation**:
  The base of the school rests on two critical anchors: **Leadership Principles** and **Core Values**. These foundational principles support every decision, interaction, and expectation across the school community.

- **The Roof**:
  Sitting above are **Daily School Mission**, **School Vision**, and **School Goals**: the guiding forces that give direction, clarity, and aspiration to your daily actions and long-term purpose.

- **The Center—SelfCulture**:
  SelfCulture is the living expression of all five other anchors combined. It is where principles, vision, mission, values, and goals come together in action. It represents how your school community experiences and lives its identity every day: in the way students are greeted, how classrooms are run, how traditions are honored, and how people feel when they walk through your halls.

This visual model helps leaders and teams:

- Ground discussions in a shared mental map
- See how each anchor is connected and interdependent
- Align future decisions with the school's SelfCulture
- Reflect on where coherence is strong and where it needs to be strengthened

Use the **SelfCulture Anchor Model** during planning sessions, team reflections, and strategic discussions. Let it guide how you think, how you lead, and how you live your school's identity from the inside out.

The Guiding Question for School SelfCulture:

If someone walked through the front doors of your school today, without reading a handbook or talking to an administrator, what would your SelfCulture tell them about who you are and what you stand for?

Transitioning to Anchor 2: School Vision

Now that you've clarified your school's SelfCulture: the foundation of identity and internal alignment, it's time to look ahead.

We next turn our focus toward the critical Inward Anchor: **School Vision**.

This anchor is the beacon that illuminates your school's **purpose**, **potential**, and **passion**. It serves as a guiding light, shaping the direction and aspirations of your educational community.

By clearly defining your School Vision, you articulate what drives your work, what you aim to achieve, and what ignites your collective enthusiasm. This vision sets the stage for a journey of alignment, transformation, and achievement: uniting you in a shared quest to realize the full potential of your school and its members.

Inward School Anchor 2

SCHOOL VISION

The Principle of Life Living

Your vision will become clear only when you can look into your own heart. Who looks outside, dreams; who looks inside, awakes.
—Carl Jung

School Vision: Embracing the Principle of Life Living to Chart Our Future

The Principle of Life Living forms the foundation of your **School Vision**. It calls us to look inward and define a future that reflects the school's highest aspirations: one that uplifts students, teachers, and families, and shapes the day-to-day culture of the school.

Life Living means creating a vision that embodies the **purpose, potential**, and **passion** of the school community. It provides direction for daily decisions while inspiring long-term achievement. A strong School Vision goes beyond words on a wall. It becomes a shared compass that aligns people, priorities, and possibilities.

A School Vision steers the school toward its ideal attainment of excellence. It projects a future where **academic achievement is celebrated, personal growth is nurtured**, and **every individual is empowered** to contribute meaningfully to the school and the world beyond.

Integrated with school anchors three through six which include Daily School Mission, School Leadership Principles, School Core Values, and School Goals, your vision becomes more than a distant dream. It becomes a cohesive, guiding force that aligns all aspects of school life, connecting identity with action.

As a main component of the Inward School Map (ISM), the School Vision ensures that your direction is not only clear and ambitious but also grounded in the collective aspirations of the community. It's not just about where the school is going; it's about who you are becoming along the way.

By embracing the Principle of Life Living, your vision remains a living force, constantly inviting reflection and renewal. It inspires each member of the school to reach beyond comfort zones, contribute with passion, and pursue a shared vision of growth, unity, and excellence. In doing so, you shape a school culture where everyone is inspired to aspire.

Purpose + Potential + Passion = School Vision

The Principle of Life Living centers on inspiring and nurturing the *purpose*, *potential*, and *passion* of every member of the school community: students, teachers, staff, leaders, and families. This principle moves the School Vision beyond a statement on paper to a dynamic force that drives meaning, energy, and aspiration throughout your culture.

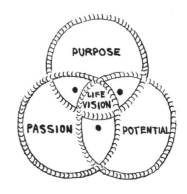

- **Purpose** reflects *why* your school exists: your foundational reason for being, rooted in your deepest beliefs and long-term impact.
- **Potential** speaks to *what your school can become*: the strengths, talents, and possibilities waiting to be cultivated and realized.
- **Passion** fuels *how you pursue that vision*: with enthusiasm, commitment, and a sense of inspiration that energizes the entire community.

When the three forces of purpose, potential, and passion are clearly defined and aligned, they become the backbone of a School Vision that guides strategic decisions and inspires both daily actions and long-term growth.

Your vision becomes a motivator and a mirror of your community's highest aspirations. In an IOU School Culture, this kind of vision is the beacon that lights the way forward, shaping not just what you do, but who you become.

Defining the Essence of a Robust IOU School Vision

A powerful School Vision is intentional. It provides focus, energizes the community, and aligns decisions with long-term aspirations. Below are the key characteristics of an IOU-aligned vision that embodies the Principle of Life Living:

- **Purpose-Driven Direction**: Clearly articulates the school's reason for being: its mission, values, and long-term aspirations, and serves as the compass for every decision and strategic initiative.
- **Future-Oriented Goals**: Suggests ambitious, yet achievable, goals that reflect where the school is headed and what success looks like in the years to come.
- **Inspirational Leadership**: Encourages leaders at all levels to champion the vision, creating unity and shared ownership across the entire community.

- **Community Engagement**: Welcomes input and involvement from students, families, staff, and community partners to build buy-in and shared commitment.
- **Alignment with Educational Programs**: Seamlessly connects the vision to academic and extracurricular programs, ensuring a consistent, principle-driven experience.
- **Community Alignment:** Reflects the unique identity of the school community and reinforces a sense of belonging, pride, and shared values.
- **Motivational Influence**: Serves as a source of energy, helping the community stay inspired, focused, and driven toward excellence and innovation.
- **Embracing Everyone:** Honors the perspectives, experiences, and contributions of all members within the school community, ensuring that the vision reflects and supports everyone.
- **Sustainability and Adaptability**: Stands the test of time while remaining flexible, capable of evolving as the school grows and new opportunities emerge.
- **Visibility and Communication**: Is consistently shared, visible, and reinforced throughout the school, including in conversations, on walls, and in daily practice.

Together, these characteristics form a vision that is forward-thinking and lived daily, guiding the entire school community toward its greatest collective future.

School Vision Mindset Question

Which type of thinking does your school use – Default or Intentional?

- **Default Thinking:**

"Things are going fine, we're doing well, so there's no urgent need to revisit our vision."

This mindset feels safe. It maintains current practices and only prompts action when something breaks. But without intentional review and refinement, your school vision risks becoming outdated, misaligned, or invisible, missing opportunities to guide culture, inspire growth, or fuel innovation.

- **Intentional Thinking:**

*"Our school's future is intentionally crafted with a clear **purpose** and **passion**, driven to maximize our **potential**."*

This proactive mindset recognizes that a compelling, shared vision is not a luxury—it's a leadership necessity. It guides strategic decisions, unites the school community, and keeps purpose, potential, and passion at the center of everything you do.

Why This Matters

When default thinking sets in, a school's vision often fades into the background: outdated, underused, or unknown by those it's meant to inspire. Over time, outside pressures or habits begin to shape direction by default, leading to drift, confusion, or misalignment across the community.

Intentional thinking invites leaders to reclaim the vision as an active, daily force. It shifts the mindset from "We have a vision statement" to "Our vision shapes who we are, what we do, and where we're going." It's about unlocking what's possible.

**Strategic Thinking Questions for
Inward Anchor 2:
School Vision**

Purpose + Potential + Passion = School Vision

Purpose:

1. *What is the fundamental purpose of our school? How can we clearly articulate this purpose to inspire all stakeholders?*

_____
_____
_____
_____
_____
_____

2. *How do we want our school to impact the lives of our students and the broader community in the next five years?*

_____
_____
_____
_____
_____
_____

3. *What core values and principles guide our daily operations and long-term goals?*

_____
_____
_____
_____
_____
_____

4. *What gives our school's existence meaning, and how do we communicate this effectively?*

_____
_____
_____
_____
_____
_____

Potential:

1. *What strengths, talents, and unique abilities exist across our school community, and how can we better use them to support our vision?*

_____
_____
_____
_____
_____
_____

2. *Where do we see the greatest potential for growth and improvement, both academically and within our school culture?*

_____
_____
_____
_____
_____
_____

3. *What intentional steps can we take to help students, staff, and families realize their full potential?*

_____
_____
_____
_____
_____
_____

4. *What systems, supports, or mindsets might we need to adjust to unlock more of our community's potential?*

_____
_____
_____
_____
_____
_____

Passion:

1. *What inspires and excites our students, staff, and families to be part of this school community?*

_____
_____
_____
_____
_____
_____

2. *How can we intentionally integrate that passion into our school vision, programs, and culture?*

_____
_____
_____
_____
_____
_____

3. *What traditions, initiatives, or learning experiences could we create to ignite and sustain enthusiasm for learning and growth?*

_____
_____
_____
_____
_____
_____

4. *How do we recognize and celebrate the passions, contributions, and successes of our school community in ways that reinforce our vision?*

_____
_____
_____
_____
_____
_____

Establishing the Foundation:
Early Drafts of Your School Vision Statement

At this point in your journey, you likely already have a vision statement for your school. You may have inherited it, helped create it, or revised it over time. Whatever the case, now is the time to look at it with fresh eyes.

Now that you've reflected on your school's **purpose, potential, and passion,** we invite you to revisit your current vision statement, or begin drafting one if it doesn't yet exist. How well does it reflect what you've just explored? What might you enhance or clarify based on your deepened understanding of your school's aspirations?

This may not be about rewriting your school's vision statement—at least not at this time. Instead, think of this exercise as an internal leadership tool, a way for your leadership team to reflect, align, and reconnect with your school's higher purpose. Use this draft process to spark meaningful dialogue, uncover assumptions, and build shared clarity. Whether or not you revise your official vision down the line, this reflection will strengthen the foundation of your leadership.

This is a working draft, not a final statement. Let it capture authentic insights about what your school is truly striving toward. Don't overthink or aim for perfection. Be bold. Be hopeful.

As you work through the remaining Inward Anchors: **Daily School Mission, School Leadership Principles, School Core Values, and School Goals**, your vision will continue to sharpen. When you return to revise this draft later, it will be even more powerful, enriched by the full picture of your school's identity.

Remember: your school vision should be aspirational and enduring. **It provides direction and inspiration for everyone in your school community**: leaders, staff, students, and families alike. But for now, let this be a reflective exercise; it will serve as a tool to realign and reenergize your school from the inside out.

For now, let this first draft be authentic, bold, and hopeful.

Initial Thoughts for Your School Vision Statement:

_____
_____
_____
_____
_____
_____
_____
_____
_____
_____
_____
_____
_____
_____
_____
_____
_____
_____

School Vision Statement Examples

The following are examples of School Vision Statements, each beginning with a memorable motto:

1. Empowering Lifelong Learners:
"Our school envisions a future where every student is empowered to become a lifelong learner, equipped with the skills and mindsets needed to thrive in an ever-changing world. We aspire to cultivate curiosity, resilience, and a love for learning, ensuring all members of our community grow with purpose, lead with integrity, and contribute meaningfully to society."

2. Inspiring Global Citizens:
"Our vision is to nurture compassionate, curious, and globally minded individuals who think critically and act responsibly. We strive to build a learning environment that embraces individual differences, fosters collaboration, and encourages students to engage with the world around them, preparing them to contribute positively to a connected and ever-evolving global society."

3. Fostering Excellence and Innovation:
"We envision our school as a hub of creativity, excellence, and forward-thinking education. Through bold ideas and a relentless pursuit of improvement, we aim to empower students and educators to lead with confidence, solve real-world problems, and shape the future with innovation, integrity, and purpose."

4. Building a Thriving Community:
"Our school aims to be a thriving community where students, staff, and parents are united by a shared commitment to excellence, respect, and mutual support. We strive to create a safe and welcoming environment that values each individual's unique talents and perspectives, fostering a strong sense of belonging and pride in our school."

5. Cultivating Leaders of Tomorrow:
"Our vision is to develop future leaders who are confident, compassionate, and driven by a sense of purpose. We seek to provide an education that not only imparts knowledge but also builds character, encouraging students to take initiative, embrace challenges, and lead with empathy and conviction."

6. Excellence Through Inquiry. Purpose Through Learning:
"Our vision is to cultivate a community of critical thinkers, problem-solvers, and lifelong learners who pursue academic excellence with integrity and purpose. We are committed to providing a rigorous and engaging curriculum that challenges every student, fosters deep inquiry, and prepares all learners to succeed in a complex, knowledge-driven world."

7. A Community of Learners, A Culture of Growth.
"Our vision is to be a community where learning is a shared pursuit and academic growth is embraced by all: students, educators, families, board members, and staff alike. Through high expectations, reflective practice, and a relentless commitment to continuous improvement, we foster a culture where every individual is both a learner and a leader."

The School Vision Anchor Model

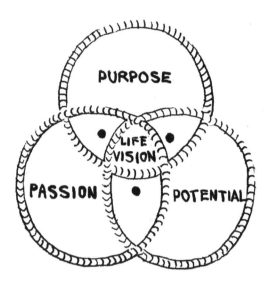

School Vision: Rooted in the Principle of Life Living

The Principle of Life Living is about leading with a clear sense of purpose, recognizing potential, and fueling passion. *Life Living* means fully engaging in the present while intentionally shaping the future. It is about living each day with meaning, direction, and a belief in growth. This principle reminds us that schools operate as living communities, shaped by belief, energy, and long-term impact. For the School Vision anchor, Life Living ensures your vision reflects more than just goals. It brings into focus the *why*, *what if*, and *what could be* that energize your school's journey forward.

Bringing Purpose, Potential, and Passion into Focus

The **School Vision Model** visually represents the essence of your school's long-term direction. Grounded in the **Principle of Life Living**, this model centers on the intersection of **Purpose**, **Potential**, and **Passion**—three essential elements that shape an intentional and aspirational School Vision.

- **Purpose** reflects your school's broader reason for being. It includes long-term hopes and the positive impact your school seeks to make in the

lives of students. It captures the 'why' that anchors your vision beyond day-to-day operations.
- **Potential** represents the unique strengths and capabilities within your school community. It reflects your belief in continuous growth and the capacity to improve and achieve excellence.
- **Passion** is the energy that drives engagement, enthusiasm, and meaning. It fuels the desire to inspire learning, foster creativity, and create a vibrant culture of contribution.

When these three forces align, they form a powerful School Vision that serves as a guiding light, informing strategic decisions, inspiring the community, and keeping the school centered through change.

This model serves as a reflection tool for leadership teams. Use it to ask:

- Are we clear on our purpose?
- Are we tapping into our community's full potential?
- Are we leading with passion and authenticity?

Keep this model visible in your planning spaces. Revisit it regularly to ensure that your strategic goals and school culture initiatives remain connected to your deeper vision.

Let this serve as both a compass and a conversation starter. It will help you lead with intention and align your entire community toward an Upward Dynamic Positive Culture.

The Guiding Questions for School Vision:

If someone asked anyone in your school, students, teachers, or parents, what your vision is and why it matters, would they know?

Could they feel it in your everyday practices and priorities?

Transitioning to Anchor 3: Daily School Mission

If your School Vision sets your destination, your long-term purpose, potential, and passion, your Daily School Mission is what propels you toward it, one day at a time. It's not just a statement on the wall; it's a living everyday commitment that answers three essential questions:

4. **Who are we impacting?**
5. **What are we doing?**
6. **And what is the byproduct we expect from our efforts?**

While **vision is future-oriented**, your **mission is present-focused**. It defines the daily actions, decisions, and interactions that bring your aspirations to life. A clear, intentional Daily School Mission ensures that every stakeholder: students, staff, and families, knows how their work contributes to the larger purpose.

This anchor challenges you to reflect on whether your mission is visible, actionable, and integrated into daily life. When your mission aligns with your vision and principles, it becomes a steady force that grounds your team and unites your school culture.

Let's explore how to craft a Daily School Mission that is clear, purposeful, and lived every single day.

Inward School Anchor 3

DAILY SCHOOL MISSION

The Principle of Intentional Actions

*A leader is one who knows the way, goes the way,
and shows the way.*
—John Maxwell

Daily School Mission: Turning Vision Into Daily Practice

The **Principle of Intentional Actions** reminds us that long-term success is shaped by short-term choices. While a compelling School Vision sets the destination, the **Daily School Mission** defines the consistent, purpose-driven actions that move a school community forward—*every day*.

This anchor reinforces that a school's mission isn't a one-time statement or a poster on the wall; it's a living, everyday commitment. It requires every student, staff member, and leader to act with clarity and intention, ensuring that the school's principles and goals are reflected in its routines, relationships, and decisions.

By placing the word *"Daily"* before *"School Mission,"* we emphasize that this anchor is about what actually happens in classrooms, hallways, and conversations every single day. It bridges vision and action through three essential questions:

- **Who are we impacting?**
- **What are we doing?**
- **What is the intended byproduct of those efforts?**

This simple formula—**Who + What + Byproduct = Daily School Mission**—serves as a clear and actionable framework for aligning your school's daily actions with its long-term vision.

As one of the 6 Essential Inward Anchors, the Daily School Mission plays a pivotal role in shaping your Inward School Map (ISM)—your internal blueprint for culture, clarity, and excellence. The ISM is not complete without this anchor, as it transforms inward identity into observable, real-time behaviors. This is how culture is lived—not just defined.

When clearly articulated and embraced, the **Daily School Mission turns school culture from aspiration into action**. It guarantees that your school's other Inward Anchors: Vision, Leadership Principles, Core Values, and Goals, are reflected in the rhythm of everyday life.

By adopting the Principle of Intentional Actions, schools commit to consistency, alignment, and meaningful impact. They create an environment where each day is an opportunity to lead, learn, and live with purpose.

Clarifying the Three Elements of the Daily School Mission

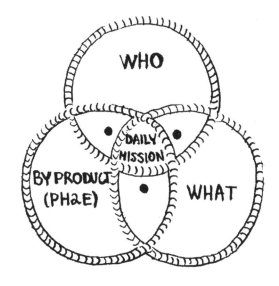

Who + What + Byproduct = Daily School Mission

To bring your Daily School Mission to life, you must define three essential components:

- **Who** – Who are the people most directly impacted by your daily efforts? While students are central, your mission should also reflect your commitment to teachers, support staff, families, and community partners.
- **What** – What are you doing intentionally and consistently to move the school forward? These include the systems, routines, conversations, and actions aligned with your principles and values.
- **Byproduct** – What results do you strive to create? Think beyond academics: include emotional safety, pride, joy, belonging, and leadership. These byproducts represent the experiences and outcomes you hope your school community feels each day.

These three elements do not exist in isolation—they intersect.

Your **Daily School Mission** lives at the center of this intersection: where *who* you serve, *what* you do, and *why* it matters all come together with clarity and purpose. When these elements are clearly defined and lived with consistency, your mission becomes a practical, energizing guide for everyday decisions and collective momentum.

Defining Features of a Robust IOU Daily School Mission

A strong Daily School Mission is not abstract; it is felt, seen, and lived in the halls, classrooms, and conversations every single day. It drives how staff members interact, how students engage, and how the community experiences school life.

Below are the defining features of a well-developed IOU Daily School Mission:

- **Focused Intentionality**: Daily actions are purposeful, not habitual. Every decision reflects the school's foundational beliefs and long-term goals.
- **Clear Objectives and Tasks**: Staff and students understand the specific actions expected each day to move the school toward its vision.
- **Daily Reflection and Adjustment**: There's space built into the culture for pausing, assessing, and course-correcting—no day is wasted.
- **Collaborative Effort**: Everyone shares responsibility for the mission. Success is collective and dependent on all individuals.
- **Student-Centered Actions**: The needs, growth, and voices of students are at the heart of daily decisions and practices.
- **Staff Engagement and Empowerment**: Staff not only execute a plan—they help shape it. Their leadership and ideas matter every day.
- **Community Involvement**: Parents and partners are invited into the mission, with opportunities to participate meaningfully in school life.
- **Effective Communication**: Clear, consistent messaging reinforces what matters most—helping everyone stay aligned in their actions.
- **Celebration of Daily Achievements**: Big wins and small steps are recognized and celebrated, fueling momentum and morale.
- **Adaptability and Flexibility**: Intentionality doesn't mean rigidity. The school adapts with awareness, responding to real-time needs without losing sight of the mission.

Together, these features form the structure of a mission that is lived rather than laminated. When embraced consistently, they help turn daily routines into a powerful expression of your school's identity, vision, and values.

> *"Your mission is not what you write—it's what you live, every day."*
> —Dr. Joe Famularo

Daily School Mission Mindset Question

Which type of thinking does your school use – Default or Intentional?

- **Default Thinking:**

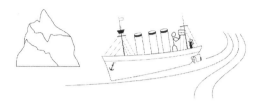

"We assume everyone is on the same page about what matters each day, so we haven't defined a Daily School Mission."

This mindset assumes alignment without verifying it. While built on trust, it often leads to disconnected efforts, inconsistent practices, and a school culture that drifts rather than everyday acts on its mission.

- **Intentional Thinking:**

"Each day is an opportunity to move closer to our vision through purposeful, shared action of our Daily School Mission."

This mindset promotes clarity, cohesion, and accountability; it turns daily routines into intentional steps forward, and every stakeholder contributes to a **living mission rooted in every action and behavior.**

Why This Matters

Most schools don't ignore their mission on purpose, it simply fades into the background. Without a clear, daily school mission that's lived out intentionally, people start to fill in the gaps. Teachers focus on their classrooms. Leaders juggle tasks. Students go through routines. And slowly, the school's direction becomes fragmented.

That's what happens when default thinking creeps in.

Without a shared daily purpose, actions become reactive, efforts are disconnected, and good intentions don't always translate into aligned results. When a school embraces the **Principle of Intentional Actions**, something powerful happens:

- Every day has **meaning.**
- Every action has **direction**.
- Everyone understands **how their work connects to the school's broader vision.**

Then the **Daily School Mission** becomes a rhythm. A habit. A compass for daily practice.

If your school resonates, even slightly, with the default mindset, that's okay. This process isn't about judgment. It's about awakening a more powerful way to lead. Through the anchors ahead, you'll build a mission that grounds your daily work in clarity, energy, and collective momentum.

Your school is already doing important work each day.
The question is: **Are those daily actions propelling you toward your vision—or just keeping things afloat?**

**Strategic Thinking Questions for
Inward School Anchor 3:
Daily School Mission**

Who + What + Byproduct = Daily School Mission

Most schools already have a mission statement, perhaps inherited, collaboratively written, or developed years ago. This anchor invites you to look at that statement with a fresh lens. By focusing on what happens *every day*, and applying the Who + What + Byproduct framework, you can begin shaping a mission that feels more grounded, practical, and alive in your school's daily rhythms.

These questions are designed to help your leadership team reflect deeply on how your school's everyday actions align with your long-term vision. Use them as a tool to begin drafting a Daily School Mission that is intentional, reflective of your values, and energizing for your entire school community.

Who:

1. *Who are the primary individuals or groups we aim to impact with our daily mission?*

_____
_____
_____
_____
_____
_____

2. *How can we ensure that our daily actions positively affect the well-being and growth of our students, staff, and the broader community?*

_____
_____
_____
_____
_____
_____

3. *Who needs the most support and attention today, and how can we address their needs effectively?*

_____
_____
_____
_____
_____
_____

4. *Who are the key stakeholders we need to engage and collaborate with daily to achieve our mission?*

_____
_____
_____
_____
_____
_____

What:

1. *What specific actions and tasks do we need to undertake today to move closer to our school vision?*

_____
_____
_____
_____
_____
_____

2. *What daily practices can we implement to foster a culture of continuous improvement and excellence?*

_____
_____
_____
_____
_____
_____

3. *What resources and tools are necessary for our staff and students to achieve our daily school mission?*

_____
_____
_____
_____
_____
_____

4. *What new initiatives or adjustments can we introduce to strengthen our daily operations and outcomes?*

_____
_____
_____
_____
_____
_____

Byproduct:

1. *What positive outcomes do we aim to achieve through our daily actions, and how can we measure these successes?*

_____
_____
_____
_____
_____
_____

2. *How can we ensure that our daily mission contributes to the overall well-being, happiness, and success of our school community?*

_____
_____
_____
_____
_____
_____

3. *What indicators will show that our daily efforts are aligned with our long-term vision and goals?*

_____

_____

_____

_____

_____

_____

4. *How can we celebrate and recognize the daily achievements and contributions of our students, staff, and community members?*

_____

_____

_____

_____

_____

_____

Establishing the Foundation:
Early Drafts of Your Daily School Mission Statement

Now that you've explored the central components of your Daily School Mission, including **Who** you serve, **What** you do, and the **Byproduct** you aim to create, it's time to begin shaping your first draft.

Just like with your School Vision, you likely already have a mission statement. It may have served your school well, but this exercise isn't about replacing it just yet. Instead, think of this as an opportunity to examine it through a new, more focused lens: *Is our mission being lived out every day? Does it reflect how we lead, learn, and serve in real time?*

This draft is not final—it's a starting point. Let your ideas flow. Capture what your school is striving to do on an ordinary day, not just in moments of big change. This is your chance to describe how your school community shows up with purpose.

As you continue developing the remaining Inward Anchors: School Leadership Principles, Core Values, and Goals, you'll gain even more clarity. You'll return to this draft with new insight and can fine-tune it to reflect your school's full identity and direction.

Right now, your goal is simple: Put words to how your school shows up each day. Picture your leadership team walking through the halls on an average day. *What are you seeing? What are you doing? What ripple effects are those actions having?*

Let this be the first step toward a Daily School Mission that is not only thoughtful—but lived, shared, and deeply felt.

Initial Thoughts for Your School Daily Mission Statement:

_____
_____
_____
_____
_____
_____
_____
_____
_____
_____
_____
_____
_____
_____
_____
_____
_____
_____
_____

Daily School Mission Statement Examples

The following are examples of School Mission Statements, each beginning with a memorable motto:

1. Cultivating a Safe and Supportive Environment:
"Today, we commit to ensuring the safety and well-being of every student and staff member. By fostering a supportive and welcoming environment, we aim to create a space where everyone feels valued and respected. Our daily actions will reflect our dedication to maintaining a secure and nurturing school community."

2. Promoting Academic Excellence:
"Our mission today is to inspire and challenge our students to reach their highest academic potential. Through engaging lessons, thoughtful feedback, and supportive resources, we will cultivate an atmosphere of curiosity and achievement, ensuring every student is empowered to succeed."

3. Fostering Positive Relationships:
Today, we focus on building and strengthening relationships within our school community. We will practice active listening, show empathy, and foster open communication to create a culture of trust and mutual respect. By prioritizing positive interactions, we aim to enhance collaboration and a sense of belonging for all members of our community."

4. Encouraging Continuous Improvement:
"Our daily school mission is to embrace a mindset of continuous improvement. We will seek opportunities to learn, grow, and innovate in our practices. By continually striving for excellence, we ensure that our school remains dynamic and responsive to the needs of our community."

5. Leading and Learning:
"Today, we commit to leading by example and fostering a culture of continuous learning. Every decision and action we take will center around leadership and education. We aim to inspire our students and staff to develop their leadership skills and pursue knowledge passionately. Through collaborative efforts and a shared dedication to personal and professional growth, we will cultivate an environment where leading and learning are at the heart of everything we do."

6. Empowering Growth, Connection, and Excellence

"Today, we empower every student and staff member to grow, connect, and lead. Through intentional instruction, meaningful relationships, and a focus on well-being, our daily mission drives us toward a school culture defined by Peacefulness, Happiness, Healthiness, and Excellence (PH2E)."

These examples demonstrate how a Daily School Mission can guide the actions and decisions of the school community, ensuring alignment with the overall School Vision and fostering an environment of continuous improvement and excellence.

The Daily School Mission Anchor Model

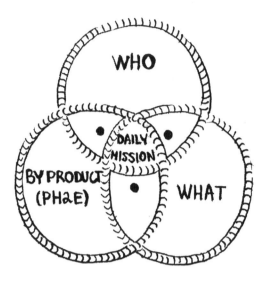

Daily School Mission: Rooted in the Principle of Intentional Actions

The Principle of Intentional Actions is about choosing to act with clarity and purpose rather than reacting by default. *Intentional Actions* mean making daily decisions that align with your values, mission, and long-term goals. It is about ensuring that what happens each day in your school is not random or routine, but deliberate and meaningful. This principle reminds us that schools thrive when daily efforts are connected to a larger purpose. For the Daily School Mission anchor, Intentional Actions ensure that every practice, routine, and interaction reflects who you serve, what you do, and the outcomes you aim to create.

Living Your Mission with Daily Intention

The **Daily School Mission Model** is a simple yet powerful visual that reinforces the structure of an effective mission. Grounded in the Principle of Intentional Actions, this model centers on the intersection of three essential components:

- **Who** – the individuals or groups your daily actions aim to support and impact (e.g., students, teachers, families, staff, or the broader community).

- **What** – the specific, intentional actions and practices you engage in each day to advance learning, growth, and well-being.
- **Byproduct** – the outcomes and experiences you hope to create as a result of those actions. These are the results you want to see more of in your school culture.

At the center of this model lies your **Daily School Mission**—the intersection of these three elements. When a school's daily efforts are aligned across who, what, and byproduct, clarity emerges. This clarity fosters consistency, purpose, and unity of effort throughout the school community.

This model provides a powerful tool for reflection, team discussions, and alignment. Leadership teams can use it to ask:

- Are we clear on who we're trying to impact each day?
- Are our daily actions aligned and intentional?
- Do we know what outcomes we're working toward, and are they consistent with our school's vision?

When these three circles come together, the mission becomes a living practice woven into every interaction, every decision, and every moment of the school day.

>
>
> ### The Guiding Questions for Daily School Mission
>
> *If someone observed your school community for one day, without reading a handbook or asking a single question, what would they see?*
>
> *What would they believe your mission is, based solely on the daily actions, interactions, and decisions they witness?*

These are the questions to revisit again and again. It keeps your focus on alignment, intentionality, and the lived experience of your mission—every single day.

Transitioning to Anchor 4: School Leadership Principles

With your Daily School Mission clarified, we now turn our attention to the beliefs that drive it: your **School Leadership Principles**. These are the timeless truths that guide how your school leads, learns, and lives.

While the Daily School Mission focuses on what you do each day, your Leadership Principles define **how you do it**: through consistency, character, and shared intent. They serve as a core navigational guide within your school's larger leadership map, anchoring actions in natural laws that transcend trends and preferences, grounded instead in universal truths.

But here's the challenge: as human beings, we all carry assumptions, opinions, and mental models that can distort our understanding of these principles. These internal distortions, however unintentional, can gradually steer your school off course. That's why this work isn't a one-time declaration, but a continuous process of checking, recalibrating, and realigning your leadership model to stay intentional and principle-centered.

As we move into the next anchor, we'll explore how to define, align, and live out your **School Leadership Principles** in a way that strengthens your school culture and accelerates your strategic journey.

Inward School Anchor 4
SCHOOL LEADERSHIP PRINCIPLES

The Principle of Life Realities

*It's a law of life—check it, and you'll see it holds true
in every situation of life.*
—Indira Gandhi

Grounding the Journey: School Leadership Principles as True Coordinates

The **Principle of Life Realities** reminds us that effective leadership is built on timeless truths rather than on trends and opinions. These enduring principles form the backbone of a school's culture, serving as the **true coordinates** that guide your vision, mission, and daily practices. They represent the foundational rules that help your school navigate with integrity, unity, and purpose.

Unlike policies that shift or personal beliefs that vary, School Leadership Principles are rooted in universal truths—reliable and time-tested. When clearly defined, taught, and lived, these principles align everyone: leaders, staff and students, around a shared framework for decision-making, behavior, and communication. They shape not just what a school does, but how it does it.

By identifying and committing to a clear set of leadership principles, your school establishes a deeply embedded culture of trust, accountability, and forward motion.

Navigating Internal Maps: Avoiding the Drift

We all carry internal maps: personal beliefs, experiences, opinions, and assumptions that shape how we see the world. Alfred Korzybski once said, **"The map is not the territory."** Our perceptions can sometimes distort reality, pulling us away from the principles we intend to live by.

In a school setting, this misalignment can cause confusion, inconsistency, or drift, where actions no longer match values, and the culture feels off-course. That's why School Leadership Principles matter so much; they serve as the **true coordinates** that help bring our internal maps back into alignment.

To lead with clarity, we must regularly reflect on how our personal viewpoints match, or clash, with our shared principles. This requires humility, curiosity, and a willingness to update our thinking. Just like a navigator adjusts their route based on new conditions, school leaders must constantly recalibrate to stay aligned with what matters most.

By anchoring your school to universal principles and committing to continuous reflection, you ensure your leadership culture remains steady, resilient, and purpose-driven—even in times of change.

Embedding Robust IOU Leadership Principles in Daily Practice

Bringing Life Realities Into Practice

Imagine stepping into a school where the very air is filled with a sense of shared purpose and commitment to excellence. Here, School Leadership Principles aren't just posters on the wall or phrases in a handbook, they're lived, felt, and seen in action. They're embedded in the way people speak, collaborate, and lead.

Schools that intentionally embed their Leadership Principles create vibrant, dynamic communities where culture isn't left to chance; it's cultivated through aligned behaviors, decisions, and beliefs.

The following examples are not a checklist of requirements. Rather, they're illustrations to inspire your thinking. Each school may focus on different principles depending on its individual needs and identity. Start with what resonates most, and remember: embedding just a few Leadership Principles with clarity and consistency can have a profound impact on the school's culture.

Culture of Integrity and Ethical Leadership
From the moment you enter, it's clear that integrity is the cornerstone of this school. Ethical leadership guides decisions at every level, and those decisions are made transparently, communicated clearly, and grounded in fairness. Students are taught and expected to act with honesty and accountability, and these values are reinforced daily by staff, families, and leadership.

Proactive and Responsible Behavior
Staff and students alike demonstrate ownership of their actions. Whether tackling a classroom task or leading a school-wide initiative, people step forward with purpose. This proactive mindset isn't accidental: it's nurtured, celebrated, and modeled from the top down.

Vision-Aligned Goals and Collaborative Efforts
Every initiative and program connects back to the school's vision. That vision is practical and actionable, guiding both long-term strategy and everyday routines. School leadership works collaboratively with students, teachers, and families to align efforts, solve problems, and stay focused on shared goals.

Respect and Belonging
You can feel it in the hallways, this is a place where everyone matters. Whether through structured programs or everyday interactions, students and staff are uplifted, honored, and heard. The school embraces differences and cultivates a deep sense of belonging for all.

Continuous Improvement and Lifelong Learning
Professional development is prioritized. Staff stay current and curious. Students are encouraged to explore, stretch, and reflect. The school's systems support innovation, and there's a common understanding that learning never stops—for anyone.

Innovative and Creative Thinking
Classrooms buzz with ideas. Students solve real-world problems, experiment with solutions, and present bold thinking. Teachers design learning experiences that prioritize creativity over compliance. The result is a culture that prizes fresh thinking and embraces the unknown.

Empathy, Compassion, and Support
Social-emotional learning is not an add-on, it's woven into the fabric of the school. There's a shared responsibility to care for each other. Staff and students feel safe, seen, and supported. Peer groups, counseling, and mentorship create a strong web of emotional support.

Accountability and Transparent Communication
Clear expectations. Consistent feedback. Open dialogue. Accountability is not punitive—it's empowering. Everyone understands their role, and there are structures in place for honest reflection and ongoing dialogue across the school community.

Resilience and Perseverance
Challenges are embraced as part of the learning process. Grit is modeled and celebrated. Whether overcoming setbacks or pursuing long-term goals, students and staff persevere together, supported by a culture that encourages effort and growth.

Environmental Stewardship and Global Awareness
Sustainability is integrated into school life: from curriculum to operations. Students learn to care about the world and act as global citizens. They explore issues that extend beyond their walls and take initiative to make a meaningful impact.

The Takeaway
Schools with embedded Leadership Principles don't just talk about leadership—they live it. Principles like **ownership, innovation, resilience, and accountability** aren't just ideals, they're practiced daily through decisions, conversations, and relationships. These lived principles elevate the learning environment and help develop the character and capacity of everyone within it.

By embracing even a few Leadership Principles with clarity and consistency, your school can begin shaping a leadership culture that is **purposeful, empowering, and aligned** with the long-term aspirations of your entire community.

School Leadership Principles Mindset Question

Which type of thinking does your school use – Default or Intentional?

- **Default Thinking:**

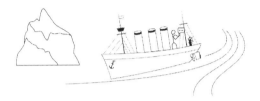

"Our school has a set of Leadership Principles or statements that are listed in our handbook and *mentioned occasionally during meetings."*

This mindset reflects a passive approach. Leadership Principles may exist on paper, but they are not embedded into daily conversations or decisions. Staff and students may have heard of them but wouldn't be able to explain or model them. The result? Inconsistent expectations missed opportunities for alignment, and a leadership culture that drifts rather than drives.

- **Intentional Thinking:**

"Our school lives its Leadership Principles and everyone knows them, uses them, and sees them in action every day."

This mindset reflects a proactive culture where Leadership Principles are clearly defined, posted, and practiced. They're integrated into professional development, student leadership, daily lessons, and decision-making. Everyone, from students to staff to school leaders, knows the principles and uses them to guide behavior, build trust, and stay aligned with the school's identity and vision.

Why This Matters

Most schools don't *intend* to drift from their Leadership Principles, but it happens. One leadership transition. One vague initiative. One year without reinforcement. Slowly, the principles that once shaped your school start to fade from daily practice. What fills the gap? Outside influences, individual preferences, or reactive decision-making.

Without intentionality, the loudest voice or latest trend can dictate direction. Leadership becomes inconsistent, and culture becomes fragmented.

But when a school anchors itself in clear, timeless principles, and uses them daily, everything changes. Decisions are aligned. Relationships deepen. Expectations are clear. And the leadership culture becomes one of trust, consistency, and shared responsibility.

These mindset questions are not meant to shame, they're here to spark reflection. If you see your school slipping into default, that's okay. This manual is here to help you realign, reset, and rebuild—principle by principle.

The question isn't whether your school *has* Leadership Principles.
The question is: Do you *live* them?

> *Leadership is not a position; it's a choice. It's not about managing people but about inspiring them to unleash their potential.*
> —Stephen M. R. Covey & David Kasperson – *Trust & Inspire*

The Importance of Clearly Defining School Leadership Principles

When **School Leadership Principles are not clearly defined**, discussed, and lived out, **a void forms**, and that void doesn't stay empty for long. In its place, **outside forces begin to fill it and define what leadership looks like**. Individual beliefs, opinions, and perceptions take over. And over time, **the culture fragments**.

Without a shared set of principles, **decisions are inconsistent. Expectations vary** from person to person. **Conflicts increase. Frustration builds.** What was once a cohesive vision becomes muddied by personal preferences, competing priorities, or reactive choices. Slowly, the school **drifts from intentional culture-building into uncoordinated effort and unclear direction**.

In this environment, even well-meaning leadership feels chaotic. **Morale dips, trust erodes**, and the school community becomes unsure of what to expect or what is expected of them. The leadership culture **loses its center of gravity**.

Intentional leadership is not optional—it's essential.

Your School Leadership Principles must be clearly defined and actively embedded into everything from classroom instruction to staff development to decision-making.

Without this anchor, your school runs on default settings, where leadership is driven by personalities, politics, or pressure rather than principle.

But when you define your School Leadership Principles with clarity, and revisit them regularly, they become a stabilizing force within your leadership framework. They bring consistency. They create alignment. And they empower every member of the school community to lead with confidence, integrity, and shared intent.

Reflecting on School Leadership Principles

Taking time to reflect on your current leadership culture, thoughtfully and intentionally, is a powerful step toward lasting change.

If your school is slipping into default thinking, you're not alone. Most schools don't drift by choice. It happens subtly, over time. This manual exists to help you realign your compass and lead with clarity.

When you adopt a principles-first mindset, you transform the foundation of your school. You shift from fragmented to focused, from reactive to intentional, from uncertain to united.

Your School Leadership Principles are not just words; they are the guardrails of your culture, the drivers of your decisions, and the fuel behind your forward motion.

Let's reflect on how your school currently lives, or overlooks, the Leadership Principles that could guide it forward.

Strategic Thinking Questions for Inward School Anchor 4: School Leadership Principles

1. *What beliefs do we want to instill in our students and staff to guide their decision-making?*

2. *How do we define effective leadership within our school, and what qualities do we believe are essential for leaders at all levels?*

3. *What principles will ensure that our school's mission and vision are reflected in our daily practices and interactions?*

4. *How can we intentionally cultivate a culture of continuous improvement and lifelong learning for both students and staff?*

_____
_____
_____
_____
_____
_____

5. *How can we foster a welcoming environment that values the differences among individuals and ensures all voices are heard and respected?*

_____
_____
_____
_____
_____
_____

6. *What strategies can we implement to encourage accountability and responsibility among students and staff?*

_____
_____
_____
_____
_____
_____

7. *How can we ensure that integrity and fairness guide every decision and interaction in our school?*

8. *What approaches can we adopt to promote collaboration, teamwork, and strong partnerships within our school community and beyond?*

9. *How can we cultivate resilience and perseverance in the face of challenges, ensuring that both students and staff develop a strong work ethic and determination?*

10. *What principles should guide our efforts to engage with and support the broader community, including parents, local organizations, and global initiatives?*

_____
_____
_____
_____
_____
_____

How to Choose and Implement School Leadership Principles

The Leadership Principles your school chooses can be any principles that your team believes will guide you to be *IOU (insert your school's name) Leaders*. These principles can be selected from the anchor principles outlined in this Leadership Manual or can be entirely new principles created by your team. The essential point is that the school Leadership Principles chosen will be posted, taught, and practiced by everyone in the school, including students, staff, and administrators, etc. See School Leadership examples later in this section.

Customizing Your Leadership Principles

- **Flexible Selection:** Choose from the anchor principles in this book or create your own. What matters most is alignment with your school's unique identity and goals.
- **Community Alignment:** Your principles should resonate with your school community. They must feel relevant, practical, and aspirational for students and adults alike.
- **Guiding Framework:** These principles should serve as a core component of your school's leadership system: providing clarity for behavior, decision-making, and culture. Think of them as the *alignment mechanism* that ensures everyone is steering in the same direction.

Bringing School Leadership Principles to Life

Once your principles are defined, they must become part of the school's everyday rhythm. That happens through intentional implementation:

- **Visible and Accessible:** Post your Leadership Principles throughout the school: in hallways, classrooms, and shared spaces. Let them be a daily reminder for all.
- **Taught and Discussed:** Integrate the principles into lessons, leadership meetings, and staff development. Use stories, role-plays, and real-life examples to bring them to life.
- **Practiced Daily:** Make your principles a filter for decisions and behaviors. Encourage staff and students to reference them when solving problems, setting goals, or collaborating.
- **Reflected On and Revisited:** Set aside regular time to assess how well your school is living its principles. Gather feedback, celebrate progress, and make adjustments to ensure they remain a living part of your culture.

By selecting and committing to specific Leadership Principles, your school will create a strong foundation for a dynamic positive school culture. These principles will guide the members of the school community towards becoming effective *IOU Leaders*, fostering an environment of continuous growth, learning, and excellence.

Initial Drafts of Your School Leadership Principles

You don't need a perfect set right away. Begin by reflecting on what your school stands for, and what it needs to thrive. Based on your earlier responses and discussions, start drafting a working list of Leadership Principles that feel right for your school.

This initial draft is just the beginning. As you continue to explore the remaining anchors, your clarity and confidence in these principles will grow. You'll revisit and refine them to ensure they align with your school's Mission, Vision, and SelfCulture.

Initial Thoughts for Your School Leadership Principles:

_____
_____
_____
_____
_____
_____
_____
_____
_____
_____
_____
_____
_____
_____
_____
_____
_____
_____
_____
_____

Examples of School Leadership Principles

The **Principle of Life Realities** serves as the foundation for our School Leadership Principles. It underscores the importance of rooting our actions and decisions in **universal truths and natural laws**: principles that are not based on trends or opinions, but on time-tested realities. These truths form a stable foundation that transcends personal viewpoints and perceptions, helping ensure your school's approach remains coherent, consistent, and aligned with enduring values.

In the district where I have had the privilege of serving in leadership roles for over two decades, we use the principles outlined in Stephen R. Covey's *The 7 Habits of Highly Effective People*. These habits have been adopted as our **School Leadership Principles** because they reflect both **individual growth** and **collective leadership** in a school setting:

1. **Be Proactive**: Encouraging personal responsibility and initiative.
2. **Begin with the End in Mind**: Emphasizing the importance of clear goals and vision.
3. **Put First Things First**: Prioritizing based on purpose, not pressure.
4. **Think Win-Win**: Promoting mutual benefit, fairness, and positive relationships.
5. **Seek First to Understand, Then to Be Understood**: Advocating for empathy and effective communication.
6. **Synergize**: Valuing teamwork and combining strengths for greater outcomes.
7. **Sharpen the Saw (Continuous Improvement)**: Committing to growth, balance, and lifelong learning.

Everyone in the school community, from students to staff, is trained in these Leadership Principles. They're not just taught; they're spoken, modeled, and lived. The language of leadership becomes part of daily routines, guiding how people think, act, and interact. Over time, proactive behavior, goal-setting, prioritization, collaboration, and continuous improvement become second nature. These principles not only enhance personal development and study habits, but also strengthen outward relationships and create a culture of consistency, trust, and growth.

Additional Examples of School Leadership Principles:

Below are additional Leadership Principles your school might choose to adopt or adapt based on your unique culture, goals, and community needs. These principles can stand alone or be blended with others (such as the 7 Habits) to form your school's guiding framework:

- **Growth Mindset**
  Promoting the belief that abilities and intelligence can be developed through dedication, effort, and reflection.
- **Ethical Leadership**
  Grounding all actions in integrity, fairness, and transparency, and modeling ethical behavior at all levels.
- **Innovation and Creativity**
  Encouraging students and staff to think critically, solve problems in new ways, and embrace bold ideas.
- **Accountability and Responsibility**
  Fostering a culture where every member of the community takes ownership for their actions, commitments, and outcomes.
- **Fairness and Respect**
  Ensuring that all voices are valued and that every individual is treated with dignity, empathy, and equal opportunity to contribute and succeed.
- **Collaboration and Teamwork**
  Creating a shared culture of trust and support by working together toward common goals.
- **Resilience and Perseverance**
  Cultivating mental toughness and determination, encouraging students and staff to overcome setbacks and push through challenges.
- **Empathy and Compassion**
  Nurturing emotional intelligence, active listening, and a deep commitment to understanding others.
- **Curiosity and Lifelong Learning**
  Inspiring a spirit of inquiry and continuous personal and professional growth for all members of the school.
- **Respect and Civility**
  Reinforcing expectations for respectful, kind, and constructive communication in all school interactions.
- **Environmental Stewardship**
  Promoting sustainability, conservation, and global responsibility through learning and daily practice.

- **Visionary Thinking**
  Encouraging forward-thinking, strategic planning, and bold leadership that shapes the future of the school.
- **Empowerment**
  Giving students and staff the opportunity, support, and confidence to take initiative and lead from where they are.
- **Data-Informed Practices**
  Using evidence and data to guide decisions, track progress, and improve outcomes.
- **Community Engagement**
  Building strong partnerships with parents, local organizations, and stakeholders to support student success.
- **Health and Well-being**
  Prioritizing the physical, emotional, and mental wellness of all community members.
- **Global Citizenship**
  Developing awareness, responsibility, and active engagement with global issues and perspectives beyond one's own community or experience.
- **Adaptability and Flexibility**
  Promoting agility in the face of change and openness to new approaches, technologies, and learning environments.
- **Purpose-Driven Leadership**
  Ensuring that all decisions and behaviors reflect the school's mission, vision, and deeper purpose.
- **Leadership Development**
  Creating intentional opportunities for students and staff to grow their leadership capacity through mentorship, practice, and reflection.
- **Student Empowerment**
  Encouraging students to take an active role in their learning journey, voice their ideas, and lead initiatives.
- **Reflective Practice**
  Embedding self-reflection and team reflection into routines to ensure continual growth and alignment with school principles.
- **Environmental Sustainability**
  Encouraging responsibility and care for the environments we live, learn, and grow in.

The School Leadership Principles Anchor Model

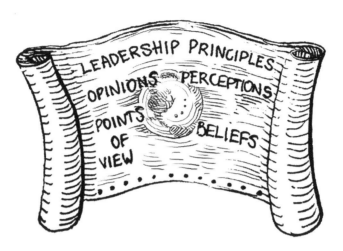

School Leadership Principles: Rooted in the Principle of Life Realities

The Principle of Life Realities reminds us that while circumstances may change, natural laws and timeless truths remain constant. *Life Realities* are the enduring principles that govern effective leadership and human behavior—truths that exist whether we acknowledge them or not. To lead with consistency and integrity, schools must align their decisions and culture with these universal truths. For the School Leadership Principles anchor, Life Realities ensure that leadership is grounded, not reactive. They act as steady coordinates that help schools navigate change, clarify expectations, and lead with purpose.

Aligning Beliefs and Behavior with Timeless Truths

The **School Leadership Principles Model** illustrates how clearly defined principles shape both our **Inward Thoughts** and **Outward Actions**. These principles are not trends or opinions; they are timeless truths, grounded in the Principle of Life Realities. They form the bedrock of a school's identity and provide consistent, trustworthy direction, even in moments of uncertainty or change.

Yet while principles are fixed, **our internal maps** (beliefs, perceptions, and assumptions) can distort how we interpret and apply them. Just as a map must be regularly updated to reflect current terrain, our leadership mindset must be examined and adjusted to remain in alignment with enduring truths.

This visual model is a practical tool designed to support **leadership team discussions**. It helps school leaders reflect on how personal or collective mindsets may be influencing (or distorting) their alignment with agreed-upon principles. When misalignment occurs, it doesn't mean failure—it signals a need for recalibration.

Much like how GPS systems update constantly to reflect construction, detours, or new roads, school leaders must regularly pause, reflect, and **update their internal maps** to stay on course. This process of realignment fuels growth, deepens integrity, and strengthens the shared leadership of the school.

Over time, these moments of reflection lead to meaningful shifts in mindset and practice, fostering a dynamic and resilient school environment where Leadership Principles are not just statements but lived realities.

The Guiding Question for School Leadership Principles

Are the decisions and behaviors across our school truly guided by our shared Leadership Principles, or are personal maps pulling us off course?

Transitioning to Anchor 5: School Core Values

With your School Leadership Principles clarified, we now turn to the next Inward Anchor: **School Core Values**.

While principles serve as the enduring truths that guide thinking and decision-making, **core values are the foundation of your school's daily interactions and relationships**. They define how people treat one another, how respect is shown, and how collaboration is built across classrooms, hallways, offices, and beyond.

This anchor focuses on the lived behaviors that bring your vision, mission, and principles to life. It asks: *What do we stand for as a school community?* And more importantly: *Are those values reflected in the way we lead, learn, and live together each day?*

By clearly defining your School Core Values, you lay the groundwork for a culture of trust, belonging, and shared expectations. A culture where every student and staff member feels seen, valued, and empowered to contribute.

Now, let's explore how to define and embed values that reflect who you are as a school—and who you aspire to be.

Inward School Anchor 5

School Core Values

The Principle of Life Character

Values are like fingerprints. Nobody's are the same, but you leave them all over everything you do.
—Elvis Presley

Living the Principle of Life Character

At the heart of every thriving school culture lies a shared commitment to character. **School Core Values**, grounded in the ***Principle of Life Character***, represent the deeply held beliefs that guide how we treat one another, how we lead, learn, and grow. These values provide a foundation of shared character: shaping everyday decisions, behaviors, and relationships.

When clearly defined and intentionally lived, School Core Values foster an environment of respect, trust, and belonging. They become the steady thread running through every classroom, hallway, and interaction: bringing consistency to expectations and helping build a culture where people feel safe, seen, and supported.

When core values are truly lived, they become the heartbeat of a positive, unified school culture.

Experiencing a School Rooted in Core Values

When you walk into a school where **Core Values** are clearly defined and deeply lived, you can feel it. There's a visible sense of respect in every interaction: among students, staff, and families. The walls are lined with purposeful displays: words like **dedication, respect, teamwork, integrity, and trust**—not just posted, but practiced.

Each core value is clearly defined and known by all. Students, teachers, and staff speak the same language, understand what the values look like in action, and hold one another accountable to them. This shared understanding ensures that the language of your values is not abstract, but accessible, consistent, and alive in the daily life of the school.

These values are present in how students collaborate with enthusiasm and kindness, in how teachers speak with care and clarity, and in how families engage with openness and pride. You see it in staff who model consistency and students who support one another without being prompted.

Because these **School Core Values** are reinforced through daily actions, common language, and shared experiences, they form a living culture. A culture where everyone feels welcomed, seen, and committed to something greater than themselves.

School Core Values: Creating a Framework for Shared Values

Anchor 5 is not about handing you a list of Core Values to adopt; it's about helping you build a framework to discover the values that are most meaningful to *your* school community. The goal is to facilitate a collaborative process where students, staff, parents, and administrators reflect together on what truly matters. Through this dialogue, your school identifies the values that reflect its vision, character, and highest aspirations.

This framework ensures that the chosen School Core Values are owned rather than imposed. They emerge from within your community and are shaped by its unique identity, experiences, and beliefs. Once defined, these values guide how people interact, how decisions are made, and how your school culture continues to grow.

While there may be many core values you admire, it's important to focus on a concise, clearly articulated set that can be consistently taught, modeled, and reinforced. These core values should be visible in the environment, present in your language, and lived out in your daily routines.

When core values are integrated into the rhythm of school life, not just referenced in documents or assemblies, they build trust, deepen relationships, and create a cohesive culture where everyone knows what your school stands for, and how to live it.

Evaluating and Refreshing Your School Core Values

If your school already has a set of core values—great. That means you've already begun the journey of defining who you are and what you stand for. But like anything truly foundational, core values need more than a one-time unveiling. They require ongoing attention, reflection, and renewal.

School Core Values are only powerful if they are current, visible, and lived. Over time, even well-intentioned values can fade into the background: printed in handbooks, posted on walls, but disconnected from the actual rhythm of school life.

This is your opportunity to pause and ask:

- **Are our values alive, or just listed?**
- **Do they still resonate with who we are and where we're going?**
- **Can students, staff, and families see them in our actions, not just our words?**

Refreshing your core values doesn't necessarily mean starting over. It means re-engaging with your community to ask whether your values are still relevant, still inspiring, and still shaping the culture you hope to cultivate.

This might involve:

- Hosting staff or student focus groups to gather perceptions.
- Using surveys to measure awareness and alignment.
- Rebranding your values visually to give them new life.
- Embedding them more intentionally into lessons, meetings, and celebrations.
- Revisiting how they're used in decision-making, discipline, and recognition.

When you engage in reflective practice, you're not **abandoning your values**; you're **breathing new life into them**. You're ensuring they evolve alongside your school community, remaining a **vibrant and active** part of your collective identity.

Dynamic schools grow. So should their values.

School Core Values Mindset Question

Which type of thinking does your school use – Default or Intentional?

- **Default Thinking**

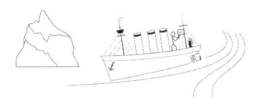

"Our school has a set of core values that are listed on our website, posted in a few areas of the school, and occasionally mentioned during assemblies."

This mindset often starts with good intentions, but over time, the core values fade into the background. They exist in writing but not in practice. Students and staff may vaguely recall the words, but they don't actively reference them. As a result, daily interactions are shaped more by habit than by shared principles, and opportunities to build a truly values-driven culture are missed.

- **Intentional Thinking**

"Our school actively embodies our core values in every interaction and decision."

In this proactive stance the core values are clearly understood, posted throughout the school, and can be recited by all stakeholders, including staff, students, and parents. All staff ensures that the core values guide behavior, shape the school culture, and influence the decision-making processes. Each member of the school community is committed to upholding the core values, which are consistently reinforced through training, communication, and daily practice.

Why This Matters

Most schools don't mean to drift from their core values, It often happens gradually. A core value is mentioned less. A new initiative takes priority. A few staff or students leave. Over time, the core values that once shaped your school's identity begin to fade from daily practice.

When that happens, culture becomes reactive, shaped more by individual preferences than collective principles. Day-to-day pressures and outside influences begin to define who you are, and the sense of **unity, clarity, and trust** starts to erode.

But when a school adopts **intentional thinking**, core values become **anchors** for the school culture. They guide decisions. They unify people. They give students and staff a shared lens for expectations, accountability, and celebration.

This section is designed to spark **honest reflection**, not judgment. If parts of your school resonate with the default mindset, you're not alone. That's exactly why this framework exists. Each anchor ahead offers a practical way to realign your school's culture around purpose and principle.

Your values are still there. The question is: **Are you intentionally living them—or unintentionally letting them drift?**

Reflecting on School Core Values

Taking time to reflect on how your core values appear, or fail to appear, across your school community is a powerful step toward **strengthening culture from within**. Core values are not meant to live in documents—they are meant to live in people.

When a school slips into default mode, values become passive. But when they're actively reinforced through modeling, language, and expectations, they create a **shared behavioral standard** that everyone understands and upholds.

Intentional core values shape culture. They shift how people treat one another, how decisions are made, and how problems are solved. **Respect** isn't just encouraged; it's demonstrated. **Collaboration** isn't just suggested; it's seen in action. **Integrity** isn't just posted—it's practiced.

This is about **alignment**. When your values are lived consistently, students and staff know what your school stands for, and how they're expected to stand together.

Ask yourself: **Are your values shaping culture—or sitting quietly in the background?**

**Strategic Thinking Questions for
Inward School Anchor 5:
School Core Values**

Reflecting on your school's core values is not just about reaffirming what's written on your walls or in your handbook. It's about ensuring they are truly lived and embedded in how people speak, treat one another, and make decisions.

By thoughtfully considering the questions that follow, your school can better define and refine the core values that shape behavior, relationships, and climate, ultimately cultivating a culture of trust, respect, and unity.

1. *What behaviors, language, and attitudes do we want to consistently see among students, staff, and families that reflect our school's core values?*

_____
_____
_____
_____
_____

2. *How do our current core values actively influence daily interactions, classroom practices, and decision-making in our school?*

_____
_____
_____
_____
_____

3. *Are our core values clearly understood, embraced, and consistently applied by all members of our school community? If not, where are the gaps, and how can we bridge them?*

_____
_____
_____
_____
_____
_____

4. *In what ways can we reinforce our core values through daily communication, staff development, and schoolwide routines?*

_____
_____
_____
_____
_____
_____

5. *Do our existing core values still reflect who we are and where we're going as a school? Is it time to revisit, revise, or reintroduce them with clarity and energy?*

_____
_____
_____
_____
_____
_____

6. *How might we integrate our core values into both academic learning and extracurricular opportunities so they become more than slogans, and instead, are truly practiced?*

_____
_____
_____
_____
_____
_____

7. *What systems or structures can we put in place to regularly recognize and celebrate actions that exemplify our core values in real time?*

_____
_____
_____
_____
_____
_____

8. *How can we involve students, staff, families, and community partners in the process of defining, living, and promoting our school's core values?*

_____
_____
_____
_____
_____
_____

9. *What challenges do we face in embedding our core values into the school culture, and how can we address these challenges?*

_____
_____
_____
_____
_____
_____

10. *How do we measure the impact of our core values on the school environment and overall community well-being?*

_____
_____
_____
_____
_____
_____

By reflecting on these questions, your school can better identify and define the core values that will improve behavior and interactions, creating a more cohesive, respectful, and supportive educational environment.

Identifying Core Values for Your School

While many values may resonate with your school community, it's essential to focus on a few that truly reflect your school's identity and aspirations. This list is not meant to prescribe the "right" values; rather, it is intended to spark reflection and dialogue.

Start by reviewing the options below as a team. Highlight the ten values that stand out most. Then, through discussion and consensus, narrow your list to **five core values** that will serve as the foundation for your school culture. These are the values you are committed to **modeling, teaching, and reinforcing** every day.

These core values should inspire and be actionable, visible, and sustainable throughout your school community.

You're also encouraged to create your own values not listed here. What matters most is that your core values feel authentic and owned by your school.

School Core Values:

- Dependable
- Reliable
- Loyal
- Committed
- Open-Minded
- Consistent
- Honest
- Efficient
- Innovative
- Creative
- Good-Humored
- Compassionate
- Adventurous
- Motivated
- Positive
- Optimistic
- Passionate
- Respect
- Courageous
- Persistent
- Dedication
- Integrity
- Trust
- Teamwork
- Positivity
- Perseverance
- Service to Others
- Welcoming

Initial Drafts of Your School Core Values

Most schools already have Core Values, but over time, they can fade into the background, becoming more symbolic than lived. This anchor invites you to bring them back to the forefront with clarity, intention, and renewed energy.

Whether you're **developing new Core Values** or **refining ones already in place**, this is your opportunity to make them meaningful, memorable, and actionable for your entire school community.

Start by identifying five values that authentically reflect your school's identity, aspirations, and desired culture. If your values are already established, use this moment to revisit and clearly define what each one means in your context. Consider creating a **short, memorable phrase for each value**, something students and staff can use, recall, and live by. You may even want to develop **visual icons or symbols** to represent each one, helping to embed them more deeply into your daily environment and routines.

This process is about choosing Core Values your school is committed to **modeling, teaching, and reinforcing** every day. The Core Values you define now will become visible guideposts, anchoring how people interact, make decisions, and build community.

Let this first draft be natural and collaborative. As you continue through the remaining Inward Anchors, your clarity will grow, and your Core Values will come into sharper focus.

This is your chance to breathe life into the values your community already believes in, and to ensure they're **seen, spoken, and lived every single day**.

Initial Thoughts for your School Core Values:

Defining and Aligning School Core Values

Once your school has identified its Core Values, the next step is to **define them clearly and intentionally**. This is essential for clarity and school unity.

Every person in your school community, students, staff, parents, and administrators, brings a unique internal map that is shaped by personal experiences, beliefs, and interpretations. Without shared definitions, these individual perspectives can cause misalignment in how your values are understood and lived.

That's why it's critical to **create a common language** around your Core Values. When each value is clearly defined and discussed, the community begins to align. Expectations become consistent. Behavior becomes purposeful. Decision-making becomes anchored.

This clarity allows your Core Values to move beyond slogans or posters to become **actionable commitments** that shape the school's culture at every level.

By regularly revisiting these definitions, through staff conversations, student reflections, and parent engagement, you reinforce what your school stands for. Over time, these values become the threads that weave trust, respect, and purpose into the everyday fabric of school life.

When values are clearly defined and consistently reinforced, they guide behavior—and build belonging.

The School Core Values Anchor Model

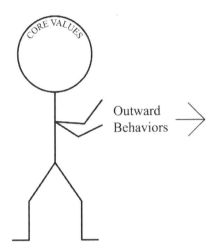

School Core Values: Rooted in the Principle of Life Character

The Principle of Life Character reminds us that who we are is reflected in what we do. *Life Character* means embodying integrity, empathy, and consistency, living from the inside out in a way that builds trust and respect. In a school, character is not only developed in students; it is demonstrated through the daily actions of every adult and leader. For the School Core Values anchor, Life Character ensures that internal beliefs are not just stated but lived. Core Values guide behavior, shape relationships, and create the dependable rhythm of how people treat one another every day.

Living What We Value, Every Day

This **visual model** features a stick figure with the words **"Core Values"** in the head and **"Outward Behaviors"** extending from the hands, symbolizing the powerful connection between what we value and how we behave.

This simple yet impactful image is a reflective tool designed to spark meaningful conversations across your school community. It visually represents how our **internal beliefs** (core values) must inform our **external actions** (behavior), ensuring that the way we treat one another reflects the shared values we uphold as a school.

Use this model to:

- Facilitate professional learning and leadership team conversations
- Support classroom lessons and student leadership discussions
- Guide schoolwide reflections on alignment between values and culture
- Address behavioral inconsistencies in a proactive, non-punitive way

This model reminds us that values are not just words on a wall; they must live in our hallways, classrooms, conversations, and decisions.

When our shared core values live in the minds of each stakeholder and extend into their daily behavior, the result is a consistent, trustworthy, and unified school culture.

By incorporating this **School Core Values Model** into regular team meetings, trainings, and student assemblies, schools can ensure that students, staff, parents, and administrators all understand the expectation:

Core Values: The Centerpiece of an IOU Dynamic Positive Culture

School Core Values, **Anchor 5**, sit at the heart of your IOU Dynamic Positive School Culture. More than just words, these values are the **active force** that connects your school's vision, mission, leadership principles, and goals to the everyday behaviors and interactions that shape your environment.

When intentionally embedded, Core Values become like glue, **anchoring how people treat one another**, make decisions, and show up each day. They clarify what the school stands for, create unity across classrooms and buildings, and serve as a dependable reference point during times of challenge or change.

A school may have a compelling vision and strategic goals, but without clearly defined and consistently practiced Core Values, the culture risks becoming fragmented or reactive. Core Values bring consistency. They ensure that every initiative, conversation, and decision is grounded in **who you are and what you believe** as a community.

As your school grows and adapts, these values will remain a stable center, **flexible enough to evolve with your needs, yet firm enough to guide your direction**. They are what keep the culture vibrant, the people connected, and the mission alive.

The Guiding Question for School Core Values:

When actions, language, and decisions are made in your school, do they echo the core values you've defined, or reveal a gap between words and reality?

Transitioning to Anchor 6: School Goals

With our School Core Values clearly defined, we now turn to the final Inward Anchor: **School Goals**. These goals transform vision and values into focused action. They give your school community something concrete to strive toward: clear, measurable objectives that reflect your mission, elevate your vision, and bring your culture to life.

School Goals serve as a forward-facing roadmap. They drive academic achievement, foster personal growth, and strengthen community connection. When aligned with your Inward School Map, these goals ensure every initiative, program, and practice is purposeful and progress-oriented.

In the next anchor, we'll explore how to craft goals that are not only strategic but inspiring, so every member of your school community understands the destination and feels empowered to help reach it.

Inward School Anchor 6

SCHOOL GOALS

The Principle of Life Aspirations

A man without a goal is like a ship without a rudder.
—Thomas Carlyle

Turning Aspiration into Aligned Action

The Principle of Life Aspirations reminds us that even the most inspiring purpose can drift aimlessly without a path. School Goals bring that path to life by turning vision into direction and inspiration into action.

When intentionally crafted, **School Goals** become directional beacons. They should motivate every member of the school community, from students and teachers to administrators, board members, and families. Whether academic, operational, or addressing school culture, these goals serve as shared milestones that unify efforts, shape priorities, and elevate performance.

By anchoring our goals in the Principle of Life Aspirations, we commit to a living process of growth and excellence, where progress is intentional, and every action moves us closer to our shared purpose.

Establishing Measurable and Monitored School Goals

Your School Goals are the **rudders** that steer your school forward, transforming vision into purposeful direction. Aligned with your School Vision and Daily School Mission, and grounded in your Core Values and Leadership Principles, these goals **bring the Principle of Life Aspirations to life**. They translate intention into action, guiding your school toward meaningful progress and sustained achievement.

School Goals are **milestones with meaning**. When designed intentionally, they provide daily direction, motivate your school community, and serve as visible markers of collective success.

For goals to drive real impact, they must be:

- **Clear and Specific** – Broad intentions become powerful when narrowed into defined priorities.
- **Measurable** – What gets measured gets focused. Each goal should have tangible indicators of progress.
- **Time-Bound** – A goal without a timeline is a wish. Establish deadlines that promote urgency and accountability.
- **Attainable, Not Delusional** – Goals should stretch your school community while remaining realistic. Overreaching undermines progress; thoughtful stretch goals inspire it.
- **Monitored and Adjusted** – Embed systems to regularly reflect, assess, and recalibrate. Course corrections are part of the journey.

Think of School Goals as a **living system of continuous improvement**. Timely reflection allows your team to celebrate successes, address challenges, and stay nimble in the face of change. School Goals should be **revisited often**, not tucked away in binders or slideshows.

Goals are only effective when they are **owned**. Every stakeholder, including students, teachers, staff, administrators, and families, should feel connected to the goals and understand their role in achieving them. Leadership teams must provide the structures, support, and encouragement needed to turn goals into **school-wide habits**.

School Goals **infuse daily life with purpose**. They ensure every step your school takes is part of a greater journey toward **growth, achievement, and excellence**.

School Goals Mindset Question

Which type of thinking does your school use – Default or Intentional?

- **Default Thinking**

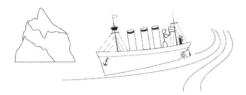

"Our school has a set of goals that are listed in our strategic plan and occasionally mentioned during meetings."

In this mindset, the school goals are not actively monitored, referenced, or integrated into daily practices. Staff and students are vaguely aware of the goals, which does not significantly impact actions or decisions.

- **Intentional Thinking**

"Our school actively pursues our goals in every action and decision."

This mindset reflects a culture where goals are **visible, shared, and lived**. Whether a goal is system-wide, school-specific, or team-based, every stakeholder, including staff, students, parents, and community members, knows their role in making it real. Goals are crafted collaboratively, communicated clearly, and reinforced consistently.

School Goals are touchpoints for planning, drivers of behavior, and motivators for reflection. Effective School Goals are **ambitious and energizing**, challenging but achievable. They serve as shared commitments that move the school forward, creating clarity, purpose, and upward momentum.

Experiencing a School with Clear and Targeted Goals: Navigating with a Goal Map

Walking into a school with clearly defined, well-communicated goals feels like boarding a ship with a detailed map; everyone knows the destination, their role in the journey, and the route they're taking together. These **Goal Maps** provide structure, clarity, and momentum. Whether you're a student, teacher, leader, or parent, you're part of the same voyage, guided by shared aspirations and visible progress.

A school with strong goal alignment doesn't just talk about goals; it lives them. Here's how that looks and feels in action:

A Purposeful Atmosphere

Customized Visual Displays:
Each goal is made visible in developmentally appropriate ways. For a school-wide literacy goal, you might find reading challenges and interactive trackers throughout classrooms and hallways. A goal focused on "Enhancing Student Support Services" may include visual resources in counseling centers or celebrations of student milestones.Administrative and leadership goals, like "Ensuring Financial Stability" or "Improving Family Engagement," are integrated into meeting agendas or highlighted on leadership dashboards, offering constant reminders of purpose and progress.

Goal-Oriented Language:
The entire school speaks a common language of progress. Students discuss their part in "Acts of Kindness" challenges, teachers tie professional development to strategic instructional goals, and leadership teams reflect openly on goals during staff briefings. The result? A shared mindset and mission.

Engaged and Motivated Students

Fun, Measurable Goals:
Big, bold, student-centered goals like "Reading a Million Minutes" or "Contributing 1,000 Kind Acts" create enthusiasm and school-wide participation. Public displays of progress, like a kindness tree in the main hallway or a reading journey mural in the library, build excitement and ownership.

Student-Driven Projects:
From designing school-wide campaigns to piloting service-learning programs, students are not bystanders; they are goal-builders. They help shape and promote the work, connecting learning to leadership.

Empowered Teachers and Staff

Professional Alignment:
Teachers participate in development experiences that directly connect to goals like "Expanding Project-Based Learning" or "Improving Differentiated Instruction." This helps align classroom practices with strategic direction.

Progress Monitoring Tools:
Staff collaborate using shared documents, visual progress walls, or digital dashboards that track momentum. These tools keep energy high and teams aligned.

A Collaborative, Goal-Aligned Community

Parent and Community Involvement:
For a goal like "Expanding Character Education," family events, service projects, and newsletters involve parents and partners in meaningful ways. These are shared community commitments.

Transparent Communication:
Digital goal dashboards, regular updates at PTA meetings, and open forums ensure stakeholders stay informed, invested, and inspired to help move the school forward.

Ongoing Monitoring and Celebration

Interactive Progress Tracking:
Attendance goals, college readiness targets, and staff wellness metrics are displayed on goal walls, celebrated in weekly bulletins, or updated through school news platforms, keeping everyone focused and motivated.

Celebrating Milestones:
Whether through assemblies, social media shoutouts, or handwritten notes, schools regularly celebrate growth and success. These recognitions reinforce belief in the process and energize the path ahead.

An Adaptive and Resilient Culture

Goal Map Updates:
Just like a GPS adjusts to real-time conditions, effective schools revisit their goals frequently. Leadership teams review data, reflect with stakeholders, and revise strategies when needed, ensuring momentum stays aligned with mission.

Flexibility with Purpose:
Obstacles are inevitable, but they don't throw the school off course. Instead, they prompt creative responses. Whether pivoting to meet a new student need or rethinking timelines, intentional schools remain agile while staying true to their destination.

Anchoring Progress: Navigating Clear School Goals with a Goal Map

A school with well-defined goals doesn't drift, it sails with direction. Clear, shared goals generate momentum, sharpen focus, and bring purpose to every classroom, office, and hallway. Like a navigational map, these goals give each stakeholder, students, staff, leaders, and families, clarity about where the school is headed and how they can contribute meaningfully to the journey.

When goals are made visible, revisited regularly, and embraced as a collective priority, they foster a culture of intentionality. Visual displays, progress checkpoints, and purposeful daily actions serve as course markers, keeping the school aligned and responsive as conditions change. The result is a dynamic, upward-moving environment where each success is a shared milestone, and every effort propels the community closer to its highest aspirations.

To help bring this vision to life, the next section introduces the **REBEL Goals™ Framework**: a practical, actionable model for setting and implementing goals in schools. It helps teams move from vague intentions to clearly defined actions, structured reflection, and community-supported progress. Whether applied to instructional initiatives, culture-building efforts, or district-wide objectives, **REBEL ensures your goals are not only written—but actively practiced and pursued.**

The REBEL Goals™ Framework

The **REBEL Goals™ Framework**, which was originally introduced in my book *IOU Life Leadership*, was designed as a universal tool to help individuals, teams, and organizations turn aspiration into aligned, actionable progress. In this Leadership Manual, the framework is applied specifically to the school setting, providing a powerful structure for setting meaningful goals, aligning efforts, and driving sustainable growth across the educational community.

The name **REBEL** is an acronym representing five essential components that make a goal inspiring, implementable and enduring.

Navigating with Purpose: A Nautical View of REBEL School Goals

*In your nautical journey, the School Goals act as the **rudders-(R)** that set your direction—your clearly defined destinations. The leader, as captain, charts the course and guides the ship toward each port, marking significant milestones along the voyage.*

*To reach these destinations, the **engine-(E)** provides the necessary power; your outward actions, daily efforts, and strategic decisions aligned with your mission. Along the way, **buoys-(B)** serve as visible checkpoints, marking your progress and helping you stay on course.*

*As you navigate, external winds and waves, such as challenges, disruptions, and resistance, will inevitably appear. Here, regular **evaluation-(E)** becomes critical, allowing your crew to assess conditions, reflect, and adjust the course as needed. And when waters become rough, your **lifeline-(L)**, the support network of your leadership partners, teams, and colleagues, keeps you connected, motivated, and resilient.*

Together, these elements guide your school steadily forward, transforming goals into meaningful achievements that energize the entire community.

The REBEL School Goals Model

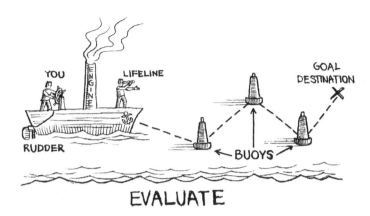

Use the **REBEL framework** to steer your school's strategic goals with clarity and impact:

- **Rudder** – *Set your direction.*
  This is your **School Goal** or your intended destination. Just as a ship's rudder determines its path, a clearly defined goal steers your school's collective energy. Write it down. Make it visible. Own it.
- **Engine** – *Ignite forward movement.*
  The engine turns the propeller representing the **Outward Actions** needed to reach your goal. These are the daily efforts, initiatives, and decisions that align with your school's mission and drive you toward your vision.
- **Buoys** – *Mark your checkpoints.*
  Buoys act as **progress indicators** which are the visual, measurable checkpoints that help track how far you've come and whether you're still on course. They give direction, pacing, and a rhythm of accountability.
- **Evaluate** – *Course-correct as needed.*
  No goal journey is perfectly smooth. **Regular evaluation** ensures you reflect, revise, and stay responsive to change. Use data, feedback, and team input to guide next steps and refine your course.
- **Lifeline** – *Stay connected and supported.*
  Every great journey requires support. **Your Lifeline is your team**—those who help you stay motivated, give honest feedback, and hold you accountable. Whether it's a leadership partner, a trusted team, or your whole staff, a strong Lifeline is essential for sustainability.

The Effectiveness of REBEL Goals:

The true power of the **REBEL Goals™ Framework** lies in its ability to turn strategic intentions into school-wide action. Each component—**Rudder, Engine, Buoys, Evaluate, and Lifeline**—brings clarity, structure, and sustainability to the goal-setting process. Together, they help schools move beyond good intentions and into intentional action that's measurable, supported, and aligned with a shared vision.

Below is a deeper look at how each **REBEL component** enhances school performance and creates lasting impact:

1. Rudder: Clarity and Direction

- **Purpose:** The **Rudder** sets the direction by defining a clear, compelling School Goal. It provides a shared destination for the entire school community.
- **Effectiveness:** When the Rudder is strong, everyone, from students to administrators, understands where the school is headed and why. This alignment helps eliminate distractions, unify energy, and ensure that every initiative supports a clearly defined purpose.

A goal without direction is like a journey without a map. The Rudder ensures your goal is not only stated, but also understood, owned, and has a clear destination.

2. Engine: Action-Oriented Strategies

- **Purpose:** The **Engine** represents the intentional actions and strategies that drive the school toward the goal.
- **Effectiveness:** By breaking the goal into manageable, clearly defined steps, the Engine transforms vision into motion. It ensures everyone knows *what to do next*, creating traction through daily, purposeful action.

Strategy without action stalls progress. The Engine transforms strategy into action, driving your mission forward.

3. Buoys: Measurable Progress

- **Purpose: Buoys** act as checkpoints along the journey, providing visual and measurable markers of progress.

- **Effectiveness:** These checkpoints create rhythm, keep the community motivated, and offer moments to reflect, recalibrate, and celebrate small wins. They prevent drift and keep momentum strong, even in stormy waters.

Without Buoys, progress is invisible. With them, growth becomes a visible, celebrated journey.

4. Evaluate: Continuous Improvement

- **Purpose:** The **Evaluate** step invites consistent reflection on progress and challenges, making adjustments as needed.
- **Effectiveness:** Schools are dynamic systems, constantly facing new circumstances. Regular evaluation builds agility into the system, ensuring schools respond to feedback, adapt to change, and stay focused on the goal without losing sight of the bigger vision.

Evaluation is about progress through insight and adjustment.

5. Lifeline: Support and Accountability

- **Purpose:** The **Lifeline** represents the support network made up of people who champion the goal, provide honest feedback, and help maintain momentum.
- **Effectiveness:** When accountability is shared, motivation multiplies. Whether it's leadership teams, student advisory groups, or community partners, the Lifeline ensures that no one is navigating alone. Encouragement, reflection, and shared responsibility make lasting impact possible.

Great goals are never achieved in isolation. Lifelines connect the vision to a village of support.

The REBEL Advantage

By adopting the **REBEL Goals™ Framework**, your school ensures that goals aren't just words on a document; they are active, living priorities. This framework brings structure, action, and passion to your goal-setting process, turning aspirations into tangible progress.

It promotes a culture of:

- **Clarity** – through clearly defined goals.
- **Consistency** – through daily actions aligned to a shared vision.
- **Celebration** – through visual progress and recognized milestones.
- **Resilience** – through ongoing evaluation and adaptation.
- **Community** – through shared ownership and accountability.

This is the power of **REBEL**—goals that are anchored in aspiration and propelled by action.

Example 1

REBEL Goal Example

Implement a School-Wide Science Enrichment Program

Implementing a science enrichment program offers an opportunity to ignite curiosity, deepen inquiry, and elevate engagement across all grade levels. Here's how the REBEL Goals™ framework can support a clear and purposeful rollout:

1. Rudder: Set the Direction

The Rudder represents the specific goal of implementing a school-wide science enrichment program.

Defined Goal:
Enhance science understanding and skills across all grade levels within one academic year.

Action:
Document the goal and communicate it clearly to all stakeholders. Ensure every member of the community understands the destination, why it matters, and their role in reaching it.

2. Engine: Power the Movement

The Engine symbolizes the actions needed to move toward the science enrichment goal.

Actions:

- Develop a comprehensive science curriculum that includes hands-on experiments, project-based learning, and inquiry-based activities.
- Conduct professional development workshops for teachers on innovative science teaching methods and the latest scientific discoveries.
- Implement weekly science labs and activities for students to apply their learning practically.
- Organize science fairs and exhibitions to encourage student participation and showcase their work.
- Engage parents and the community by inviting them to science events and providing resources to support science learning at home.

3. Buoys: Mark the Milestones

Set measurable checkpoints to monitor and celebrate progress throughout the year.

Checkpoints:

- **Buoy 1:** By the end of Quarter 1, students will have completed their first major science project and demonstrated an improved understanding of the scientific method.
- **Buoy 2:** By mid-year, students will have participated in a school-wide science fair, with projects evaluated by teachers and community members.
- **Buoy 3:** By Quarter 3, students will have completed at least three hands-on lab activities and shown measurable growth in applying scientific concepts.
- **Buoy 4:** By year's end, students will demonstrate significant improvement in their science skills through final assessments and project presentations.

4. Evaluate: Monitor and Adjust

Regularly assess the program's effectiveness and refine strategies based on data and feedback.

Actions:

- Collect and analyze data from student assessments, project outcomes, and teacher feedback.
- Identify gaps or challenges in the implementation process.
- Adjust instructional strategies and provide additional support where needed.
- Celebrate progress to maintain motivation and momentum.

Reflection Prompt:
Are students more engaged in science? Are teachers feeling more confident in their delivery? Evaluation is both about outcomes and insight.

5. Lifeline: Build Support Systems

Establish a team of accountability partners to support the successful implementation and long-term sustainability of the program.

Actions:

- Form a science enrichment committee made up of teachers, administrators, parents, and community members.
- Schedule regular meetings to share progress, discuss surface challenges, and collaborate on solutions.
- Encourage open communication and shared leadership across roles.
- Provide ongoing resources and encouragement to keep energy and focus high.

Reminder:
The Lifeline ensures the initiative is not the responsibility of a single individual, but a shared commitment embraced by a unified team.

Example 1: Summary and Reflection

1. **Rudder:** *Enhance science understanding and skills across all grade levels within one academic year.*
2. **Engine:** Develop a hands-on curriculum, train teachers, host science fairs, run weekly labs, and engage the community.
3. **Buoys:** Set quarterly checkpoints such as projects, science fair participation, lab activities, and improved assessments.
4. **Evaluate:** Track data, gather feedback, refine instruction, and celebrate wins.
5. **Lifeline:** Create a support team to monitor progress and ensure consistent collaboration.

By applying the **REBEL Goals™ model**, the science enrichment initiative evolves from a standalone program into a dynamic part of the school's learning identity. This approach deepens curiosity, builds scientific thinking, and creates moments of wonder that ripple across classrooms. In doing so, the school fosters a culture where inquiry becomes a habit, not an event.

Example 2

REBEL Goal Example

Implementing a New Character Education Program

Implementing a character education program offers a powerful opportunity to embed core values into every corner of the school experience. Here's how the REBEL Goals™ framework can guide this initiative from vision to reality:

1. Rudder: Set the Direction

The Rudder represents the specific goal of implementing a school-wide character education program.

Defined Goal:
Promote and integrate shared core values of respect, integrity, teamwork, perseverance, and compassion into daily school life.

Action:

- Write down the goal and communicate it to all stakeholders, ensuring everyone understands the destination and the importance of this initiative.

2. Engine: Power the Movement

The Engine symbolizes the actions needed to achieve the character education goal.

Actions:

- Develop a curriculum that includes lessons, activities, and projects focused on the core values.
- Conduct professional development workshops for teachers on how to effectively teach and model these values.
- Implement weekly character education sessions using discussions, role-playing, and collaborative learning.
- Create a recognition program (e.g., "Character Champions") to celebrate students and staff who exemplify the core values.
- Engage families and the community by providing tools and resources.

3. Buoys: Mark the Milestones

Set measurable checkpoints to track the progress of the program.

Checkpoints:

- **Buoy 1:** By the end of Quarter 1, each class completes and presents a project highlighting one of the core values.
- **Buoy 2:** By mid-year, students participate in a school-wide assembly showcasing activities related to the values.
- **Buoy 3:** By Quarter 3, students submit written reflections and participate in peer feedback to demonstrate application of the core values.
- **Buoy 4:** By year's end, the school hosts a community celebration honoring student and staff growth in character development.

4. Evaluate: Monitor and Adjust

Regularly assess the program's impact and refine as needed.

Actions:

- Collect and analyze data from student reflections, teacher observations, and community feedback.
- Identify implementation gaps and adjust strategies accordingly.
- Offer additional support or training where needed.
- Celebrate growth milestones to reinforce engagement and motivation.

5. Lifeline: Build Support Systems

Establish a team of accountability partners to support and guide implementation.

Actions:

- Form a Character Education Committee that includes teachers, administrators, parents, and community members.
- Hold regular meetings to discuss progress and troubleshoot challenges.
- Maintain open communication to encourage transparency and collaboration.
- Provide ongoing resources to ensure long-term success and sustainability.

Example 2: Summary and Reflection

1. **Rudder:** Goal – *Promote and integrate shared core values of respect, integrity, teamwork, perseverance, and compassion into daily school life.*
2. **Engine:** Develop curriculum, train staff, run weekly sessions, recognize role models, and engage families.
3. **Buoys:** Track progress quarterly through class projects, assemblies, reflections, and a culminating celebration.
4. **Evaluate:** Gather feedback, analyze data, adjust actions, and acknowledge growth.
5. **Lifeline:** Form a character education committee, promote shared responsibility, and offer sustained support.

The REBEL Goals™ framework helps character education move beyond bulletin boards and pledges by turning values into visible, daily behaviors. As students and staff consistently model shared principles, the school culture becomes more cohesive, compassionate, and empowered. What begins as a character initiative becomes a way of life that strengthens every relationship and every interaction.

Example 3

REBEL Goal Example

Improve District-Wide Student Academic Performance

Boosting academic performance across an entire district requires unified vision, strategic action, and consistent support. The REBEL Goals™ framework offers a clear structure to guide this journey, turning goals into collective momentum and results.

1. Rudder: Set the Direction

The Rudder represents the specific goal of improving district-wide student academic performance.

Defined Goal:
Increase the overall academic performance of students in the district by implementing targeted instructional strategies and support systems within one academic year.

Action:
Write down the goal and communicate it clearly to all stakeholders. Ensure that every educator, parent, and community partner understands the shared destination and their role in helping students reach it.

2. Engine: Power the Movement

The Engine symbolizes the actions needed to drive progress toward the academic goal.

Actions:

- Develop and implement a district-wide professional development program focused on effective instructional strategies.
- Introduce data-driven instructional practices to identify and close student learning gaps.
- Enhance student support services, including tutoring, counseling, and after-school enrichment programs.
- Foster collaboration among schools to share best practices, tools, and resources.
- Engage parents and the broader community in student learning through targeted workshops and consistent communication.

3. Buoys: Mark the Milestones

Measurable checkpoints help monitor progress and make necessary course corrections throughout the year.

Checkpoints:

- **Buoy 1:** By the end of Quarter 1, conduct baseline assessments to identify performance gaps and establish targeted improvement areas.
- **Buoy 2:** By mid-year, implement targeted instructional strategies and support systems across all schools; initial assessments should show signs of progress.
- **Buoy 3:** By Quarter 3, conduct mid-year assessments to evaluate impact, gather feedback, and adjust plans where needed.
- **Buoy 4:** By year's end, conduct final assessments and compare results with baseline to measure growth and effectiveness.

4. Evaluate: Monitor and Adjust

Regular assessment ensures alignment, accountability, and the ability to course-correct in real time.

Actions:

- Collect and analyze data from student assessments, teacher feedback, and usage of support services.
- Identify implementation gaps or barriers affecting progress.
- Adjust instructional or support strategies to better meet student needs.
- Celebrate successes at every stage to build morale and maintain momentum.

Reflection Prompt:
Are all schools demonstrating improvement? Where is support most needed? What strategies are making the biggest impact?

5. Lifeline: Build Support Systems

The Lifeline is your network of accountability partners that ensures shared responsibility and momentum.

Actions:

- Form a district-wide academic improvement committee with principals, teachers, parents, and community members.
- Schedule regular check-ins to share progress, collaborate on solutions, and adjust plans.
- Promote transparent communication and gather input from all stakeholders.
- Offer continuous support and professional learning to fuel sustained progress.

Reminder:
The Lifeline is not about monitoring alone; it is about empowering a unified team to stay connected to the goal and committed to the journey.

Example 3: Summary and Reflection

1. **Rudder:** Increase overall academic performance by implementing targeted strategies and support systems within one academic year.
2. **Engine:** Provide professional development, use data-driven practices, expand student supports, encourage school collaboration, and engage families.
3. **Buoys:** Use quarterly assessments and implementation milestones to measure impact and guide adjustments.
4. **Evaluate:** Monitor progress, reflect on outcomes, adjust strategies, and celebrate growth.
5. **Lifeline:** Form a district improvement committee, encourage shared accountability, and provide the tools and trust needed for success.

Using the REBEL Goals™ framework, this effort becomes a shared pursuit of growth and community building. The structure brings clarity, while the collective ownership builds momentum. Together, schools, staff, and families unite to raise the bar—and lift every student along with it.

Strategic Goal Topics

Every thriving school needs clear strategic goals that blend immediate priorities with long-term aspirations. A well-crafted set of school goals functions as this roadmap, aligning daily efforts with the broader mission and vision. These goals are intentional anchors that **guide progress, foster unity, and create a culture of continuous improvement.**

Your strategic goals should reflect both the unique identity of your school community and the areas of growth that will most meaningfully impact student learning and well-being. Some may be short-term in focus, while others will chart a long-range course. Together, they shape the future you are striving to build.

Here are common **Strategic Goal Topics** that may appear on a Strategic School Map:

- Academic Excellence
- Enhanced Student Support Services
- Professional Development for Staff
- Technology Integration
- Community and Parental Engagement
- Safe and Welcoming School Environment
- Curriculum and Instructional Improvement
- Student Leadership and Extracurricular Activities
- Sustainable Practices and Environmental Education
- College and Career Readiness
- Financial Stability and Resource Management
- Student Attendance and Engagement

Each of these topics represents a pillar of school success and a path to building a stronger, more aligned learning community.

The following pages provide strategic goal topics, objectives, and examples that could appear in a Strategic School Map (SSM). Each example is designed to help you develop broad categories into actionable goals with clear objectives, timelines, and accountability structures. Use these ideas to design a Strategic School Map that reflects your highest aspirations, and empowers every stakeholder to play a meaningful role in bringing your school's vision to life.

Strategic School Goals Examples:

- **Academic Excellence**
    - **Objective:** Improve student academic performance and achieve higher standardized test scores.
    - **Example:** Increase the percentage of students meeting or exceeding state proficiency standards in reading and math by 10% over the next three years.

- **Enhanced Student Support Services**
    - **Objective:** Provide comprehensive support services to address the academic, social, and emotional needs of students.
    - **Example:** Implement a school-wide counseling program to support students' mental health and well-being, reducing the student-to-counselor ratio to 250:1 within two years.

- **Professional Development for Staff**
    - **Objective:** Invest in the professional growth of teachers and staff to improve instructional practices.
    - **Example:** Offer quarterly professional development workshops focused on innovative teaching methods and classroom management, with at least 80% of teachers participating annually.

- **Technology Integration**
    - **Objective:** Integrate technology into the curriculum to enhance learning and prepare students for the digital age.
    - **Example:** Ensure that every classroom is equipped with up-to-date technology and provide training for teachers to effectively use digital tools in instruction within the next two years.

- **Community and Parental Engagement**
    - **Objective:** Foster strong relationships between the school, parents, and the community to support student success.

- o **Example:** Increase parent participation in school events and activities by 25% over the next three years through targeted outreach and engagement initiatives.

- **Safe and Welcoming School Environment**

  - o **Objective:** Create a safe, welcoming, and supportive school environment for all students and staff.
  - o **Example:** Implement a comprehensive anti-bullying program and reduce reported bullying incidents by 50% over the next two years.

- **Curriculum and Instructional Improvement**

  - o **Objective:** Continuously improve the curriculum and instructional practices to meet the varied student needs.
  - o **Example:** Revise the curriculum to include more project-based and experiential learning opportunities, with at least 75% of teachers incorporating these methods within the next three years.

- **Student Leadership and Extracurricular Activities**

  - o **Objective:** Develop student leadership skills and increase participation in extracurricular activities.
  - o **Example:** Establish a student leadership program and increase student participation in clubs and sports by 20% over the next two years.

- **Sustainable Practices and Environmental Education**

  - o **Objective:** Promote sustainability and environmental awareness within the school community.
  - o **Example:** Implement a school-wide recycling program and integrate environmental education into the curriculum, with at least 50% of students participating in sustainability projects annually.

- **College and Career Readiness**

  - o **Objective:** Prepare students for post-secondary education and career success.
  - o **Example:** Increase the percentage of graduating seniors who are accepted into college or vocational training programs by 15% over the next three years.

- **Financial Stability and Resource Management**

    o **Objective:** Ensure the school is financially stable and resources are managed efficiently.
    o **Example:** Develop a comprehensive budget plan that reduces operational costs by 10% over the next three years while maintaining quality education services.

- **Student Attendance and Engagement**

    o **Objective:** Improve student attendance rates and engagement in learning.
    o **Example:** Implement initiatives to reduce absenteeism and achieve a 95% attendance rate within the next two years.

Why This Matters

These strategic school goals offer a clear and actionable path for schools to pursue excellence across every facet of the educational experience. By identifying focused objectives and supporting them with measurable, community-driven examples, schools can foster a welcoming, energized, and forward-moving culture that benefits all stakeholders: students, staff, families, and the broader community.

Setting Your Sights Higher: Charting Goals That Stretch Your School's Horizon

> *Your goal should be just out of reach, but not out of sight.*
> —Denis Waitley and Remi Witt

You've mapped out your destination and set your rudder firmly toward your strategic school goals. Now it's time to ensure those goals are truly worthy of the journey ahead. As you navigate forward, distinguishing between goals that are too comfortable, just right, or overly ambitious becomes crucial to sustained progress. Like a seasoned captain scanning the horizon, you'll use the REBEL Goals™ Framework to pinpoint goals that inspire meaningful growth, stretching your team without overwhelming them.

Let's explore how to identify goals that live in the sweet spot, just beyond easy reach, yet clearly visible and attainable.

The Goal Setting Circle

Finding the "Just Right" Challenge

In a school's Strategic Map, there are three types of goals you can set: **Comfort Goals**, **Stretch Goals**, and **Delusional Goals**. The key is to aim for the *"just right"* target, one that pushes your school to a higher level while still being achievable.

1. Comfort Goals: Too Comfortable

These are goals that fall well within your school's current capabilities. If you accomplish them and nothing visibly improves, it sends the message that goal setting isn't worth the effort. These goals feel safe, but they don't challenge your school community to grow. Everyone stays on autopilot, going through the motions.

2. Stretch Goals: Just Beyond Reach

Stretch Goals sit just outside your comfort zone, but with intentional effort, collaboration, and support, they can be reached. These are the goals that push your school to stretch and grow.

Martin Seligman, one of the founders of Positive Psychology, emphasized that achieving a Stretch Goal creates a sense of accomplishment, fulfillment, and happiness. According to his research, the act of setting and reaching meaningful goals is essential to building self-esteem and boosting well-being at both the individual and collective levels.

A Stretch Goal might require recalibration along the way. That's okay. The goal is to challenge your team in a way that is motivating, not overwhelming.

3. Delusional Goals: Out of Reach

These goals are well beyond the current capacity of the school and risk causing frustration or burnout. For example, aiming to be the top-performing school in your region may be inspiring, but expecting it to happen within a single year, without significant changes or resources, is unrealistic. Many smaller Stretch Goals must be set and accomplished along the way to reach this larger aspiration.

The Zone of Proximal Development: Where Stretch Lives

Russian psychologist **Lev Vygotsky** developed the concept of the **Zone of Proximal Development (ZPD)**, the area just outside what a person (or school) can do independently, but within reach with effort, guidance, and collaboration.

You can think of it this way:

- **Comfort Goals** sit **within** your current abilities.
- **Stretch Goals** sit **just outside** your current capacity, within your Zone of Proximal Development (ZPD).
- **Delusional Goals** sit **far outside** your ZPD and can lead to stress or discouragement.

When you set goals in your Stretch Zone, you create forward momentum. These goals **inspire, energize, and satisfy**, moving your school closer to its destination in meaningful, measurable ways.

Using the REBEL Goals™ Framework to Stretch Every Component

Once you've identified a Stretch Goal, the next step is to make sure every part of that goal, its direction, action plan, checkpoints, evaluation process, and support systems, is designed to stretch thinking without slipping into overwhelm. That's where the **REBEL Goals™ Framework** and **Goal Setting Circle** come into play.

Each REBEL component—**Rudder, Engine, Buoys, Evaluate, and Lifeline**—can be approached with either a **Comfort**, **Stretch**, or **Delusional** mindset. This section helps you apply the **Stretch Zone mindset** to every part of your goal, ensuring it's not only well-defined but also well-supported, well-paced, and well-monitored.

The goal is full alignment: a clear direction, purposeful actions, meaningful progress markers, ongoing reflection, and the right level of accountability and support—all calibrated to challenge your team just beyond their current capacity, where real growth happens.

1. Rudder (Defining the Goal)

- **Comfort Goal**: The goal is safe and easily attainable. It does not require major changes or inspire new thinking.
- **Stretch Goal**: The goal demands innovation, effort, and vision. It challenges current practices and pushes the school forward.
- **Delusional Goal**: The goal is so ambitious that it feels disconnected from current realities and available resources.

2. Engine (Action-Oriented Strategies)

- **Comfort Goal**: Requires minimal action, relying mostly routine steps already in place.
- **Stretch Goal**: Involves new strategies, significant collaboration, and consistent execution by all stakeholders.
- **Delusional Goal**: Demands actions that exceed what is realistic or sustainable given time, staffing, or funding constraints.

3. Buoys (Measurable Progress)

- **Comfort Goal**: Checkpoints are easy wins that are unlikely to stretch capacity or drive improvement.
- **Stretch Goal**: Checkpoints are bold and meaningful, requiring focused effort and ongoing monitoring.
- **Delusional Goal**: Checkpoints are so far out of reach they risk discouragement or disengagement.

4. Evaluate (Continuous Improvement)

- **Comfort Goal**: Little evaluation is needed, and few changes are ever required because little is being challenged.
- **Stretch Goal**: Regular evaluation leads to important course corrections and momentum-building progress.
- **Delusional Goal**: Evaluation shows repeated setbacks or little advancement, despite strong effort, pointing to an unrealistic goal.

5. Lifeline (Support and Accountability)

- **Comfort Goal**: Needs minimal support. The goal can be achieved with little collaboration or accountability.
- **Stretch Goal**: Requires robust support structures and clear accountability systems to succeed.
- **Delusional Goal**: Needs more support than the school can realistically provide, placing undue pressure on the system.

Final Thought:

When your **REBEL components align within the Stretch Zone**, your school is poised for **real and measurable growth**.

Stretch Goals are where **vision meets action**, and where **confidence, capacity, and community** thrive.

Example of a Stretch Goal with the REBEL Format

Improve literacy skills across all grade levels within one academic year.

Summary

This REBEL Goal focuses on improving literacy through clearly defined objectives, actionable strategies, progress checkpoints, and ongoing support. By setting a **Stretch Goal** and using the REBEL framework, the school fosters a culture of reading, collaboration, and achievement that benefits all learners.

1. Rudder (Defining the Goal)

Goal: Clearly define the objective, such as "Improve literacy skills across all grade levels within one academic year."

This serves as the clear destination that will guide all instruction, planning, and collaboration.

2. Engine (Action-Oriented Strategies)

The Engine outlines the actions that will drive progress toward the goal.

Actions:

- Develop a comprehensive, vertically aligned literacy curriculum across all grade levels.
- Conduct professional development workshops focused on reading instruction, assessment strategies, and differentiation.
- Implement targeted reading programs (e.g., structured phonics instruction, decodable text practice, fluency-building activities) to support student engagement and fluency.
- Create literacy-rich environments with classroom libraries, student authorship opportunities, and reading celebrations.
- Engage parents through take-home reading resources, literacy nights, and family reading challenges.

3. Buoys (Measurable Progress)

These checkpoints will monitor progress and provide opportunities to adjust.

Checkpoints:

- **End of Quarter 1**: Complete initial literacy assessments and analyze baseline data.
- **Mid-Year**: Conduct mid-point assessments to evaluate growth and identify gaps.
- **End of Quarter 3**: Review student work and assessment trends to fine-tune interventions.
- **End of Year**: Use final assessments and portfolio reviews to measure overall literacy improvement.

4. Evaluate (Continuous Improvement)

Frequent review ensures the initiative stays on course.

Evaluation:

- Collect and analyze literacy data at each checkpoint (e.g., reading levels, comprehension scores).
- Survey teachers and students on the effectiveness of strategies.
- Adjust instruction based on data and feedback.
- Celebrate growth through assemblies, student showcases, and recognitions to maintain motivation.

5. Lifeline (Support and Accountability)

Support systems and collaboration keep the goal alive.

Support System:

- Form a literacy improvement committee that includes reading specialists, teachers, and administrators.
- Hold monthly meetings to review progress and share best practices.
- Involve parents through consistent communication and engagement tools.
- Provide resources, mentoring, and coaching to support implementation across classrooms.

The School Goals Anchor Models

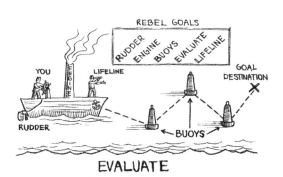 

School Goals: Rooted in the Principle of Life Aspirations

The Principle of Life Aspirations is about striving to become your best, reaching for higher levels of growth, and pursuing meaningful goals with purpose and passion. *Life Aspirations* inspire individuals and teams to look beyond the present and work toward something greater. In schools, this principle fuels progress, continuous improvement, and the desire to create lasting impact. For the School Goals anchor, Life Aspirations guide leaders and teams in setting intentional, focused, and energizing goals, ones that reflect who they want to become, what they want to achieve, and how they will grow together. Goal setting is the strategic engine that turns aspiration into direction, direction into action, and action into excellence.

Putting Aspirations into Motion

Now that you've explored how to set meaningful school goals, this section brings everything together in one place. Consider this your ready-to-use goals model, perfect for sharing with your leadership team, using in staff meetings, or guiding strategic planning sessions.

School goals are most effective when they're not just written—but *fully lived.* To bring them to life, schools need models that go beyond checklists and transform strategic planning into shared momentum. Two such models—the **REBEL Goals™ Framework** and the **Goal Setting Circle**—help turn vision into motion and ideas into impact. These visuals serve as navigational tools for reflection, alignment, and real-time progress monitoring.

1. The REBEL Goals™ Framework

This framework uses the metaphor of a boat at sea to represent the strategic journey toward achieving a meaningful school goal. Each REBEL component plays a unique role in navigating your school's path with clarity, consistency, and purpose:

- **R – Rudder (Direction)**
  Your **goal** is the rudder, and it sets your direction. Just like a ship without a rudder drifts aimlessly, a school without clear goals loses focus. The rudder provides clarity about *where you're going* and ensures everyone on board understands the destination.
- **E – Engine (Action)**
  The **engine** represents the day-to-day **actions** and initiatives that drive the school forward. This is where effort meets execution. When your actions are aligned with your mission and vision, the engine propels your culture and progress.
- **B – Buoys (Checkpoints)**
  Buoys are measurable **progress indicators** along the way, such as benchmarks, milestones, or data points that help you track whether you're on course. They provide timely feedback, allow for pacing, and promote accountability.
- **E – Evaluate (Reflection)**
  Like any good navigator, a leader must constantly **evaluate** the journey. This means reviewing progress, analyzing what's working, identifying obstacles, and adjusting course as needed. Evaluation turns intention into *informed action.*
- **L – Lifeline (Support & Accountability)**
  No school leader succeeds alone. The **lifeline** represents the **team, partnerships, and support systems** that sustain progress. Whether it's your staff, a leadership team, a PLC, or community partners, your lifeline offers encouragement, reflection, and shared ownership of the journey.

When used with your leadership team or school staff, the REBEL Goals™ Framework becomes a living tool for *propelling* meaningful progress. It encourages goal-setting that is clear, collaborative, and sustainable, anchoring your daily actions in long-term vision.

2. The Goal Setting Circle

The **Goal Setting Circle** is a simple yet powerful visual that helps school teams assess the level of challenge embedded in their goals. It uses concentric circles to map where a goal falls in relation to a school's current capacity and ambition. The goal isn't just to set any goal—but to set the *right* goal.

At the center of the model is a central dot labeled **"You Are Here,"** representing your current state, including the skills, systems, and supports your school already has in place.

Surrounding this center are three concentric rings:

- **Comfort Goals** (Inner Circle): These are safe and easily attainable. They keep the school within its current capacity, requiring little innovation or risk. While they offer a sense of accomplishment, they often produce limited growth and can reinforce a status quo mindset. If goals feel like "business as usual," they likely fall here.
- **Stretch Goals** (Middle Circle): These are goals that push your school just beyond its current capacity, within reach, but not without effort. Stretch Goals inspire creativity, collaboration, and continuous improvement. They're challenging enough to spark momentum and rewarding enough to build confidence and collective pride when achieved. This is the **zone of growth.**
- **Delusional Goals** (Outer Circle): These goals may sound visionary, but they are unrealistic given your current time, resources, or capacity. While they may stem from good intentions, they can lead to frustration, burnout, or disillusionment when the gap between ambition and reality becomes too wide. Schools must be cautious here. Big dreams are encouraged, but they need to be scaffolded with achievable steps.

Why It Matters:

The Goal Setting Circle helps leadership teams set expectations wisely and align their efforts with what is possible—*with a stretch*. When used in tandem with the REBEL Goals Framework, it becomes easier to gauge not just *how* to pursue a goal, but *whether* that goal is set at the right level of challenge to inspire meaningful progress without overwhelming your team.

> *"A goal that stretches you without breaking you activates potential you didn't know was there."*
> —Dr. Joe Famularo

Strategic Goal Development Using the Visual Goal Models

The **REBEL Goals Framework** and the **Goal Setting Circle** are powerful tools for fostering clarity and collaboration in the goal-setting process. These visual models help leadership teams move from abstract intentions to clearly defined, actionable, and measurable goals, while also ensuring the right level of challenge.

By embedding these tools into your strategic planning sessions, your team can navigate the complexities of school improvement with a shared language and framework. Here's how to make the most of these models:

1. Introduce the Models with Purpose

Begin by walking your leadership team through both models, **the REBEL Goals Framework** and the **Goal Setting Circle**. Explain their components, why they matter, and how they can be used to sharpen focus and build alignment. Use real examples from your school context to bring the concepts to life.

2. Facilitate Interactive Goal-Setting Sessions

Use the **REBEL Goals™ Framework** during planning workshops, staff meetings, or leadership retreats to collaboratively develop schoolwide, team, or department goals. Break into small groups and have each team brainstorm:

- **Rudders** – What is the goal? Is it clear and directional?
  - Is this goal challenging enough to inspire growth without becoming overwhelming?
- **Engines** – What specific actions will move us toward it?
  - Are these actions bold, intentional, and beyond business-as-usual?
- **Buoys** – What checkpoints or metrics will show our progress?
  - Do our benchmarks reflect meaningful progress that pushes us to grow?
- **Evaluate** – How and when will we assess progress and adjust course?
  - Are we committed to regular reflection that sparks improvement—not just compliance?
- **Lifelines** – Who will provide support and help maintain focus?
  - Do we have strong enough systems and relationships in place to sustain a Stretch Goal?

End each session with a team dialogue grounded in the **Comfort–Stretch–Delusional lens**:

- *Are we aiming just beyond reach—but still within the zone of possibility?*
- *Have we pushed our thinking to design a goal that challenges us—without setting us up to fail?*

By visualizing goals with REBEL and involving your full team in the process, your strategic planning becomes collaborative, focused, and truly culture-driven.

3. Use Large Visual Aids

Create enlarged visuals of both models and post them on whiteboards, digital boards, or large wall posters in your meeting space. Invite participants to add sticky notes or write directly on the models as they define goals and plot their course forward. These visual anchors support clarity, collaboration, and group memory.

4. Revisit Often—Not Just Once

These models are not one-time tools. Refer back to them regularly during staff meetings, leadership check-ins, or mid-year reviews. They can be used to assess progress, celebrate milestones, and recalibrate if necessary.

Make it the norm to ask:

- Where are we on the REBEL map?
- Are we still working within our Stretch zone, or have we slipped into comfort or veered into delusion?

By incorporating the REBEL Goals Framework and the Goal Setting Circle into your strategic development process, you create a shared system that is both rigorous and motivating. These models turn abstract planning into purposeful action, guiding your school community toward continuous growth, alignment, and excellence.

**Strategic Thinking Questions for
Inward School Anchor 6:
School Goal**

Here is a list of strategic thinking questions to help guide your reflection when developing meaningful school goals. These questions are designed to promote clarity, alignment, and intentional action, ensuring your goals are rooted in authentic needs, informed by strengths, and directed toward measurable impact. As you reflect, consider whether your goals live in the **"Stretch Zone,"** ambitious yet achievable, and how each element connects to the **REBEL Goals™ Framework**. This process will help you set goals that are not only strategic, but also sustainable, supported, and truly lived across your school community.

Needs and Priorities

- What current challenges or gaps are most pressing in our school or district?
- What data or trends suggest this area needs targeted improvement?
- Which student, staff, or community needs are not yet fully addressed?

Strengths and Opportunities

- What existing strengths or successful practices can we build on?
- Who or what within our community can help propel this goal forward?
- What recent successes can serve as a launchpad for this work?

Purpose and Relevance

- Why is this goal worth pursuing now?
- How does this goal align with our school's vision, mission, and core values?
- Will this goal inspire meaningful participation and commitment from stakeholders?

Stretch and Challenge

- Does this goal push us just beyond our comfort zone?
- Are we aiming high enough to inspire progress, but not so high that it feels unachievable?
- How does this goal reflect the qualities of a Stretch Goal in the Goal Setting Circle?

Clarity and Direction (Rudder)

- Is the goal stated clearly and concisely?
- Can every stakeholder understand what this goal is and why it matters?
- Is it written in a way that reflects a shared destination?

Action and Alignment (Engine)

- What specific actions will bring this goal to life?
- How will we ensure these actions align with our core values and leadership principles?
- Are responsibilities clear across teams and departments?

Milestones and Metrics (Buoys)

- What does success look like at key checkpoints along the way?
- How will we know if we are making progress?
- Are our milestones both measurable and motivating?

Evaluation and Adjustment (Evaluate)

- How will we monitor progress and gather feedback?
- What structures will we use to reflect, recalibrate, and improve?
- How often will we revisit this goal to ensure it remains relevant?

Support and Accountability (Lifeline)

- Who will help lead, support, and sustain this goal?
- What accountability systems are needed to keep the work moving forward?
- How will we build a culture of shared ownership and responsibility?

Now that you've reflected using these strategic thinking questions, take a moment to capture your school or district's emerging priorities, challenges, and opportunities. Use the space on the next page to jot down your initial goal ideas. This is your draft zone. Don't worry about perfect wording just yet.

At the end of this chapter, and in Appendix C, you'll use the **REBEL Goals™ Framework Template** to shape these ideas into purposeful, actionable, and community-supported Stretch Goals that align with your Strategic School Map.

Initial Thoughts for Your School Stretch Goals:

The Guiding Question for School Goals

Are your current school goals at the forefront of your culture, actively guiding daily decisions and actions, or are they tucked away in a binder?

If your goals aren't visible, shared, and lived, your Strategic School Map lacks the direction needed to move your school forward. Every effective plan needs goals that are clear, motivating, and aligned with your school's highest aspirations.

REBEL Goals Framework: Strategic Goal-Setting Template

School/District Name:
Goal Title:
Date:

RUDDER – Defining the Goal

- **Goal Statement:**
  Clearly define the objective in one focused sentence.
- **Why this Goal Matters:**
  Explain how this goal aligns with your school's vision, mission, or strategic priorities.

ENGINE – Action-Oriented Strategies

Identify the key steps and initiatives needed to propel your school toward this goal.

- Action 1:
- Action 2:
- Action 3:
- Action 4:
- Action 5:

BUOYS – Measurable Progress Checkpoints

Establish clear, trackable checkpoints to monitor progress and celebrate wins.

- Buoy 1:
- Buoy 2:
- Buoy 3:
- Buoy 4:

EVALUATE – Continuous Improvement

Outline how you will review progress and adapt strategies when needed.

- Collection Methods:
- Frequency of Review:
- Adjustment Strategies:

LIFELINE – Support and Accountability

Define the people and systems responsible for sustaining momentum.

- Accountability Partners / Committees:
- Stakeholder Engagement Strategies:
- Communication Channels:

Stretch Goal Zone Check

Use the Goal Setting Circle to determine whether your overall goal and each REBEL component are appropriately challenging.

Goal Type	Indicators	Check
Comfort Goal	Too easy, low effort, minimal change	Yes No
Stretch Goal	Ambitious but achievable, pushes growth	Yes No
Delusional Goal	Unrealistic given current resources or timeframe	Yes No

Reflection Notes:
Review your current strategies. Do they match the level of challenge you intend? If not, revise your REBEL components to bring them into the Stretch Zone.

*This template is designed to help schools create intentional, impactful, and inspiring goals using the REBEL Goals™ Framework. It serves not only as a planning tool but as a strategic map that guides your school community toward shared success. A printable version is available in **Appendix C** for ongoing use in planning, goal-setting, and team reflection.*

Chapter 5

Developing Your Inward School Map (ISM)

Mapping the School's Foundational Identity

After exploring the 6 Inward School Anchors—**School SelfCulture, School Vision, Daily School Mission, School Leadership Principles, School Core Values,** and **School Goals**—it's time to bring these foundational elements together into one cohesive framework: your **Inward School Map (ISM).**

This chapter guides you through the process of assembling, displaying, and applying your ISM. This map is more than a summary; it's a **living representation** of your school's identity: the beliefs, priorities, and aspirations that drive your culture from the inside out. It acts as an internal compass for leadership and a strategic blueprint for the entire community. When fully realized and applied, your ISM ensures that daily actions align with long-term intentions, allowing every decision, behavior, and conversation to reflect the school's deepest convictions.

As you begin this process, you'll explore how to:

- Visually and meaningfully display your school's key messages.
- Elevate your School Vision and School Mission through powerful, repeatable mottos.
- Integrate each anchor into the daily rhythm of school life.
- Use your SelfCulture Statement as a leadership lens for clarity and direction.
- Communicate and manage your School Goals for visibility and impact.

Now that you've journeyed through the 6 Inward Anchors, this next phase shifts your focus from individual anchor development to **collective integration** by pulling everything together into one unified, strategic foundation. The **six steps** that follow will help you thoughtfully construct and begin using your Inward School Map.

Let's begin mapping your school's **foundational identity** by laying the internal **structure** for a culture of clarity, consistency, and collective purpose.

6 Steps to Build and Launch Your Inward School Map

Step 1: Reflect on Your Journey

Before assembling your Inward School Map (ISM), take time to pause and reflect on the journey you've just completed through the 6 Inward Anchors. These reflections are an essential checkpoint. Each anchor you've explored represents a piece of your school's internal DNA: the beliefs you hold, the purpose you pursue, and the principles you live by.

Ask yourself:

- What new clarity has emerged about your school's identity?
- Which anchor(s) sparked the most conversation, energy, or alignment?
- Are there areas that still need refinement or deeper discussion?

Use this moment to gather your notes, drafts, and team reflections. Whether you've fully developed each anchor or are still refining your ideas, this is the time to step back and see the larger picture taking shape. The ISM process is about progress, intentionality, and anchoring your school's culture in clearly defined, principle-based direction. This reflection serves as the foundation for developing your ISM, where clarity, focus, and alignment set the tone for the entire process.

The stronger your foundation, the more purposeful your map. And the clearer your map, the more unified your team's journey forward will be.

Step 2: Integrate the Inward Anchors

Now it's time to bring all 6 Inward Anchors together into one cohesive and strategic framework, your Inward School Map (ISM). This is where clarity becomes direction.

Each anchor you've developed represents a vital spoke on your school's leadership wheel, with the SelfCulture Anchor at the center. Together, they form a balanced, principle-driven structure that strengthens your entire school culture from the inside out.

When fully realized and applied, your **ISM** serves as an internal compass for leadership, ensuring that daily actions align with long-term intentions and that every decision, behavior, and conversation reflects the school's deepest convictions.

The **ISM** is a **living, evolving** representation of your school's foundational identity. It serves as an internal compass, constantly adjusting as your school's culture grows.

- **School SelfCulture Statement** – Your foundation and identity.
- **School Vision Statement** – Your long-range aspiration.
- **Daily School Mission Statement** – Your everyday purpose in action.
- **School Leadership Principles** – Your internal guideposts for leadership.
- **School Core Values** – Your shared commitments that shape behavior.
- **School Goals** – Your focused objectives that move your school forward.

As you review each element, ensure they align, not just in language, but in spirit. Do they reinforce one another? Are they grounded in the same beliefs and aspirations? When viewed together, these anchors should feel like a tightly constructed wheel, with each part supporting the others all turning in unison.

A strong Inward School Map means your leadership foundation is ready to drive the school forward with clarity, consistency, and momentum.

Step 3: Display Key Anchors Everywhere: Embedding the School's Identity into Daily Life:

To create and sustain a unified school culture, it is essential to display the foundational school anchors—your **School Vision, Daily School Mission, School Leadership Principles, and School Core Values**—throughout the school environment. The mottos for the Vision and Mission, along with the School Core Values and Leadership Principles, should be displayed in multiple visible locations around the school to inspire and align the community. The full statements for the Vision and Mission should be displayed in strategic, high-traffic areas to reinforce the deeper meaning and intentionality behind them. These foundational inward anchors define the school's identity and brand, connecting and creating a bond among all stakeholders. By prominently showcasing these elements, the school's values and priorities are not just communicated but are embedded into daily life, guiding actions and interactions across the community.

Foundational Anchors to Display

- **School Vision Statement:** A clear and inspiring articulation of the school's long-term aspirations. It represents what the school strives to achieve and motivates the entire community to work toward a shared future.
- **School Vision Motto:** A succinct phrase that captures the essence of the school's vision. It should be displayed widely throughout the school to inspire and align all stakeholders.
- **Daily School Mission Statement:** A concise statement outlining the school's daily purpose and commitment. It provides focus and clarity for day-to-day actions, connecting them to the larger vision.
- **Daily School Mission Motto:** A short, impactful phrase that represents the school's daily mission. It should be prominently placed in many areas to keep the school community focused on daily actions aligned with the mission.
- **School Leadership Principles:** The guiding principles that shape leadership behaviors and decisions. These principles reflect the school's core beliefs and provide a framework for intentional and effective leadership.
- **School Core Values:** The fundamental values that define the school's culture and priorities. These shared values shape interactions, decision-making, and the overall atmosphere of the school community.

Where to Display These Foundational Anchors

1. **Classrooms and Hallways**: Place posters or banners with the anchors prominently in spaces where students and teachers spend the most time, reinforcing the school's identity throughout the day.
2. **School Website and Digital Platforms**: Feature these statements on the homepage, staff portals, and newsletters to ensure they are accessible to both internal and external audiences.
3. **Calendars and Agendas**: Print the Vision and Mission Statements on school calendars, planners, and agendas so they remain central to daily and long-term planning.
4. **Creative Spaces**: Embed these anchors into murals, floor designs, or staircases, and even in unexpected places such as gym walls or bathroom mirrors, creating moments of inspiration throughout the school.
5. **Administrative and Staff Areas**: Display the anchors prominently in faculty lounges, meeting rooms, and leadership offices as reminders of the shared goals and principles that drive decisions and collaboration.
6. **Outdoor and Common Spaces**: Place large-scale displays in high-visibility areas like the main entrance, cafeteria, gymnasium, or auditorium to signal a unified identity as soon as anyone enters the school.

Why Display These Foundational Anchors

1. **Reinforces Identity**: By displaying these foundational elements, the school ensures that every stakeholder internalizes and connects with its identity and purpose.
2. **Creates Alignment**: Visual reminders keep everyone focused on shared priorities and goals, fostering consistency across all areas of the school.
3. **Encourages Ownership**: Publicly visible anchors inspire pride and commitment among students, staff, and the broader school community.
4. **Supports Decision-Making**: Whether in leadership meetings, classrooms, or parent interactions, having the school's Vision, Mission, Principles, and Values prominently displayed ensures they guide every action and decision.

By embedding the School Vision Statement, Daily School Mission Statement, School Leadership Principles, and School Core Values into the daily fabric of the school, these elements become a driving force of the school culture, inspiring every action and interaction across the community.

Step 4. Utilize the School SelfCulture Statement as an Internal Leadership Tool

Aligning Identity with Every Decision

Your School SelfCulture Statement is a **strategic anchor**. Crafted from the 6 Inward Anchors, this unified narrative reflects your school's identity, foundational beliefs, and long-term aspirations. It brings together your **vision, mission, principles, values, and goals** into a single, guiding reference point.

But its real power lies in how it's used.

This statement should live at the center of leadership conversations, strategic planning sessions, and collaborative decision-making. Just like the center anchor in a captain's wheel, it keeps your direction steady when external pressures push and pull. When your leadership team regularly returns to the SelfCulture Statement, it ensures that every action, no matter how small, flows from shared beliefs and reinforces your culture from the inside out.

Why It Matters

- **Clarifies Identity**: It reminds your team who you are, what you stand for, and where you're headed.
- **Aligns Decisions**: It serves as a filter to ensure that initiatives, programs, and responses remain true to your core.
- **Fosters Consistency**: Whether onboarding a new staff member or launching a new goal, the statement creates coherence across time and leadership changes.
- **Strengthens Culture**: When used with intention, it builds trust, unity, and purpose because decisions feel rooted, not reactive.

Use your School SelfCulture Statement as the anchor that grounds your leadership and the steering force that propels your school forward with clarity and conviction.

Step 5. Display and Evolve School Goals

Flexibility in Practice, Focus in Purpose

While your **Vision, Mission, Leadership Principles,** and **Core Values** serve as **steady principled anchors**, **school goals** are **intentionally dynamic** and designed to evolve with your school's **priorities and progress**.

Whether or not these goals are displayed publicly should depend on their purpose and the audience they're meant to inspire or inform.

When to Display School Goals?

For goals that involve or energize the broader school community, public visibility becomes a powerful strategy. Consider displaying goals like:

- *Improving Literacy Skills Across All Grade Levels*
- *Creating a Safe and Welcoming Environment*
- *Increasing Student Engagement Through Project-Based Learning*

Visible displays on hallway boards, classroom posters, or digital platforms spark excitement, clarify focus, and foster a sense of shared responsibility. They make progress **tangible** and turn abstract ambitions into **community action.**

When to Keep Goals Internal

Not all goals need to be raised like a flag. Some are best managed behind the scenes, focused and strategic yet deeply aligned. Internal goals may include:

- *Enhancing Professional Development for Staff*
- *Refining Data-Informed Instruction*
- *Improving Financial Resource Management*

These may be tracked through:

- Internal dashboards
- Team goal sheets
- Leadership meeting agendas
- Digital calendars with milestones

This approach keeps the core team focused, without diluting broader communication or overloading stakeholders with unnecessary detail.

A Balanced Approach

- **Display for Unity:** Goals that touch the whole community deserve visibility. They build momentum, inspire participation, and showcase progress.
- **Keep Focused:** Goals that are strategic, technical, or in early planning stages may benefit from internal clarity before becoming public-facing.
- **Anchor to What's Enduring:** While goals shift with time, your Vision, Mission, Principles, and Core Values should always remain **prominently displayed** as your school's stable anchors amid evolving priorities.

By thoughtfully balancing public celebration with internal focus, your school can **turn its goals into sails**, adjusting to catch the right wind while always steering toward a shared horizon.

Step 6: Implement and Observe

Bring Your Inward School Map (ISM) to Life

You don't have to wait for perfection to take meaningful action.

Once you've drafted your ISM, even if some pieces are still evolving, take the powerful step of putting it into practice. Begin sharing it with your school community. Introduce it during leadership meetings, staff gatherings, and school-wide events. Post it in places where it can be seen, discussed, and lived daily.

Then observe.

Watch how language begins to shift, how decisions become more intentional, how culture starts aligning with your anchors. Listen for echoes of your School Mission in hallway conversations, see your Core Values show up in classroom norms, and feel your SelfCulture statement reflected in staff collaboration.

This stage is about awareness.

- What's resonating?
- Where are the sparks of alignment?
- Where is more clarity or reinforcement needed?

The ISM is not a final product; it is a living framework. And now that it's in motion, you can refine, adapt, and strengthen it with the feedback and energy it generates. In this step, culture begins to move from concept to reality.

More Than Words: Why Vision and Mission Mottos Are Essential for School Culture

Creating a motto for both your School Vision Statement and Daily Mission Statement is a critical step in defining and reinforcing your school's culture. **A motto is a succinct and memorable phrase** that captures the essence of your school's vision and mission in a way that resonates with all stakeholders.

Whenever I speak at workshops for school leaders, I often ask participants to share their school's vision or mission statement. The common response is, "Can I look it up?" or "It's on our website." Most leaders can recall only a few words or concepts, often because these statements are lengthy paragraphs rather than concise, actionable phrases. If leaders themselves struggle, it's likely that stakeholders such as teachers, students, and parents will find it even harder to recall or internalize these guiding statements. This is why **creating a motto is so important**: it **distills the vision and mission into an accessible, meaningful phrase** that everyone can understand, remember, and live by.

Why Mottos Matter

1. **Clarity and Focus**
   A motto takes the complexity of a full vision or mission statement and simplifies it into a clear and focused expression. By boiling down your school's purpose into a concise statement, you make it easy for everyone to remember and apply in daily interactions.
2. **Identity and Unity**
   A well-crafted motto fosters a sense of identity and unity. It serves as a rallying cry for the entire school community, bringing students, teachers, staff, and parents together around a common purpose.
3. **Inspiration and Motivation**
   A motto acts as a constant source of inspiration and motivation. Whether it's spoken at assemblies, displayed in hallways, or included in communication, it keeps the school's core values and goals top of mind, encouraging excellence and positivity.
4. **Communication and Branding**
   Your motto becomes a cornerstone of your school's brand. It's ideal for use in newsletters, promotional materials, social media, and even on T-shirts or banners. A memorable motto strengthens your school's identity and makes it easily recognizable within and beyond your community.

5. **Guidance for Decision-Making**
   A motto serves as a quick reference point for decision-making. When evaluating policies, programs, or behaviors, leaders and stakeholders can ask, "Does this align with our motto?" This ensures that all actions support the school's core vision and mission, creating consistency and integrity.

These reasons underscore why mottos aren't just decorative; they are directional. Let's look at how this plays out in real schools.

Examples of Mottos in Action

Imagine a school with a vision statement about fostering lifelong learning and a mission focused on empowerment and innovation. Their mottos might be:

- **Vision Motto:** "Learn Today, Lead Tomorrow."
- **Mission Motto:** "Every Voice, Every Dream, Every Day."

These mottos encapsulate the school's aspirations and make it easy for stakeholders to internalize and repeat. They are short, memorable, and packed with meaning, making them perfect tools for fostering a dynamic and cohesive school culture.

By creating meaningful mottos, your school can elevate its vision and mission, ensuring they are not only written statements but lived experiences for everyone in the community.

The Leadership Role in Keeping the Culture Alive

As leaders, it is crucial that we consistently use these mottos in our daily language, whether in conversations, meetings, or public addresses. By constantly referring to them, we not only reinforce their importance but also model the behaviors and mindset we want to cultivate. When leaders consistently live by and speak the vision and mission, the entire school culture will begin to reflect those values. The power of repetition, alignment, and intentionality cannot be overstated. So, be sure to say it, live it, and watch your school's culture and brand grow stronger each day.

Steps to Create a Motto Include:

1. **Reflect on Your Vision and Mission:** Review your School Vision Statement and Daily Mission Statement. Identify the key themes that you want to highlight.
2. **Keep it Short and Memorable:** A motto should be concise and easy to remember. Aim for a phrase that is no more than a few words long.
3. **Incorporate Key Values:** Ensure that your motto reflects the fundamental principles and aspirations of your school. It should resonate with the entire school community and encapsulate what makes your school unique.
4. **Involve the Community:** Engage students, teachers, and staff in the process of creating the motto. This can foster a sense of ownership and ensure that the motto resonates with everyone.
5. **Test and Refine:** Once you have a draft motto, test it out. Get feedback from different members of the school community and refine it until it perfectly captures your school's vision and mission.

By creating mottos that succinctly capture the essence of your School Vision Statement and Daily Mission Statement, you can effectively communicate your school's core values and aspirations. These mottos will serve as a guiding light, inspiring and unifying the entire school community.

"Mottos. Post them. Say them. Live them. Repeat!"
—Dr. Joe Famularo

Inward School Map (ISM) Examples and Template

Below, you'll find a full example of a completed ISM followed by a template your leadership team can use to draft and refine your own. These tools are designed to spark meaningful conversation and provide a structured foundation for crafting your school's Inward School Map.

Inward School Map (ISM) Examples

- **School Vision Statement & Motto**

    "Inspire to Aspire"
    "Our vision is to create a welcoming and empowering educational environment where every student is inspired to reach their full potential and contribute positively to society."

- **Daily School Mission Statement & Motto**

    "Empowering Potential, Fostering Excellence"
    "Our mission is to provide a safe, nurturing, and dynamic learning environment that fosters academic excellence, personal growth, and the development of a strong sense of character and leadership every day."

- **School Leadership Principles**

  1. Lead with integrity and transparency.
  2. Foster collaborative decision-making.
  3. Empower and support staff and students.
  4. Model continuous learning and improvement.
  5. Prioritize the well-being and development of every individual.

- **School Core Values:**

  1. **Respect:** Valuing each person's unique contributions and treating everyone with dignity.
  2. **Excellence:** Striving for the highest standards in all endeavors.
  3. **Integrity:** Upholding honesty and ethical behavior.
  4. **Collaboration:** Working together to achieve common goals.
  5. **Innovation:** Encouraging creativity and forward-thinking solutions.

- **Incorporating Branding Elements:**

  - **Logo**: A stylized lighthouse with a bright beam of light shining outward, symbolizing guidance, clarity, and the school's mission to illuminate the path for students. The lighthouse represents the role of the school in providing direction and inspiration for every student's journey.
  - **Mascot**: The **Star**, representing each student as a shining star with unique potential. The mascot is depicted in a dynamic, upward pose, symbolizing growth, ambition, and the school's commitment to helping students shine brightly in every aspect of their lives.
  - **School Colors**: **Navy Blue and White**
    - **Navy Blue** represents stability, wisdom, and integrity.
    - **White** symbolizes clarity, simplicity, and a bright future, reflecting the school's commitment to academic excellence and personal growth.
  - **Visuals**:
    - Feature the lighthouse and star logo in prominent locations such as entryways, leadership documents, and student recognition displays to emphasize guidance and aspiration.
    - Use images of the star mascot in various poses, such as shining brightly, reaching toward the sky, or guiding others, on school banners, spirit wear, and classroom walls to inspire a sense of unity, pride, and determination.

- Incorporate **navy blue** and **white** in all ISM materials, from posters to digital displays, ensuring a cohesive and recognizable brand that reinforces the school's values and vision.

By prominently displaying these anchor elements, you create a clear and shared understanding of your school's identity, guiding everyone towards a cohesive and dynamic school culture.

School SelfCulture Statement

This statement provides an overarching narrative of the school's culture for internal use; however, it may also be shared with the broader community.

"Inspire to Aspire: A Community of Leaders and Learners"

Central to our school lies a commitment to fostering a dynamic and empowering educational environment where every individual feels valued, supported, and inspired to reach their full potential. Guided by our vision to create a welcoming space where students contribute positively to society, we strive daily to live out our mission: to provide a safe, nurturing, and innovative learning atmosphere that cultivates academic excellence, personal growth, and social responsibility.

Our Leadership Principles emphasize integrity, transparency, and collaboration. We lead by example, empowering staff and students to continuously improve while prioritizing the well-being and growth of each individual. Our shared Core Values—**Respect, Excellence, Integrity, Collaboration, and Innovation**—are the foundation of our SelfCulture, driving every decision and action to create a community of learners who embody these ideals.

Branding is integral to our identity and culture. Our school logo and mascot symbolize unity and pride, while our school colors and visual elements reinforce our collective spirit. Together, these elements represent a cohesive and recognizable culture that connects our community and celebrates our achievements.

As we lead and learn together, our SelfCulture statement serves as a compass, ensuring every action, interaction, and decision reflects our vision, mission, values, and principles, anchoring us in purpose and guiding us toward a brighter future.

School Goals

1. **Academic Excellence**
   - Increase student proficiency in core subjects by X% over the next academic year.
   - Implement project-based learning to enhance critical thinking skills.
   - Achieve a Y% graduation rate within the next Z years.

2. **Personal Growth**
   - Develop and implement a student mentorship program to support personal and academic growth.
   - Increase student participation in extracurricular activities by X%.

3. **Community Engagement**
   - Strengthen partnerships with local businesses and organizations to provide more opportunities for student internships and community service.
   - Host quarterly community forums to engage parents and stakeholders in school activities and decision-making processes.

4. **Staff Development**
   - Provide ongoing professional development opportunities focused on innovative teaching strategies and student engagement.
   - Increase staff satisfaction and retention rates by X% over the next Y years.

5. **School Environment**
   - Enhance school facilities to create a more welcoming and conducive learning environment.
   - Implement a school-wide sustainability initiative to reduce the school's carbon footprint.
   - Increase student proficiency in reading and math by X% by the end of the academic year.

Note:
You may insert the comprehensive details of your goals here or attach them to your Inward School Map (ISM). Use the **REBEL Goals™ Framework** to ensure each goal includes clear direction, actionable steps, measurable progress, ongoing evaluation, and sustained support.

Inward School Map (ISM) Template

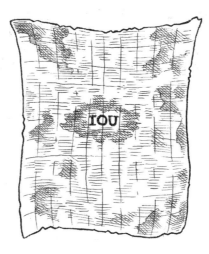

 Inward School Map (ISM) Statements:

Note: The 4 Foundational Inward Anchors
These 4 Foundational Inward School Anchors (School Anchors: 2,3,4,5) should be prominently displayed along with the school's/district's branding elements to reinforce and communicate the school's foundational principles to all members of the community.

1. **School Vision Statement & Motto:**
   - [Insert School Motto Here]
   - [Insert School Vision Statement Here]

2. **Daily School Mission Statement & Motto:**
   - [Insert School Motto Here]
   - [Insert Daily School Mission Statement Here]

3. **School Leadership Principles:**
   - [Insert Leadership Principle 1 Here]
   - [Insert Leadership Principle 2 Here]
   - [Insert Leadership Principle 3 Here]
   - [Insert Leadership Principle 4 Here]
   - [Insert Leadership Principle 5 Here]

4. **School Core Values:**
   - Core Value 1: [Insert Definition Here]
   - Core Value 2: [Insert Definition Here]
   - Core Value 3: [Insert Definition Here]
   - Core Value 4: [Insert Definition Here]
   - Core Value 5: [Insert Definition Here]

Incorporating Branding Elements:

- Logo: [Insert School Logo]
- Mascot [Insert School Mascot]
- School Colors: [Insert School Colors Here]
- Visuals: [Insert Visual Descriptions Here]

School SelfCulture Statement:

This statement provides an overarching narrative of the school's culture for internal use; however, it may also be shared with the broader community.

- [Insert School SelfCulture Statement Here]

School Goals:

Goals should be discussed in meetings and shared with school leaders, staff, and parents, as appropriate. Each goal should be specific to the individual or group responsible for its implementation.

- [Insert School Goal 1 Here]
- [Insert School Goal 2 Here]
- [Insert School Goal 3 Here]
- [Insert School Goal 4 Here]

Note:
You may insert the comprehensive details of your goals here or attach them to your Inward School Map (ISM). Use the **REBEL Goals™ Framework** to ensure each goal includes clear direction, actionable steps, measurable progress, ongoing evaluation, and sustained support.

For convenience, this ISM template is also included in **Appendix B**.

Encouragement for the Path Forward:

Your ISM is a living document that will continue to evolve as your school grows and progresses. Regularly revisit and refine it to ensure it remains aligned with your school's journey. By continuously enhancing these foundational elements, you will reinforce a dynamic, and positive school culture that inspires and empowers every member of your community.

As you move forward, let your ISM serve as a guiding light, illuminating the path towards an Upward Dynamic Positive Culture. Embrace the principles of inward living, and let them drive your actions and decisions, fostering a thriving and harmonious school environment. This is the beginning of the IOU process for developing an IOU School Culture.

Transition to the 6 Outward School Anchors: Enhancing Relationships and Interactions

The next focus is the **6 Outward School Anchors**. While the Inward Anchors have provided a robust framework for understanding and shaping the internal culture of the school, the Outward Anchors will delve into the vital relationships and interactions among students, staff, parents, and the broader community. These anchors emphasize the importance of collaboration, communication, and mutual respect, reinforcing and enhancing **a school culture centered on trust.**

The 6 Outward School Anchors are:

1. **Inspire IOU Trust:** The Principle of Life Relationships
2. **Practice Positive Communication:** The Principle of Outward Understanding
3. **Create Common Language:** The Principle of Outward Effectiveness
4. **Construct a Cohesive Environment:** The Principle of Outward Connectedness
5. **Establish Everlasting Traditions:** The Principle of Life History
6. **Model a Mindset of Propelling PH2E**: The Principle of Life Gifts

It's important to understand that while the insights and results gained from the Outward Anchors will significantly contribute to the overall school culture, as with the Inward Anchors, you do not need to establish all of them before you start implementing your Strategic School Map. You can begin sharing and executing your Strategic School Map now, and gradually integrate the Outward Anchors as you go. This approach allows you to start making immediate progress, while also providing time for thoughtful integration of the Outward Anchors.

As you explore and implement each Outward Anchor, engage in discussions with your team. These anchors will seamlessly reinforce the work you have already completed with the Inward Anchors, creating a more cohesive and dynamic school environment. By focusing on the 6 Outward School Anchors, you will strengthen the foundation established by the Inward Anchors, enhancing trust and positive relationships throughout the school community.

This next chapter promises to further propel the school's ship toward a culture of excellence and mutual support, where every relationship becomes part of the wind in your sails, guiding your journey toward lasting impact.

Chapter 6

The IOU 6 Outward School Anchors

Launching the Outward Journey

An Overview of the Outward School Anchors: Relationships within an IOU School Culture

Having explored the 6 Inward School Anchors that shape a school's foundational identity and developed the school's ISM, we now transition to the **Outward School Anchors**, which focus on the relationships, interactions, and culture we build together. While the Inward Anchors define who we are, **the Outward Anchors determine how we live that identity out loud by connecting with others, collaborating with purpose, and leading with intention in our daily school life.**

Rooted in the **Principle of Life Relationships**, the 6 Outward Anchors emphasize the intentional, relational work that sustains a thriving IOU School Culture. These outward practices build the connective tissue of trust, communication, and shared purpose that empowers every member of the community.

As you move through this section, the message of **"Inspire to Aspire"** continues to serve as a guiding principle, encouraging you to create a school environment that is outwardly dynamic, positive, and deeply connected.

The 6 Outward School Anchors

These anchors are designed to build trusting relationships, cultivate shared language, and reinforce a cohesive and vibrant culture. Together, they form your **Outward School Map (OSM)**—the counterpart to your **Inward School Map (ISM)**.

1. **Inspire IOU Trust** (*Principle of Life Relationships*)
   Build trust through consistent, transparent, and supportive interactions.

2. **Practice Positive Communication** (*Principle of Outward Understanding*)
   Foster open, honest, and constructive dialogue across the school.

3. **Create Common Language** (*Principle of Outward Effectiveness*)
   Establish shared vocabulary and understanding that drive clarity and collaboration.

4. **Construct a Cohesive Environment** (*Principle of Outward Connectedness*)
   Develop a welcoming culture where every voice is valued and every individual feels connected.

5. **Establish Everlasting Traditions** (*Principle of Life History*)
   Build traditions that celebrate your community, reinforce identity, and create continuity.

6. **Model a Mindset of Propelling PH2E** (*Principle of Life Gifts*)
   Live and model the pursuit of **Peacefulness, Happiness, Healthiness, and Excellence** in all aspects of school life.

Together, these 6 Outward Anchors work in harmony with the ISM to form your **Strategic School Map (SSM)**, a complete, Inside-Out framework for building and sustaining a Dynamic Positive School Culture.

The Foundational Outward Anchor: Inspire IOU Trust

Principle of Life Relationships

> *Trust is the glue of life. It's the foundational principle that holds all relationships.*
> —Stephen M. R. Covey, *The Speed of Trust*

Trust is the foundation upon which all 6 Outward School Anchors are built. Without trust, communication breaks down, collaboration weakens, and the culture becomes fragmented. But when trust is intentionally nurtured, it creates the conditions for every other Outward Anchor to thrive, **serving as the invisible thread that connects people**, strengthens relationships, and builds shared momentum.

In an IOU School Culture, trust is not assumed; it is actively built through consistent, transparent, and supportive actions. It shows up in every hallway conversation, staff meeting, and parent interaction. It's present when students take risks, when teachers collaborate, and when leaders follow through. Trust is the foundation of a healthy school.

Why Trust Comes First

Trust is the anchor that holds the others outward anchors in place:

- **Positive communication** flourishes in an environment of trust.
- **Common language** only matters if people believe in and use it with authenticity.
- **Cohesive environments** grow stronger when people feel safe and supported.
- **Traditions endure** when they're built on genuine community bonds.
- **PH2E is modeled and multiplied** when trust gives people the freedom to be their best selves.

Actions → Relationships → Trust

Every outward action you take and every interaction with a student, colleague, or parent, either strengthens or weakens trust. That's why **trust-building must be intentional**, embedded in the small moments as well as the big initiatives. This anchor challenges leaders and teams to make trust a daily priority.

As we continue into the upcoming chapter on the Outward Anchors, we'll explore how to build IOU Trust within your school community using practical models, questions, and strategies that align with your Inward School Map. Remember: **the more trust you build, the more capacity your school has to grow, connect, and achieve.**

Navigating School Culture: An Overview of the 6 Outward School Anchors

As we shift from defining who we are (Inward School Anchors) to how we live and lead together (Outward School Anchors), we focus on the critical components that shape our interactions, build relationships, and influence the collective experience of the school community. **These Outward Anchors extend the inward work and reflect it through action.**

Each of the 6 Outward School Anchors is rooted in timeless principles, offering a practical framework for cultivating trust, fostering connection, and sustaining a positive and dynamic school culture.

1. Inspire IOU Trust
Building the Foundation of Life Relationships

Trust is the cornerstone of a thriving school culture. It is built through consistent, transparent, and supportive interactions that affirm each stakeholder's value and dignity. When trust is present, students feel safe to take risks, staff feel supported in their growth, and families feel welcomed as partners. Trust unlocks openness, vulnerability, and full participation, creating the foundation for every other Outward Anchor to thrive.

2. Practice Positive Communication
Enhancing Outward Understanding

Positive communication strengthens relationships and fosters mutual understanding. When schools prioritize open, honest, and respectful dialogue, they empower students and staff to express themselves clearly and listen actively. This principle elevates the quality of collaboration and problem-solving across the community and sets the tone for a culture rooted in empathy and clarity.

3. Create Common Language
Promoting Outward Effectiveness

A shared language builds bridges. When schools intentionally establish common words, phrases, and frameworks, whether for leadership, core values, or behavior expectations, they reduce confusion and increase alignment. A common language helps everyone move in the same direction with purpose, deepening collaboration and unity.

4. Construct a Cohesive Environment
Fostering Outward Connectedness

Cohesion is both felt and seen. A cohesive school environment is one where the physical spaces are welcoming, and the relationships are respectful. From the tone of conversations to the condition of the hallways, everything reflects the community's commitment to belonging. A cohesive environment allows individuals to thrive and the school to function as a unified whole.

5. Establish Everlasting Traditions
Embracing Life History

Traditions are the cornerstone of school identity. They create continuity, celebrate progress, and connect generations of learners. Whether it's a monthly assembly, a graduation walk, or a community celebration, meaningful traditions build pride, reinforce values, and shape a lasting sense of belonging.

6. Model a Mindset of Propelling PH2E
Uplifting Life Gifts

Peacefulness, Happiness, Healthiness, and Excellence (PH2E®) are the ultimate outcomes of a thriving IOU School Culture. Modeling a mindset that continuously propels PH2E means intentionally aligning daily actions with your highest aspirations. It's about growth, contribution, and well-being, and creating a ripple effect that inspires others to lead lives of balance, joy, and impact.

Immediate Implementation: Building and Boosting School Culture as You Go

It's important to reiterate that you don't have to wait until every anchor is finalized before you start implementing your Strategic School Map.

As you and your team work through each anchor, start integrating the ideas and strategies into your daily routines and school conversations. This is especially true for the Outward Anchors. Begin fostering trust, enhancing communication, and building a cohesive environment right away, as these actions can immediately uplift the culture and energy of your school.

Once your **Inward School Map (ISM)** is defined, let it guide your school forward. It becomes the identity foundation from which all other practices and relationships take shape. The **Outward Anchors** then act as powerful boosters, amplifying the ISM's impact and propelling your school into a dynamic, trust-filled, and connected environment where everyone can thrive.

Each anchor you implement adds momentum. Whether you start with a conversation, a hallway display, or a leadership meeting, small intentional actions lead to big shifts in mindset and behavior. This gradual, integrated approach allows your team to build culture in real time by adapting, reflecting, and growing with purpose.

Remember: school culture is never static. It's a living journey. As you define, implement, and refine your **Strategic School Map (SSM)**, each step strengthens the bonds within your community. As each anchor is activated, your school becomes a more aspirational, resilient, and empowering place, where staff and students are proud to belong, grow, and lead.

Harnessing the Power of Anchor Models: Inspiring Collaborative Strategy and Action

As introduced at the start of Part II, each of the following Outward Anchors includes a **visual model**, a powerful tool designed to support strategic conversations, bring clarity to abstract concepts, and spark creative solutions.

These anchor models are not just for display; they are for dialogue.

Use them in leadership meetings, professional development sessions, and collaborative planning discussions. Place them where teams can interact with them, physically or digitally, to reflect on how each anchor shows up in your school and where it needs to grow.

These models help you:

- Facilitate deep, focused discussions with clarity.
- Align efforts across departments, teams, and stakeholder groups.
- Develop a shared understanding of each anchor's impact.
- Translate ideas into action in real-time.

As you explore each anchor in the coming chapters, allow the models to be your visual compass. They provide direction, inspiration, and a shared visual language to unite your team around building a cohesive IOU School Culture.

Together, the **ISM + OSM = SSM** framework, paired with these strategic models, will guide your school not only to articulate what it stands for—but to live it, lead it, and grow it every day.

The Integrated Approach: ISM + OSM = SSM

The Outward School Map (OSM) is not separate from the inward work; it is its extension. When combined with the Inward School Map (ISM), the result is a unified **Strategic School Map (SSM)**. This integrated framework aligns your school's identity, actions, and aspirations into one cohesive journey.

"Outward actions reveal the truth of your inward beliefs."
—Dr. Joe Famularo

Outward School Anchor 1
INSPIRE IOU TRUST

The Principle of Life Relationships

*The first job of a leader—at work or at home—is to inspire trust.
It's to bring out the best in people by entrusting them with meaningful
stewardships, and to create an environment in which high-trust
interaction inspires creativity and possibility.*
—Stephen M.R. Covey

Inspire IOU Trust: Cultivating the Highest Form of Trust in Your School Community

At the center of every vibrant and healthy school culture lies **trust** as a way of living and leading. The first Outward Anchor, **Inspire IOU Trust**, is grounded in the **Principle of Life Relationships**, which emphasizes the foundational role of trust in every connection and interaction within your school.

Trust in an IOU School Culture is not surface-level or conditional; it is **deep-rooted, enduring, and lived daily**. It's the kind of trust that fuels meaningful relationships, empowers leadership at every level, and holds the community steady through both calm and storm. Trust in an IOU culture flows in three essential directions: Inward, Outward, and Upward. Each builds on the other to create a culture of authenticity, connection, and growth.

This anchor focuses on cultivating what we call the **highest form of trust**: **Inward-Outward-Upward Trust (IOU Trust)**. This begins with **Inward Trust**: trusting oneself, your values, your integrity, and your intent. Only when we establish inner trust can we extend authentic, consistent **Outward Trust** to others. The natural byproduct of this alignment is **Upward Trust**, the kind of trust that elevates the entire community and fosters Peacefulness, Happiness, Healthiness, and Excellence (PH2E).

Trust is the **cornerstone of all relationships** in a thriving school. Whether in the classroom, the staff room, leadership meetings, or family partnerships, trust shapes the tone, expectations, and possibilities. It enables open dialogue, encourages vulnerability, and builds unity.

To inspire trust is to **lead with alignment**, where your inward intentions and outward behaviors match. When this alignment is consistently modeled and reinforced, it not only builds relationships but creates the conditions where individuals feel safe, valued, and empowered to contribute their best.

Cultivating Trust in Your School Community

Trust is the invisible thread woven through every interaction in a school. It shapes how we communicate, how we lead, how we collaborate, and ultimately, how we thrive together. But trust doesn't appear automatically. It must be intentionally built through **alignment between our Inward Thinking and our Outward Actions**.

For trust to grow, people must not only hear your values but also see them in action.

Stephen R. Covey reminds us that trust is built on two essential pillars: **character and competence**. Character speaks to your integrity and intent. Competence reflects your skills, judgment, and ability to follow through. When both are present and aligned, trust becomes the glue that strengthens relationships and fuels a collaborative culture.

Inspire IOU Trust, the first of the 6 Outward Anchors, is rooted in the **Principle of Life Relationships**. This principle calls on us to lead with integrity by ensuring our internal values match our external behaviors. When our intent is sincere, and our actions are consistent, we create an environment where trust is not only felt—but inspired.

This anchor lays the foundation for all other outward practices. Without trust, communication breaks down, collaboration falters, and school culture weakens. But when trust is present, every conversation, initiative, and relationship becomes a building block in a **dynamic and positive school culture**.

Trust in Practice: Living the School Culture of Inspire IOU Trust

A school that embodies the **Principle of Life Relationships** through the **Inspire IOU Trust** anchor will reflect trust not just in words, but in the daily rhythms of its people and practices. This type of school culture radiates alignment, authenticity, and mutual respect—elevating everyone it touches.

Schools grounded in Inspire IOU Trust often exhibit the following characteristics:

- **High Character and Competence:**
  School leaders, teachers, and staff demonstrate strong moral integrity and professional excellence. They lead by example, serving as role models for students and one another.

- **Consistency Between Words and Actions:**
  Trust grows when what is promised is what is delivered. In high-trust schools, people do what they say—and say what they mean.

- **Mutual Respect and Support:**
  Interactions across the school community are marked by genuine listening, empathy, and encouragement. Differences are honored, and every voice is valued.

- **Transparent Communication:**
  Open, honest, and timely communication builds confidence. When information is shared clearly and without hidden agendas, trust flourishes.

- **A Collaborative Spirit:**
  Teamwork is not just a value; it's a lived experience. Staff, students, and families work together, recognizing that progress happens when everyone contributes.

- **A Safe and Welcoming Space:**
  Physical, emotional, and psychological safety are prioritized. Everyone feels seen, supported, and free to be their authentic selves.

- **Commitment to Collective Excellence:**
  There is a shared drive for continuous improvement. Every success is celebrated as a community achievement, and every challenge is faced together.

This is what it means to Inspire IOU Trust where people are able to flourish together. When trust is the foundation, everything else becomes possible.

Inspire IOU Trust Mindset Question

Which type of thinking does your school use – Default or Intentional?

- **Default Thinking:**

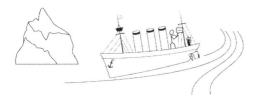

"We say we trust each other, but there's an unspoken need to micromanage tasks and double-check everything because we assume others won't follow through."

In this mindset, trust is more of a surface-level word than a practiced principle. Actions are frequently second-guessed, leading to inefficiency, frustration, and a fragmented culture where collaboration lacks depth.

- **Intentional Thinking:**

"We proactively build and sustain trust every day, recognizing it as the foundation of our school culture."

This mindset prioritizes consistency between words and actions. Trust is not assumed; it is earned and cultivated through transparency, reliability, and respect. All stakeholders, including leaders, staff, students, and families, understand that meaningful progress begins with mutual trust and shared responsibility.

Why This Matters

When trust is absent or inconsistent, schools drift toward fear-based behaviors such as micromanagement, blame, and control. This creates emotional distance and limits potential. But when trust is inspired intentionally, people feel safe to share ideas, take initiative, and support one another. The result is a culture where collaboration thrives, leadership multiplies, and everyone feels empowered to bring their best to school every day.

The Inspire IOU Trust Model for Schools

The **Inspire IOU Trust Model** outlines three essential components for cultivating the highest levels of trust across a school community: **Inspiration, Influence, and School Principles Alignment**. Trust doesn't develop by chance; it is navigated with intention. Like a captain steering a ship, building trust requires clear direction, steady leadership, and consistent action across the school.

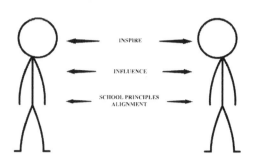

Just as mariners rely on wind, current, and charts to stay on course, school leaders must draw upon these three forces to build trust throughout the organization:

- **Inspiration**
  Inspiration is the emotional heartbeat of trust. It is the reciprocal motivation and admiration that develops when people lead with authenticity, character, and clarity of intent. As a lighthouse provides light and direction through uncertain conditions, inspiration helps illuminate the path to connection, safety, and shared purpose. It nurtures belief in one another and uplifts the entire school community.

- **Influence**
  Influence is the intellectual side of trust. It involves mutual impact, where ideas, actions, and attitudes positively shape one another. Like the currents that carry a ship forward, influence creates momentum. It builds when individuals consistently demonstrate competence, share knowledge generously, and invite others into meaningful dialogue and decision-making.

- **School Principles Alignment**
  This is the foundational structure of trust. When a school's vision, mission, and leadership principles are clear and consistently lived out, it acts like a nautical chart, giving everyone a shared sense of direction. With aligned principles, the community avoids leadership drift, unites around common goals, and navigates challenges with integrity and focus.

When these three components, **inspiration, influence, and alignment**, are present and intentionally cultivated, a school develops the conditions for deep and lasting trust. Trust is no longer assumed or conditional; it becomes a shared responsibility and a defining feature of the school's culture.

Like a ship navigating confidently toward its destination, a school anchored in **Inspire IOU Trust** moves forward with unity, confidence, and purpose—no matter what storms may come.

Strategic Thinking Questions for Outward School Anchor 1: Inspire IOU Trust

1. *What actions can we take to begin cultivating trust across all areas of our school community? How can we ensure that trust becomes a visible and intentional part of our culture?*

   _____

   _____

   _____

   _____

   _____

2. *How can we model alignment between our internal intentions and outward behaviors to build deeper, lasting trust? What routines or expectations can support this consistency?*

   _____

   _____

   _____

   _____

   _____

3. *What communication practices should we establish to promote openness, clarity, and transparency among all stakeholders?*

   _____

   _____

   _____

   _____

   _____

4. *How can we teach and reinforce high character and professional competence as cornerstones of trust within our school?*

_____
_____
_____
_____
_____
_____

5. *What specific steps can we take to create a safe and welcoming environment for every student, staff member, and family?*

_____
_____
_____
_____
_____
_____

6. *How might we intentionally design opportunities for collaboration, so that trust and mutual support grow naturally among students, staff, and families?*

_____
_____
_____
_____
_____
_____

Initial Drafts of Your Inspire IOU Trust Statement

Now that you've explored the building blocks of Inspire IOU Trust and reflected on the strategic thinking questions, you're ready to begin shaping a powerful trust statement that captures your school's highest aspirations for connection, character, and collaboration.

This statement should reflect your highest vision for how trust *should* look, feel, and function across your school community. It's not about where you are now, but about where you want to go. Consider this your guiding vision for cultivating trust that is deeply rooted in transparency, character, and collaboration.

Use the space on the following page to let your initial thoughts flow naturally. Don't focus on perfect language. Just capture what you believe trust should look like in your school when it's intentionally inspired, lived, and shared.

How do we want trust to look, sound, and feel in our school? What will it look like when trust is intentionally built and consistently lived out by all members of the school community?

This will serve as a foundational step in defining trust as a living priority within your school's culture and outward identity.

Chapter 6: The IOU 6 Outward School Anchors   **217**

Initial Key Thoughts for Your School IOU Trust Statement

_____
_____
_____
_____
_____
_____
_____
_____
_____
_____
_____
_____
_____
_____
_____
_____
_____
_____
_____
_____

Examples of School Trust Statements

Below are sample trust statements, each accompanied by a motto, that illustrate how schools can define and express their commitment to fostering a culture of trust. Each example highlights a different aspect of Inspire IOU Trust, providing you with a range of approaches to guide the development of your own school's trust statement.

1. *Cultivating Mutual Respect and Integrity*

"In our school, we commit to fostering an environment where mutual respect and integrity are the cornerstones of all relationships. We believe that trust is earned through consistent actions, open communication, and a genuine commitment to supporting one another. By prioritizing honesty and transparency, we create a safe space where everyone feels valued and trusted."

2. *Building a Community of Trust and Collaboration*

"Our school is dedicated to building a community grounded in trust and collaboration. We strive to ensure that every student, teacher, and staff member feels confident in the reliability and integrity of their peers. Through our daily interactions, we emphasize the importance of trustworthiness and teamwork, creating a cohesive and supportive environment where everyone can thrive."

3. *Fostering Transparent and Honest Communication*

"We are committed to fostering a culture of transparent and honest communication within our school. We understand that trust is built on clear and open dialogue, where every voice is heard and respected. By encouraging active listening and constructive feedback, we aim to strengthen the bonds of trust and enhance the overall well-being of our school community."

4. *Promoting Trust through Consistency and Accountability*

"At our school, we believe that trust is rooted in consistency and accountability. We hold ourselves and each other to the highest standards of integrity, ensuring that our actions align with our words. By consistently demonstrating reliability and taking responsibility for our actions, we create a trustworthy and dependable school environment."

5. *Nurturing a Safe and Trusting Environment*

"Our school is dedicated to nurturing a safe and trusting environment for all members of our community. We prioritize the emotional and physical well-being of our students and staff, fostering a culture where trust and safety go hand in hand. Through our commitment to respect, support, and understanding, we create a foundation of trust that empowers everyone to reach their full potential."

6. *Inspiring Trust through Leadership and Example*

"In our school, we inspire trust through strong leadership and leading by example. We recognize that trust is built through actions that reflect our values of respect, honesty, and integrity. By modeling these behaviors, our leaders set the standard for trustworthiness and create an environment where everyone feels confident and supported."

7. *Enhancing Trust with Community Engagement*

"We are dedicated to enhancing trust within our school through active community engagement. By involving students, parents, teachers, and staff in decision-making processes, we ensure that every voice is valued and heard. This collaborative approach fosters a deep sense of trust and ownership, strengthening our school community."

8. *Creating a Culture of Trust and Empowerment*

"Our school is committed to creating a culture where trust and empowerment are at the forefront of our interactions. We believe that trust empowers individuals to take risks, innovate, and grow. By fostering an environment where trust is given and received freely, we enable our students and staff to pursue excellence with confidence."

9. *Trust as the Foundation for Learning and Growth*

"In our school, trust is the foundation upon which learning and growth are built. We recognize that a trusting environment is essential for academic success and personal development. By cultivating trust in every relationship, we create a supportive atmosphere where students and staff are motivated to achieve their best."

10. *Trust through Empathy and Understanding*

"Our school values trust as a vital component of our community. We strive to build trust through empathy and understanding, recognizing the unique perspectives and experiences of each individual. By practicing kindness and compassion, we create a culture where trust flourishes and everyone feels valued and respected."

The Inspire IOU Trust Anchor Model

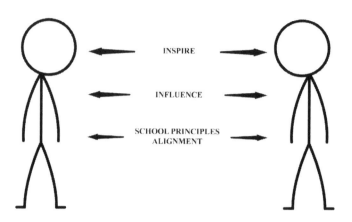

Inspire IOU Trust: Rooted in the Principle of Life Relationships

The Principle of Life Relationships reminds us that meaningful connection is at the heart of every thriving school culture. *Life Relationships* are built on trust, respect, and mutual investment in each other's growth. In schools, this principle comes alive through intentional efforts to create safe, authentic, and reciprocal interactions. For the Inspire IOU Trust anchor, Life Relationships emphasize that trust is not given once—it is nurtured daily. Trust grows when people feel seen, valued, and connected, and when relationships are shaped by consistent inspiration, positive influence, and shared principles.

The Dynamics of Reciprocal Trust

The **Inspire IOU Trust Model** is brought to life through a visual that depicts two figures, representing members of the school community, connected by three double-sided arrows. These arrows represent the **continuous, reciprocal interactions** that build trust through **Inspiration, Influence, and Alignment with School Principles**.

This visual reminds us that **trust is not static—it flows**. Like the steady rhythm of waves, **trust is strengthened through daily, mutual exchanges** rooted in shared values and meaningful connection. Each interaction, when grounded in **inspiration,**

positive influence, and principled action, reinforces the bond between individuals and the larger school community.

This model underscores an essential truth: **trust is not a one-sided transaction; it is created together**. It deepens when it is **both given and returned**. When every person in a school is **both a contributor to and recipient of trust**, it becomes **the lifeblood of a healthy culture**, flowing freely, **reinforcing relationships**, and **elevating collective well-being**.

Inspire

The first arrow reflects the **emotional side of trust**: the mutual inspiration that occurs when people demonstrate authenticity, integrity, and belief in one another. When we are inspired by the values and actions of others, and when our own behavior inspires in return, we generate trust that is heartfelt and motivating. Inspiration creates the emotional foundation of connection and fuels a shared sense of possibility.

Influence

The second arrow represents **intellectual trust**: the two-way exchange of ideas, support, and constructive feedback. In a trust-filled school, influence is not about control; it's about empowerment. Teachers learn from students. Students learn from teachers. Staff members shape each other's thinking through collaboration and mutual encouragement. Trust grows when each voice is heard and valued.

School Principles Alignment

The third arrow highlights the **structural component of trust**: shared principles that guide decisions and behaviors. When school leaders, teachers, students, and families align around clear values such as respect, responsibility, and excellence, trust becomes embedded in the culture. This alignment provides a dependable framework that holds the school steady, especially during times of uncertainty or change.

When schools model *Inspire IOU Trust*, they create a current of consistency, connection, and character that moves the entire community forward with shared purpose and confidence

> *"Trust anchors the culture. Action gives it weight."*
> —Dr. Joe Famularo

Leadership Snapshot: Trust in Action at Summit High

When Dr. Ayers stepped into the role of principal, she inherited more than a school; she inherited a culture of disconnection. Staff meetings were transactional. Student voices were muffled. Parents felt like spectators. The phrase "we're in this together" sounded more like a slogan than a reality. At Summit High School, trust didn't exist—it had to be carefully built from the ground up.

*Dr. Ayers knew trust couldn't be mandated; it had to be modeled. She began with quiet but powerful **inspiration**, connecting with the hearts of those around her. She visited classrooms not to observe, but to listen. She wrote handwritten notes to students who showed leadership in small ways. She opened each meeting with a moment of gratitude or reflection. Her leadership wasn't loud, but it was felt. Staff began to mirror her tone. Students started to lean in. The emotional climate shifted.*

*That emotional spark led to **influence**, where her knowledge and guidance began to shape actions. Teachers across departments began collaborating on interdisciplinary projects, exchanging ideas and expertise. Seniors started mentoring freshmen, not because it was required, but because they wanted to share what they had learned. Parents stepped up to co-lead community nights, bringing their own skills and insights to the table. The school became a place where knowledge was shared, ideas flowed, and people listened. Trust was no longer a goal—it was a way of operating.*

*But what made it last was the school's **alignment of principles**. Dr. Ayers led the community through a process to clarify three guiding principles: **Respect, Empowerment, and Belonging**. These weren't simply framed and posted; they were embedded in how people greeted each other, how conflicts were resolved, and how celebrations were held. Students started using the language themselves. Teachers referenced the principles in lessons and feedback. Parents echoed them at home.*

*The results? Student engagement soared. Discipline referrals dropped. Surveys showed that students felt **seen, heard, and safe**. The hallway energy changed from chaotic to collaborative. Classrooms became places of connection, not just instruction. Students spoke up more, led more, and smiled more.*

*Summit High didn't just get better; it became alive. Because when trust is inspired, influence is mutual, and principles are aligned, a school doesn't just function—it **thrives**.*

When trust is high, communication is easy, instant, and effective.
—Stephen M. R. Covey - *The Speed of Trust*

Emphasizing the "Inspire" in Inspire IOU Trust

Central to *Inspire IOU Trust* is the word **"inspire,"** which means to fill someone with the desire or ability to do or feel something meaningful. In a school community, this means creating an environment where students, staff, leaders, and families are encouraged to be their best selves, motivated by the example and support of those around them.

This form of inspiration is **emotional**, not just instructional. It arises when we lead with character, act with care, and demonstrate a deep belief in others. But just as trust is reciprocal, so too is inspiration. The most impactful school cultures are those where inspiration **flows both ways**, from leaders to students, students to staff, staff to families, and back again. When people see the good in others and strive to reflect it themselves, a cycle of trust and growth emerges.

Inspire IOU Trust is not passive. It is a deliberate commitment to showing up with authenticity, aligning our actions with our values, and modeling the kind of trust we hope to receive in return. When we do this, we create not just a school but a thriving, principled community that uplifts everyone it touches.

The Guiding Question for Inspire IOU Trust

Are we creating a school culture where trust and inspiration flow freely in all directions, lifting every voice and unleashing the full potential of every person?

Transitioning to Outward Anchor 2: Practice Positive Communication

With trust as the foundation, we now move to **Outward Anchor 2: Practice Positive Communication**. Communication is the daily expression of our values, the bridge between intention and impact, and a vital tool for cultivating relationships grounded in respect and trust.

This anchor challenges us to move beyond routine exchanges and embrace communication as a deliberate, empowering act. By fostering open dialogue, active listening, and constructive feedback, we not only prevent misunderstandings but also strengthen the connections that hold our school community together.

Let's carry forward the trust we've built and use it to shape a culture where every voice is heard, every conversation builds understanding, and every interaction moves us closer to our shared goals. It's time to explore how positive communication can elevate both individuals and the collective spirit of your school.

Outward School Anchor 2

PRACTICE POSITIVE COMMUNICATION

The Principle of Outward Understanding

*Listening is where love begins: listening to ourselves
and then to our neighbors.*
—Fred Rogers

Practice Positive Communication: Embracing the Principle of Outward Understanding

Outward Anchor 2—**Practice Positive Communication**—is grounded in the **Principle of Outward Understanding**, which reminds us that communication is more than words. It's about how we listen, interpret, and respond with empathy, presence, and intention. In a thriving school culture, positive communication builds trust, strengthens relationships, and creates a safe space where everyone feels seen, heard, understood, and valued.

To communicate positively is to lead with heart. It means using our words and actions to connect, not divide; to build, not break. It's about showing up fully in conversations and creating space for others to do the same.

When a school practices positive communication, it empowers every member of its community, including students, teachers, staff, and families, to contribute to a culture that is welcoming, respectful, and aligned with a shared vision.

This anchor is supported by two essential practices:

- **WholeHearted Listening** – Listening without judgment, with full presence and an open mind.
- **High Tide Safe Talk** – Creating a psychologically safe space for open, honest, and courageous conversations.

Together, these practices elevate everyday interactions into opportunities for connection, clarity, and community. When practiced consistently, they help shape a school culture where trust flows freely, and communication becomes a tool for growth and alignment.

The Importance of Positive Communication in School Culture

Positive communication is a shared leadership practice. It reflects how a school chooses to treat people, solve problems, and share its story. In a culture where communication is practiced intentionally, trust deepens, empathy is felt, and every interaction becomes a step toward alignment and belonging.

When positive communication is a priority:

- Gaps between students, staff, and families begin to close through understanding and shared language.
- Conflicts are not avoided; they are approached with courage, clarity, and compassion.
- Every voice, regardless of role, is valued and empowered to contribute to the school's goals.

This kind of culture doesn't happen by accident. It's the result of modeling, reinforcement, and a shared commitment to the values that sit at the heart of your Strategic School Map.

A school that lives the **Principle of Outward Understanding** doesn't just communicate—it connects. It listens with intention, speaks with care, and inspires trust with every conversation.

Practice Positive Communication Mindset Question

Which type of thinking does your school use – Default or Intentional?

- **Default Thinking:**

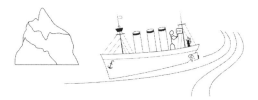

"We communicate regularly through emails, memos, and meetings and address miscommunications when they come up."

This mindset treats communication as a task to manage, not a culture to nurture. It's reactive, relying on information delivery without deeper engagement. While messages may be sent, meaningful connection is often missed. Trust erodes, misunderstandings linger, and people hesitate to share openly.

- **Intentional Thinking:**

"Our school prioritizes positive communication, actively fostering an environment of understanding and trust with all interactions."

This mindset sees communication as the foundation of school culture. Leaders and staff model **WholeHearted Listening**, make space for risk-free sharing through **High Tide Safe Talk**. These concepts will be explored in more detail in the following sections. They approach every conversation with presence and purpose. Communication is used as a tool to grow relationships, reinforce values, and align the community around a shared mission.

Why This Matters

Reflecting on your school's communication mindset reveals how relationships are shaped every day. Adopting an intentional approach is more than managing information; it is about creating an environment where empathy, clarity, and trust guide every interaction.

When communication is **thoughtful and intentional**:

- Trust deepens
- Collaboration strengthens
- Innovation becomes possible

A school that leads with communication doesn't just speak; it connects, inspires, and grows together.

The Importance of WholeHearted Listening

When asked what makes for strong communication, most people point to speaking skills such as clarity, brevity, or staying on topic. But **Outward Anchor 2: Practice Positive Communication** reminds us that effective communication starts with something deeper: **listening**.

At the heart of this anchor is **WholeHearted Listening**, the kind of listening that precedes understanding, trust, and authentic connection. This echoes the timeless principle shared by Stephen Covey in *The 7 Habits of Highly Effective People*: **"Seek first to understand, then to be understood."**

In many school settings, conversations often center on being heard by making a point, delivering a message, or moving things forward. But true school culture is built in the quiet spaces, when we pause, put aside our agenda, and genuinely listen.

WholeHearted Listening means engaging fully with the speaker, not just their words, but their **tone**, **emotion**, and **body language**. It's about suspending judgment, staying present, and seeking to understand. When practiced consistently, it creates a culture where individuals feel seen, respected, and valued, and it deepens every relationship in the school community.

Mastering Outward Listening in Schools: Navigating the Waves of Communication

Just as a seasoned captain must study the tides, currents, and winds before setting sail, educators and school leaders must practice intentional listening to navigate the ever-changing dynamics of a school community.

Think of every conversation as a voyage. The tides are the speaker's emotions. The waves are their words. The wind is the underlying context you can't always see, but can certainly feel. A skilled communicator listens not only to the message but to the meaning beneath it, adjusting course as needed to steer the conversation toward connection and clarity. This is **Outward Listening**, and it's more than just hearing. It's the anchor of collaboration and understanding. It requires effort, awareness, and presence.

In the next section, we'll explore **the Four Levels of Outward Listening**, using a nautical lens to illustrate how educators can master the art of communication and steer every conversation toward deeper trust and alignment.

The Four Levels of Outward Listening

In the journey of school culture, how we listen determines how well we lead. Just like navigating a ship, true understanding requires full attention, presence, and skill. **The Four Levels of Outward Listening** provide a clear path for developing more **intentional and empathetic communication** in schools.

Each level is paired with a nautical analogy and a school-based context, helping educators and leaders visualize how listening behaviors shape relationships, trust, and culture.

Level 1: WholeHearted Listening

Nautical Analogy:
Like a seasoned captain who studies every wave and current to steer safely through open waters, WholeHearted Listening is full attention in motion. It's listening with intention, presence, and care, navigating not just what is said, but how it's said.

In the School Context:
WholeHearted Listening means listening with your entire heart and mind, striving to understand the speaker's perspective without judgment. This level of listening is crucial in a school setting, where understanding students' and colleagues' emotions and perspectives can foster a supportive and empathetic environment.

Examples:

- A teacher sits beside a student who's visibly upset after recess, listens without rushing, and reflects back: "It sounds like today felt unfair for you. Want to walk me through what happened?"
- A principal invites a team of teachers to share concerns about a new initiative and says, "I really want to understand your experience. What's been most challenging so far?"

Key Phrases for WholeHearted Listening:

- "What I'm hearing is..."
- "It sounds like you..."
- "You seem... [frustrated, excited, unsure, etc.]"

"Wholehearted Listening is not about agreeing or disagreeing—it's about understanding."
—Dr. Joe Famularo

Level 2: HalfHearted Listening

Nautical Analogy:
Imagine a captain who glances at the water but doesn't track the waves closely, missing subtle shifts that could steer the ship off course. That's HalfHearted Listening: partial attention, limited engagement.

In the School Context:
This level includes some effort to listen, but it's undermined by internal judgments or pre-loaded conclusions. The result? Missed nuance, damaged trust, and missed opportunities for connection.

Examples:

- An administrator nods through a teacher's concern about staffing coverage but quickly replies, "We're all stretched thin," without asking any follow-up questions or offering validation.
- During a parent meeting, a school leader listens just long enough to interject, "We've had similar complaints before," shutting down the conversation instead of exploring it further

Level 3: Reply Listening

Nautical Analogy:
This is the captain who hears just enough to shout back directions but doesn't fully assess the sea. They're managing, but not leading. The risk? Shallow understanding and repeated missteps.

In the School Context:
Reply Listening involves paying minimal attention, just enough to catch the gist of what is being said, but primarily focusing on preparing a response. This type of listening does not foster deep understanding or connection.

Examples:

- A teacher shares ideas in a leadership meeting, but the principal immediately shifts focus, saying, "That's good, but here's what I think we should do," without acknowledging or exploring the input.
- A student explains a conflict with a peer, and an assistant principal responds with, "We've talked about this before. What did you do this time?" instead of fully hearing the student's side.

Level 4: Distracted Listening

Nautical Analogy:
A distracted captain, eyes on the horizon but mind elsewhere, invites disaster. The ship drifts. Critical signals go unnoticed. Safety and direction are compromised.

In the School Context:
This is the lowest level of listening, characterized by superficial engagement and often masked by nods or polite smiles. The speaker walks away feeling dismissed or invisible.

Examples:

- A school leader asks for staff feedback at a meeting but types on their laptop while responses are shared, nodding occasionally but offering no meaningful engagement.
- A teacher approaches the assistant principal with a time-sensitive issue, but the leader glances at their watch and says, "Send me an email," clearly disengaged from the moment.

Summary: The Four Levels of Outward Listening

Listening Level	Listening Style	Impact on Culture
Level 1: WholeHearted	Full presence and empathy	Builds trust, connection, and belonging
Level 2: HalfHearted	Partial attention, distracted	Weakens relationships, erodes depth
Level 3: Reply	Listening to respond, not to understand	Misses meaning, blocks collaboration
Level 4: Distracted	Pretending to listen	Damages trust, creates disconnection

Exercise: A Check on Your Listening Level

After reading through the Four Levels of Outward Listening, try this simple exercise the next time you're having a conversation:

1. **Ask yourself, "Which level is the other speaker at?"**
   Pay attention to the speaker's level of engagement, energy, and the quality of their communication. Are they speaking with full presence and empathy? Or are they distracted or only half-listening?
2. **Ask yourself, "Which level am I at?"**
   Reflect on your own level of listening. Are you fully present and engaged? Or are you preparing your response while the other person is speaking, or perhaps distracted by other thoughts?

This exercise is a helpful tool for self-improvement and understanding where others are at in their level of engagement. It's not something to use in every conversation, but it can offer valuable insights into your listening habits and the dynamics of your interactions. Over time, you'll improve your ability to listen intentionally and empathetically, fostering deeper connections and better communication.

Working with Your Team or Staff:
This exercise can also be applied to team meetings or staff interactions. Encourage your team to reflect on their listening levels and create space for open conversations about improving communication. By discussing and practicing this together, you can foster a culture of active listening, empathy, and deeper collaboration. Over time, as a team or staff, you'll be better equipped to navigate challenges and build stronger connections through intentional and empathetic communication.

Closing Reflection:

Listening isn't passive; it's one of the most powerful outward actions we can take as leaders and educators. **WholeHearted Listening anchors trust**. It opens the doors to collaboration, empathy, and progress. As we move through each level, we grow our capacity to lead with understanding and to navigate school culture with clarity and care.

Creating a Safe Environment for Communication

Positive communication isn't just about how we listen; it's also about how we speak. The words we choose, the tone we use, and the emotional safety we create in our interactions can either invite trust or shut it down. In any school setting, these dynamics have a powerful ripple effect. A single moment of unsafe talk can close someone off; a single moment of safe talk can open them up.

Continuing with our nautical analogy, there are two levels of communication environments schools often create: **High Tide Safe Talk** and **Low Tide Unsafe Talk**.

Level 1: High Tide Safe Talk

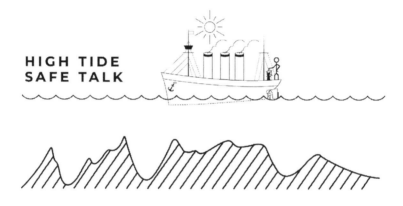

Nautical Analogy:
High tide is the safest time to navigate a vessel because the water is at its highest level, well above any dangerous obstacles like sand bars, objects or rocks beneath the water. Similarly, **High Tide Safe Talk involves creating a communication environment where others feel safe to share their deepest thoughts and concerns without fear of judgment.**

In the School Context:
High Tide Safe Talk happens when the climate of trust is so strong that people feel emotionally safe to speak honestly. Whether it's a student sharing a mistake, a teacher expressing a concern, or a leader inviting feedback, the space feels encouraging and respectful.

Examples:

- A teacher cultivates a classroom where students know it's okay to be wrong because learning is celebrated, not perfection.
- A principal opens staff meetings by asking, "What's one thing we could be doing better as a team?" Everyone then listens with full presence.
- A student support staff member hears a difficult concern and responds with calm affirmation: "Thank you for sharing that with me.

Strategies for High Tide Safe Talk:

- Use positive, respectful, and encouraging language.
- Ask open-ended questions that demonstrate curiosity and care.
- Offer feedback that builds confidence and fosters growth.
- Avoid rushed conversations by allowing time and space for meaningful dialogue and reflection.

Level 2: Low Tide Unsafe Talk

Nautical Analogy:
Low tide reveals every hidden obstacle, such as sharp rocks, sandbars, debris. In the same way, **Low Tide Unsafe Talk exposes others to emotional risk.** It makes communication feel hazardous, unpredictable, or unsafe, often resulting in silence, disengagement, or resentment.

In the School Context:
Low Tide Unsafe Talk is reactive, dismissive, or judgmental. People avoid speaking up. Students withhold their voices. Staff feel like feedback isn't welcomed. Trust erodes quietly—and sometimes permanently.

Examples:

- **A teacher** responds to a student's honest question with sarcasm or dismissiveness, unintentionally discouraging future participation and signaling that vulnerability is unsafe.
- **An assistant principal** quickly shuts down a staff member's suggestion in a meeting without inviting discussion or considering the intent behind the idea, leading others to hesitate before speaking up.
- **A district administrator** shares performance data at a principals' meeting in a way that emphasizes shortcomings without context or support, creating an atmosphere of blame rather than collaboration and improvement.

Strategies to Avoid Low Tide Unsafe Talk:

- Choose words that invite conversation, not shut it down.
- Be mindful of body language, including eye-rolling, sighing, crossed arms, or speaking loudly.
- Replace sarcasm or judgment with curiosity and kindness.
- Address tough issues, but do so with tact and empathy.

Creating a High Tide Safe Talk Environment

High Tide Safe Talk is more than a communication tactic; it's a **trust building practice.** It's what makes someone feel like your school is the **safest ship to board**. In this environment, people don't just speak up—they **open up**.

Ask yourself:

- Are your words **High Tide Positive**?
- Do others feel **stronger, seen, or more empowered** after conversations with you?

When **WholeHearted Listening** and **High Tide Safe Talk** are practiced together, **relationships deepen, trust strengthens**, and a powerful culture of understanding emerges. These practices unlock a level of connection that not only improves communication but also enhances the entire school climate.

As researcher Brené Brown wisely reminds us, effective communication also requires vulnerability. She encourages us to "rumble," to engage in real, honest dialogue with courage, humility, and care. Brown emphasizes that vulnerability is not a weakness, but a strength. It is the willingness to show up fully, listen deeply, and share our authentic thoughts and feelings. This kind of dialogue fosters connection, allowing both parties to be seen and heard without judgment or defensiveness. It is a process that requires emotional openness, where trust is built and continuously reinforced.

And just like high tide, these conversations can't be forced or rushed. The timing matters. Creating a safe environment where people feel comfortable being vulnerable requires awareness, patience, and the readiness to navigate complexity with compassion. It is about allowing the conversation to unfold naturally, without pressure, so that true understanding can take root. When done thoughtfully, these discussions lead to deeper empathy, stronger relationships, and a more cohesive, supportive school culture.

Enhancing School Communication

When school leaders and staff understand and consistently practice the full spectrum of outward listening and speaking, communication shifts from routine exchanges to relationship-building experiences. The ultimate goal is to make **WholeHearted Listening** and **High Tide Safe Talk** the standard for daily communication. These practices foster trust, mutual respect, and collaboration, which are cornerstones of any thriving school environment.

Here are several intentional strategies schools can use to embed these practices into daily routines:

- **Model the Mindset**
  Leadership sets the tone. Administrators and staff should consistently model **WholeHearted Listening and High Tide Safe Talk** in all conversations, whether with students, colleagues, or families. Nothing shapes school culture more powerfully than what is modeled by those in leadership.
- **Professional Learning and Development**
  Offer ongoing training on effective communication strategies. Include sessions that dive into listening styles, verbal and nonverbal cues, and

emotional intelligence. The goal is not just to inform, but to transform communication habits.
- **Practice Through Role-Play**
Create space for teams to practice real-world communication scenarios. Role-playing builds confidence and gives staff the tools to respond intentionally, especially in challenging or emotionally charged conversations.
- **Establish Feedback Loops**
Develop systems for students, staff, and families to reflect on and share their communication experiences. Whether through surveys, listening sessions, or feedback boxes, this input provides insight and helps leaders fine-tune their efforts.

By embedding these strategies, schools can build a culture where communication is intentional, welcoming, and deeply authentic. The result? A connected school community where every voice is valued, and every conversation moves the culture forward.

What Positive Communication Looks and Feels Like in a School

A school that embodies positive communication consistently demonstrates the following characteristics:

- **Open and Honest Dialogue:** Conversations are encouraged at all levels, between students, teachers, staff, and families, where individuals feel safe to express their thoughts and feelings without fear of judgment or dismissal.
- **WholeHearted Listening:** Listening is practiced with intention, empathy, and full presence, fostering genuine understanding and connection.
- **Constructive Feedback:** Feedback is delivered in a growth-oriented way that builds confidence and promotes learning, not fear or defensiveness.
- **Transparency and Clarity:** Communication from leadership is open, timely, and clear, ensuring everyone is aligned and informed.
- **Respectful Interactions:** Kindness, patience, and dignity guide every conversation, whether in the hallway, the classroom, or the boardroom.

Leadership Snapshot: A Culture That Listens First

At Horizon High School, communication isn't something people do—it's part of who they are.

It starts every morning in the front office. The principal greets staff not with announcements, but with intention: "What do we need to talk about today that will help us move forward together?"

Staff don't flinch. They lean in. They've learned that this is a place where honesty is welcomed, not punished. Where saying, "I'm overwhelmed," is met with, "Let's figure this out."

At the midweek leadership team meeting, a department chair voices concerns about a new grading policy. In another school, this could feel like tension. At Horizon, it's trust in action.

"Thanks for speaking up," the principal responds, with eye contact and calm. "Let's rumble with this together. What's behind the concern?"

No one talks over each other. No one shuts down. WholeHearted Listening is modeled from the top. High Tide Safe Talk is the water they all choose to sail in.

In a ninth-grade classroom that same day, a student breaks down quietly during group work. The teacher kneels beside him, not to fix, but to listen. After class, the teacher thanks the student for being open and walks with him to the counselor's office. No big scene. Just big humanity.

Later that week, a parent receives a handwritten card in the mail:

"Thank you for your thoughtful email. Your voice matters. Let's keep working together to make this the school every child deserves."

This is what communication looks like when trust is the foundation and empathy is the compass. There's no fear in expressing uncertainty, no shame in asking for help, no hesitation in telling the truth.

At Horizon, communication doesn't just pass information—it builds people. And those people are building something extraordinary—together.

Why This Anchor Matters

The story of Horizon High School reveals what's possible when a school commits to *intentional communication as a schoolwide expectation*. When WholeHearted Listening is modeled by leadership and High Tide Safe Talk becomes part of the daily rhythm, communication shifts from being basic and routine to meaningful and impactful.

In schools where this anchor is fully embraced, trust deepens across every layer of the community. Staff meetings become safe places for problem-solving, not performance. Classrooms become spaces of openness, not silence. Families feel like partners, not outsiders.

Positive communication is the conduit through which relationships grow, conflicts are resolved, and ideas take flight. It's a lived experience, renewed with every conversation, every email, every hallway check-in.

This anchor matters because:

- Miscommunication is often the root of school culture breakdowns.
- Listening is the fastest way to show others they matter.
- Safe talk fuels creativity, courage, and collaboration.
- When communication improves, everything improves: morale, engagement, and student success.

If trust is the foundation, communication is the framework that holds it all together.

Inspire to Aspire doesn't happen in silence—it happens in dialogue. And it begins with how we choose to listen and speak every day.

Strategic Thinking Questions for Outward School Anchor 2: Practice Positive Communication

1. *What kind of communication culture do we want to create in our school?*

2. *How can we create spaces where everyone feels safe to speak openly and honestly?*

3. *What actions can we take to make WholeHearted Listening a daily habit across our school?*

4. *How can we embed High Tide Safe Talk into classrooms, meetings, and conversations?*

_____
_____
_____
_____
_____
_____

5. *What strategies will help us give and receive feedback in a constructive, respectful way?*

_____
_____
_____
_____
_____
_____

6. *How can we ensure that communication across the school is clear, consistent, and transparent?*

_____
_____
_____
_____
_____
_____

7. *What language and behaviors will help promote empathy and respect in every interaction?*

_____
_____
_____
_____
_____
_____

8. *How can we empower all members of our community to play an active role in improving communication?*

_____
_____
_____
_____
_____
_____

9. *How can we recognize and repair communication breakdowns in a way that builds trust, not blame?*

_____
_____
_____
_____
_____
_____

10. What routines or rituals can we establish to reinforce positive *communication daily?*

_____
_____
_____
_____
_____
_____

Drafting the Practice Positive Communication Statement

After reflecting on the principles, mindset shifts, and strategic thinking questions, along with the key practices of WholeHearted Listening and High Tide Safe Talk, it's time to articulate a **Positive Communication Statement for your school.**

This statement is a reflection of **your school's communication identity in practice**. It should express your school's highest aspirations for creating a communication environment where every member of the community, including students, staff, families, and leaders, feels heard, valued, and understood.

Think of this as your school's communication promise:

- How do you want people to speak and listen to one another?
- What should a conversation sound like in your classrooms, offices, and meetings?
- How will communication uplift your culture and deepen trust?

Let this first draft be a starting point. Capture the spirit of WholeHearted Listening and High Tide Safe Talk. Emphasize empathy, clarity, and openness. Write with vision and intention so your statement inspires and guides every interaction.

Initial Thoughts for Your Positive Communication Statement:

Positive Communication Statement Examples

1. Fostering Open Dialogue:
"We commit to creating a culture where open, honest dialogue is not only welcomed—but expected. Every voice matters, and by fostering an environment of psychological safety, we ensure that ideas, concerns, and celebrations can be shared without fear. Through High Tide Safe Talk and a spirit of mutual trust, we build a stronger, more connected school community."

2. Encouraging Constructive Feedback:
"In our school, feedback is not a correction—it's a gift. We promote a culture where feedback is shared respectfully, received openly, and used to inspire individual and collective growth. Through consistent practice of WholeHearted Listening, we ensure that feedback strengthens relationships and drives excellence."

3. Prioritizing Active Listening:
"We believe that truly hearing one another is the foundation of trust. Active, WholeHearted Listening is a daily practice that helps us better understand, support, and uplift each other. We listen to learn, not just to respond, ensuring all voices are valued and every conversation strengthens our sense of belonging."

4. Maintaining Transparency and Clarity:
"We are committed to transparency and clarity in all forms of communication. Clear expectations, timely information, and honest conversations ensure everyone feels informed, included, and respected. We believe that transparency builds trust and unity, helping our community move forward together."

5. Promoting Respectful Interactions:
"Respect is the tone of our culture. Whether in classrooms, hallways, offices, or online spaces, we engage each other with dignity and care. By choosing words and actions that reflect empathy, kindness, and thoughtfulness, we ensure that every member of our community feels safe to express themselves and fully participate in the life of the school."

6. Modeling Safe and Intentional Communication
"We believe that how we communicate shapes who we become. Our leaders model intentional communication by creating safe spaces where vulnerability is met with empathy, and questions are welcomed as much as answers. Through High Tide Safe Talk, we establish a culture where trust is built daily, and every interaction among all members of the school community reflects our commitment to clarity, respect, and shared purpose."

The Practice Positive Communication Anchor Model

Practice Positive Communication: Rooted in the Principle of Outward Understanding

The Principle of Outward Understanding is about seeking to understand others before being understood yourself. It's the foundation of trust, empathy, and collaboration. *Outward Understanding* calls on us to approach communication with open minds, compassionate intent, and respectful attention. In schools, this principle comes to life when every conversation, between students, staff, and families, is grounded in mutual respect and emotional safety. For the Practice Positive Communication anchor, Outward Understanding ensures that communication builds people up, bridges differences, and strengthens relationships across the entire school community.

Every Conversation Counts: Building Culture Through Communication

To build a school culture where communication fuels connection, collaboration, and trust, it's essential to anchor our efforts in two guiding practices: **WholeHearted Listening** and **High Tide Safe Talk**. These models are everyday behaviors that shape how we interact with one another. They reflect the **Principle of Outward Understanding** and serve as daily reminders to lead with empathy, clarity, and respect in every conversation.

1. **WholeHearted Listening:**
   Engage Fully. Listen Deeply. Understand First.

WholeHearted Listening means being fully present in mind, body, and heart. It's not just hearing words, but also noticing tone, body language, and unspoken emotions. It's about listening without preparing your reply or judging what's being said. This level of listening creates an atmosphere of safety and significance, where people feel truly seen and understood.

In schools that practice WholeHearted Listening, every relationship between students, staff, families, and leaders is strengthened by the simple yet profound act of giving someone your full attention.

High Tide Safe Talk:
Speak Safely. Share Freely. Build Together.

High Tide Safe Talk occurs when communication is grounded in trust and emotional safety. Like navigating during high tide, when the waters are safest, this kind of talk happens in environments where people feel safe to speak their truth without fear of judgment, ridicule, or retribution. It includes language that encourages, questions that invite, and responses that validate.

Whether it's a teacher meeting with a concerned parent, a student asking for help, or a leader addressing the team, High Tide Safe Talk creates the conditions for growth, vulnerability, and problem-solving.

Together, **WholeHearted Listening** and **High Tide Safe Talk** form the backbone of the **Practice Positive Communication** anchor. These practices elevate communication from routine exchanges to intentional, relationship-building acts. They foster a culture where every member of the school community, regardless of role, feels empowered to contribute, collaborate, and aspire toward a shared vision of success and well-being.

The Guiding Question for Practicing Positive Communication

Is our school culture sailing on High Tide Safe Talk, where trust and clarity lead the way, or are we stuck in low tide waters where connection struggles to stay afloat?

Transitioning to Outward Anchor 3: Creating Common Language

From Dialogue to Shared Meaning

As we move from Outward Anchor 2: Practice Positive Communication into **Anchor 3: Create Common Language**, we shift from *how* we communicate to *what* we communicate. Communication thrives when it's not only open and respectful but also consistent and shared.

Create Common Language emphasizes the importance of developing **a unified vocabulary** with clear definitions for values, principles, and key terms that guide daily practice and decision-making. When everyone speaks the shared language of leadership, understanding deepens, collaboration strengthens, and confusion diminishes.

This anchor builds upon the trust and listening habits established in Anchor 2 by ensuring that **our words carry shared meaning**. It empowers schools to move from reactive clarification to proactive alignment, where students, staff, and families know exactly what we mean when we talk about leadership, respect, collaboration, or excellence.

In the next section, we'll explore how schools can **intentionally develop this shared language** and why it becomes a cornerstone of lasting culture change.

Outward School Anchor 3
CREATE COMMON LANGUAGE

The Principle of Outward Effectiveness

Everyone hears only what he understands.
—Johann Wolfgang von Goethe

Create Common Language: Embracing the Principle of Outward Effectiveness

At the center of effective collaboration is a shared understanding, an agreed-upon vocabulary that turns abstract values into everyday actions. That's the essence of **Outward Anchor 3: Create Common Language**, rooted in the **Principle of Outward Effectiveness**. When schools speak the same principled schoolwide language, they increase clarity, reduce misunderstandings, and build a stronger sense of unity.

Creating common language isn't about conformity—it's about alignment. It enables students, staff, and families to communicate with clarity, purpose, and consistency. When we define what our core values, like *leadership, integrity, collaboration, and excellence,* look like in practice, those words no longer remain abstract. They align the culture, reinforcing the mission and strengthening our collective purpose. These words move beyond mission statements and mottos, becoming tangible in classrooms, hallways, emails, and everyday conversations, shaping the way we work and interact together.

Why Common Language Matters in School Culture

A school culture built on shared language:

- **Clarifies Expectations:** Everyone knows what behaviors and mindsets are expected because they've been named and discussed.
- **Promotes Belonging:** When language is welcoming and consistent, every voice can contribute. No one feels like an outsider in the conversation.
- **Strengthens Collaboration:** Common terms eliminate the need for repeated explanations. With fewer misunderstandings, teams work more efficiently and respectfully.
- **Accelerates Culture Building:** Culture is shaped by the words we use. When those words are shared, so is the vision.

When everyone knows the language and its meaning, it builds culture. A few powerful words, when clearly defined and consistently used, can carry tremendous weight. In an IOU School Culture, we don't just say "Be respectful." We have defined and articulated what that looks like in action, at every level of the school community. This becomes the language of alignment.

Create Common Language Mindset Question

Which type of thinking does your school use – Default or Intentional?

- **Default Thinking:**

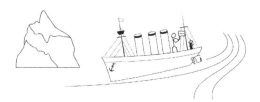

"We don't emphasize common language. When misunderstandings arise, we address them individually."

This mindset is reactive, addressing communication issues only when they become problematic. It often leads to inconsistencies, misunderstandings, and a lack of alignment among school members.

- **Intentional Thinking:**

"Our school prioritizes the creation and use of a common language, actively fostering a positive environment. We intentionally define and adopt shared terms, values, and principles every day."

This proactive approach ensures continuous improvement in communication, building stronger relationships and a more cohesive school community.

Reflecting on these mindsets and their influence is essential for understanding the role of common language in your school's strategic development. Adopting an intentional thinking approach can fundamentally transform the educational landscape of your school, setting a course that achieves innovation and excellence. This common language-oriented mindset ensures that the school is continually aligned with its highest aspirations, embedding clarity, unity, and effectiveness into every facet of its operations and long-term objectives.

Leadership Snapshot: Speaking the Same Language

The principal and leadership team at Willow Ridge Middle School were always looking for meaningful ways to strengthen school culture.

They started noticing something curious. Staff and students were already using phrases that packed a punch. A few words here and there, like "Own it," "Stay curious," or "Lead by example," seemed to carry big meaning. People understood them, felt them, and used them in ways that shaped how they showed up each day.

That's when the leadership team leaned in.

Instead of adding new programs, they started naming and nurturing what was already happening. What began informally soon became intentional. The team introduced one phrase each month, like "Be Proactive," "Walk the Talk," or "Seek First to Understand." These weren't just decorative slogans on posters. They were modeled in staff meetings, practiced in classrooms, and echoed in parent newsletters. Students started using them in reflection journals. Teachers began anchoring feedback in them. Even custodians and aides embraced the language: "Synergize" became a call for collaboration across all roles.

Then came a turning point. During a peer mediation session, a sixth grader calmly said,

"I think we forgot to begin with the end in mind."
The room paused, not because it was profound, but because everyone understood exactly what it meant.

That's the power of common language.

At Willow Ridge, shared phrases became leadership language anchors. They guided behavior, inspired leadership, and fostered unity. Misunderstandings decreased. Connection deepened. Learning accelerated.

Today, when someone walks into the school, they don't just hear words—they hear belonging.
They hear values in action.
They hear a school that speaks the same language—together.

Strategic Reflection Prompt:

What shared language is already quietly shaping our culture, and how can we bring it to life with intention?

Every school has phrases, values, and behaviors that circulate informally through staff meetings, classroom routines, or hallway conversations. These organic touchpoints hold power. By identifying them and building on them, we can transform unspoken habits into intentional, unifying language that fosters clarity, connection, and collaboration.

- What key phrases or values do we hear repeated by students, teachers, and staff?
- How might we elevate and define these as part of a schoolwide common language?
- What are the risks of not being intentional with our language, and what are the opportunities if we are?
- What systems (newsletters, reflections, announcements, etc.) could help embed this language into daily practice?

Let's move from speaking in fragments to speaking with unity. Let's give our school a language that builds culture—on purpose.

Common Language in Schools: Building Unity Through Shared Words

When a school embraces a common language, communication becomes more than efficient; it becomes a catalyst for culture. Shared language fosters clarity, reduces confusion, and strengthens collective identity. It's not about uniformity of thought, but about unity of purpose.

A school that intentionally develops and lives by a common language will exhibit these defining characteristics:

- **Unified Communication:**
  Everyone: students, teachers, administrators, and families, uses shared phrases and terms that express the school's core values, principles, and goals. A few powerful words carry deep meaning because they've been discussed, defined, and lived out together.

- **Welcoming Language:**
  The common language reflects all voices, backgrounds, and perspectives of the school community. It invites belonging, ensures that all feel seen and heard, and fosters unity through empathy, understanding, and shared respect.
- **Consistency and Clarity:**
  Language is used intentionally and consistently across classrooms, meetings, and messaging. This clarity reduces misunderstandings and keeps the school aligned and focused on what matters most.
- **Collaborative Development:**
  The creation and refinement of the common language is a shared process. Students, families, and staff are actively involved in naming, shaping, and practicing the language, making it authentic and lasting.
- **Continuous Improvement:**
  Just as school culture evolves, so should its language. Schools committed to growth revisit and refine their common language regularly to ensure it stays relevant, meaningful, and empowering.

 **Strategic Thinking Questions for Outward School Anchor 3: Create Common Language**

1. *How can we intentionally use common language to clearly communicate and reinforce our school's shared vision, principles, values, and goals across all settings?*

___

2. *What specific phrases, principles, or leadership habits do we want to embed into our school culture to represent who we are and what we stand for?*

___

3. *How can we ensure that the language we use in classrooms, meetings, and community events is simple, clear, and consistently understood by all?*

___

4. *What strategies can we use to involve students, teachers, staff, and families in creating a meaningful and unifying shared language?*

_____
_____
_____
_____
_____
_____

5. *How can we routinely reflect on and refine our common language to ensure it evolves with the needs of our school community?*

_____
_____
_____
_____
_____
_____

6. *What role can each member of our school community play in fostering a dynamic and positive culture through shared language?*

_____
_____
_____
_____
_____
_____

7. *How will we know if our common language is truly taking root across the school, reflected in conversations, behaviors, and shared understanding?*

_____
_____
_____
_____
_____
_____

8. *What intentional practices can we build into our routines to regularly review, reflect on, and evolve our common language as our school community grows?*

_____
_____
_____
_____
_____
_____

9. *How can we make our common language more visible, meaningful, and actionable across all areas of school life?*

_____
_____
_____
_____
_____
_____

Initial Drafts of Your Common Language Statement

As you reflect on the strategic thinking questions for this anchor, begin drafting a **Common Language Statement** that captures your school's vision for shared communication. This statement should outline the terminology, key phrases, Leadership Principles, and mottos that will unify your school community and strengthen community-wide understanding.

Your initial draft does not need to be perfect—it's a **starting point**, a working framework that can evolve as you continue to develop the remaining Outward Anchors. The purpose of this statement is to provide clarity and cohesion. It should help ensure that across classrooms, hallways, and meetings, the language used consistently reflects your school's vision and principles.

Be sure to include:

- Signature terms or mantras that reflect your leadership approach (e.g., *"Be Proactive," "Think Win-Win," "Aim for Excellence"*).
- School leadership principles and core values that everyone should understand and use in daily practice.
- Any **unique language** or expressions already being used in your school that positively reinforce your culture are natural foundations to build on.

As you draft, ask yourself:
What do we want our students, staff, and families to hear—and feel—when they walk through our doors?

Your common language is more than words. It's a mirror of your culture and a map for where you're headed.

Initial Thoughts for Your Common Language Statement:

Common Language Statement Examples

1. **Building a Unified Communication System**
"We commit to cultivating a common language that reflects our shared values and guiding principles. When everyone speaks the same language, rooted in clarity and purpose, we strengthen understanding, foster collaboration, and move forward as one unified community."

   Initial Common Language:
   - Be Proactive
   - Collaborate to Elevate
   - Speak with Purpose
   - Clear and Kind Communication

2. **Promoting Unity Through Language**
"Our school will develop a welcoming and unifying common language, one that reflects the voices of our students, staff, and families. This shared vocabulary will cultivate belonging, bridge understanding, and affirm that every voice matters."

   Initial Common Language:
   - We Are One
   - Every Voice Counts
   - Shared Purpose
   - Together We Thrive

3. **Ensuring Consistency and Clarity**
"We will prioritize consistency and clarity in our communication. By using defined terms and shared phrases, we minimize misunderstandings, build trust, and ensure every member of our school is aligned with our mission and daily practices."

   Initial Common Language:
   - Clarity Above All
   - Stay on the Same Page
   - Clear Intentions, Clear Actions
   - One Message, One Voice

4. **Collaborative Language Development**
   "Our language will be shaped by the whole community. We believe that involving students, staff, and families in developing our common language ensures it resonates deeply and authentically with our collective identity and aspirations."

   Initial Common Language:
   - Together We Grow
   - Shared Understanding
   - Voices United
   - Collaboration Drives Success

5. **Commitment to Continuous Improvement**
   "We pledge to reflect on and refine our common language regularly. As our school grows and evolves, so will our words, always guided by the belief that language is a living part of culture and a catalyst for progress."

   Initial Common Language:
   - Strive for Excellence
   - Continuous Growth
   - Learn, Improve, Lead
   - Embrace Change, Lead Forward

Examples of Common Language in Schools

Common language is a **shared mindset that shapes how people think, speak, and act within the school community.** When used intentionally, these phrases become anchors that guide behavior, reinforce expectations, and build unity.

The examples below can be used across classrooms, staff meetings, and leadership conversations to foster leadership development, support behavioral expectations, and promote academic and personal growth. Select the phrases that best align with your school's vision, values, and voice, and consider embedding them into everyday routines, reflections, and recognition practices.

Leadership & Character Building

- Be Proactive
- Lead by Example
- Model Integrity
- Walk the Talk

- Demonstrate Accountability
- Promote Fairness
- Build Trust
- Think Win-Win
- Seek First to Understand
- Synergize

Learning Behaviors & Study Skills

- Manage Your Time
- Prioritize Your Work
- Balance Your Schedule
- Stay Curious
- Practice Persistence
- Adapt Your Strategies
- Seek Help When Needed
- Reflect on Your Learning
- Aim for Excellence
- Sharpen the Saw

Communication & Relationship Building

- Engage in Discussions
- Seek Feedback
- Practice Self-Reflection
- Communicate with Clarity
- Show Empathy and Compassion
- Foster Collaboration

Growth & Mindset Culture

- Maintain a Positive Mindset
- Embrace Change
- Encourage Innovation
- Reflect and Adjust
- Continuous Improvement
- Commit to Personal Growth

When these phrases become part of the fabric of your school's language, from hallway conversations to morning announcements, they move beyond buzzwords. They become common ground. By cultivating a culture rooted in shared language, schools empower every voice and align every action with their core beliefs and purpose.

The Create Common Language Anchor Model

Create Common Language: Rooted in the Principle of Outward Effectiveness

The Principle of Outward Effectiveness is about using intentional language to build clarity, consistency, and unity in how we interact with one another. In schools, this principle is reflected in our spoken words, shared phrases, and daily conversations. It shows up in how we greet one another, how we teach, how we lead, and how we work together. For the Create Common Language anchor, Outward Effectiveness means openly identifying the vocabulary we value, aligning it with our shared beliefs, and using it across classrooms, meetings, and schoolwide interactions. When this language is co-created, clearly defined, and spoken regularly, it becomes a powerful connector that strengthens relationships and supports a culture of shared purpose and understanding.

Clarifying Communication. Unifying Culture.

A school's common language is **a reflection of shared understanding, aligned actions, and a unified culture.** When language is intentionally created and consistently used, it becomes a powerful tool to reinforce vision, inspire belonging, and streamline communication across every level of the school.

This model is designed to spark meaningful conversations among your school team about the language already being used, and how it can be refined, expanded, and aligned to strengthen your IOU School Culture.

Use this model as a guiding framework during planning meetings, leadership retreats, or Professional Development sessions. Ask:

- *What words do we want echoing through our hallways?*
- *Which phrases capture who we are, and who we aspire to be?*

"When common language is co-created and lived out daily, it becomes the connective tissue that holds a dynamic, positive school culture together."
—Dr. Joe Famularo

The Guiding Question for Creating Common Language

What language already exists in our school that reflects our best culture, and what language do we still need to create to reflect our highest aspirations?

This question encourages teams to identify strengths already present in their communication patterns, while also highlighting areas for growth. It emphasizes intentionality: defining what matters, saying it clearly, and saying it together.

Transitioning to Outward Anchor 4: Construct a Cohesive Environment

With a strong common language taking root, the next step in cultivating a dynamic, positive school culture is to **build the environment where that language, and those principles and values, can thrive**.

Outward Anchor 4—**Construct a Cohesive Environment**—focuses on intentionally shaping the **physical and relational spaces** of your school. This anchor is grounded in the idea that a sense of belonging doesn't happen by accident; it is built through daily interactions, shared experiences, and spaces that reflect unity, care, and purpose.

By creating a Cohesive Environment, schools don't just feel safe and welcoming; they become places where **students, staff, and families are connected**, aligned, and inspired to contribute to something greater than themselves.

In the next section, we'll explore how to intentionally design that environment, where everyone feels seen, supported, and proud to belong.

Outward School Anchor 4

CONSTRUCT A COHESIVE ENVIRONMENT

The Principle of Outward Connectedness

Alone, we can do so little; together, we can do so much.
—Helen Keller

Construct a Cohesive Environment: Embracing the Principle of Outward Connectedness

Thriving school cultures are cultivated through connection. The essence of Outward School Anchor 4: **Construct a Cohesive Environment** is the **Principle of Outward Connectedness**, which calls on us to create school environments rooted in safety, character, and competence.

This anchor invites leaders to look beyond individual classrooms or departments and consider how the entire school community, including students, staff, families, and visitors, experiences the environment, **both physically and relationally.** When these environments are intentionally designed to reflect shared values and support purposeful interactions, a sense of **cohesion** begins to take root.

Constructing a Cohesive Environment means creating spaces where people feel a deep sense of **belonging, contribution, and shared purpose**. When school members feel connected, collaboration strengthens, motivation increases, and the vision becomes a shared journey.

The Importance of a Cohesive Environment in School Culture

A Cohesive Environment is the dynamic force that links a school's vision, mission, and values to the daily experiences of its people. It manifests in two interconnected realms:

- **The Physical Environment** reflects the identity and priorities of the school. When intentional, the design and layout of spaces can inspire, guide behavior, and communicate belonging without a word being spoken.
- **The Relational Environment** is how people treat one another, including the tone of conversations, the consistency of support, and the strength of trust. It is the emotional atmosphere of the school.

When both physical and relational elements are aligned, the environment becomes more than a backdrop; it becomes a force for unity, positivity, and purpose. It signals to every person who enters: *You belong here. You are part of something meaningful.*

Leadership Snapshot: More Than Just Walls

When Dr. Morales became principal of Brighton Middle School, she didn't begin with new rules, new furniture, or a fancy initiative. She began with something simple—and powerful.

A walk.

With a clipboard in hand and a small group of staff and students beside her, she moved slowly through the halls, noticing, feeling, asking one bold question:

"What does this space say about who we are becoming?"

They stopped often.

A faded vision statement no one could recite. Dusty bulletin boards filled with old flyers. Hallways lined with silence instead of purpose. More than what they saw, *it was what they* felt. *They sensed disconnection, neutrality, and survival. The building functioned, but it didn't* inspire.

Dr. Morales didn't point fingers. She extended an invitation:

"Let's make this place speak for us—and to us."

And so began a transformation—not of paint and posters, but of **culture by design**.

- *A **welcome center** was created in the front office, run by student ambassadors who greeted visitors with pride.*
- ***Shared leadership quotes** and **student artwork** filled the halls, aligned with the school's core values.*
- *A **"Wall of Gratitude"** was added near the staff lounge, where students left sticky notes recognizing a teacher, coach, or custodian.*
- *Each classroom doorway was framed with the school's three guiding principles, chosen by the staff during a retreat:* Be Kind. Be Curious. Be Connected.

But the true shift was relational.

- *Morning announcements featured staff and student "shoutouts" and weekly "mission moments."*
- *The 6th-grade hallway adopted "House Crews," small multi-grade teams that tackled service projects and led assemblies.*

- *A custodian named Mr. Jake proposed a student mural project—and led it. His idea? "Let's paint our journey, not just our walls."*

Over time, the school's energy spoke for itself.
Visitors didn't just see the changes; they felt them, often commenting on the welcoming spirit that was evident within moments of arriving.

And that was the point.

The building began to reflect the beliefs. The environment told the story.

Today, when you walk into Brighton Middle School, it doesn't just look different. It feels different. The walls speak purpose. The people echo it. The space and spirit are finally aligned.

It's more than just a school—it's a living map of who they are… and who they are becoming.

Construct a Cohesive Environment Mindset Question

Which type of thinking does your school use – Default or Intentional?

- **Default Thinking:**

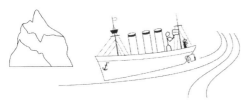

"Our physical environment hasn't changed in years. Everyone seems comfortable with it, so we haven't felt the need to revisit or realign it."

This reactive mindset accepts the status quo until problems become too big to ignore. Physical spaces may be cluttered with mixed messages. Relationships may be siloed or transactional. While things may function on the surface, there is little alignment beneath it. Without cohesive design and connection, the school culture can become fragmented, missing daily opportunities to inspire, unite, and elevate.

- **Intentional Thinking:**

"We are continually reimagining and refining our physical and relational environments to actively reflect and reinforce our shared principles, values, and mission. Every space, interaction, and design choice is viewed as an opportunity to strengthen connection, inspire belonging, and align with our collective purpose."

This proactive mindset recognizes that environment is not neutral; it's a constant communicator. Every wall, hallway, and interaction sends a message. Schools that intentionally construct a Cohesive Environment don't leave culture to chance. They curate it by shaping spaces and relationships to foster trust, teamwork, and belonging.

Why This Matters

Your school's environment is a living map of your culture. It tells the story of what you value, how you work together, and whether people feel seen and supported.

When physical spaces align with relational principles and values, a powerful synergy emerges:

- Students feel emotionally safe and connected.
- Adults collaborate more effectively.
- Families experience belonging from the moment they walk in.

This is what it means to Construct a Cohesive Environment—on purpose, with purpose.

Assessing Culture: The "Enter Your Building" Exercise

One of the most revealing ways to assess your school's culture is to experience it as if for the first time. This simple, yet powerful exercise invites leaders to step into their own school, or any school in their district, as a curious observer rather than a daily participant.

Start by walking out the front doors, then re-enter slowly and intentionally. **Pause in the main lobby for 10–15 seconds** and take in everything with fresh eyes.

Ask yourself:

What do I feel immediately?
Is it warmth, welcome, and energy? Or is it silence, tension, or indifference? Your gut response is more than intuition—it's culture speaking.

As you scan the environment, focus on two key dimensions:

- **Physical Environment:**
  What do you see? Are the school's principles, values, mission, and vision visible and lived through artwork, colors, photos, and displays? Is the space inviting, cared for, and aligned with the culture your school aspires to? Every wall, bulletin board, and hallway communicates something, whether intentional or not.

- **Relational Environment:**
  What do you hear and experience in people's interactions? Are there smiles, greetings, and a sense of openness? Do staff, students, or office personnel make eye contact or acknowledge your presence? These micro-moments reflect the relational climate of the school, its unspoken norms around connection, support, and hospitality.

This exercise offers a practical, real-time snapshot of your school's current schoolwide energy and alignment. It complements the strategic reflection questions in this anchor, helping you ground conversations about cohesion in lived experience, not just theory. When school leaders make a habit of seeing their buildings through fresh eyes, they lead with greater empathy, awareness, and clarity.

This can be done by you as the leader or a team... a powerful exercise that will make a difference.

**Strategic Thinking Questions for
Outward School Anchor 4:
Construct a Cohesive Environment**

1. *How can we intentionally design our physical environment to reflect and reinforce our school's vision, mission, principles and values?*

___

2. *What visual and sensory elements can we introduce or elevate to create an inspiring and cohesive atmosphere across all areas of our school?*

___

3. *What relational practices will help build stronger daily connections among students, staff, and families?*

___

4. *How can we foster deeper collaboration and teamwork among all members of our school community?*

_____
_____
_____
_____
_____
_____

5. *What opportunities can we create for students, staff, and families to co-design and contribute to a unified school environment?*

_____
_____
_____
_____
_____
_____

6. *How can each member of our school community become a steward of both our physical and relational environment?*

_____
_____
_____
_____
_____
_____

7. *How can we measure the effectiveness of our efforts in constructing a Cohesive Environment?*

8. *What steps can we take to continuously refine and enhance our Cohesive Environment?*

Initial Drafts of Your Cohesive Environment Statement

As you reflect on the importance of Outward Connectedness, now is the time to begin drafting your **Cohesive Environment Statement**, a working blueprint for cultivating a unified, welcoming, and purpose-driven school culture.

This statement should outline initial ideas and actionable steps to:

- **Design intentional physical spaces** that reflect your school's vison, mission, principles, and core values.
- **Strengthen relational connections** across all levels, including students, staff, families, and community partners.
- **Promote fairness, collaboration, and belonging** in both the visual and interpersonal culture of the school.

Begin with what you already observe and aspire to improve. Think about:

- What does a cohesive school feel like the moment someone walks through the doors?
- Where are the gaps in interactions or physical spaces that need better alignment?
- What simple changes could signal unity, trust, and shared purpose?

Remember, this is just the beginning. As you work through the remaining Outward Anchors, revisit and refine your plan to ensure it reflects your evolving insights, team feedback, and school-wide priorities.

A strong Cohesive Environment Statement acts not only as a guide, but as a visible commitment to building a school culture where everyone feels **seen, supported, and connected.**

Initial Thoughts for your Cohesive Environment Statement:

Cohesive Environment Statement Examples

- **Creating a Welcoming Atmosphere**
  "Each day, we intentionally create a school atmosphere where everyone feels seen, valued, and welcomed. Our physical and relational spaces reflect our shared principles and foster a culture of belonging, kindness, and respect."
- **Fostering Teamwork and Collaboration**
  "We design our environment to encourage connection, with spaces that invite conversation, and relationships that spark collaboration. Together, we build a culture where teamwork is not an event but a daily way of working and learning."
- **Promoting Safety and Well-Being**
  "We believe that trust begins with safety. From secure and calming spaces to empathetic and respectful interactions, we commit to an environment where every person feels emotionally and physically safe to grow and contribute."
- **Enhancing Learning and Growth**
  "Our learning spaces are designed with intention to reflect creativity, inspire curiosity, and support the whole child. Relationally, we cultivate trust and encouragement so every learner can thrive in both academic and personal growth."
- **Building a Positive School Culture**
  "We intentionally align our environment with our core values, where walls speak our mission and interactions echo our principles. This alignment builds a school culture that is not only positive, but purposefully united."
- **Establishing a Supportive Environment**
  "Today and every day, we work to shape a cohesive environment where support is not a program but a way of being. Our spaces, systems, and relationships empower every voice, lift every learner, and celebrate every contribution."
- **Prioritizing Connection Through Design**
  "Our school spaces are designed to spark collaboration and build community. By pairing purposeful layout with a culture of respect and kindness, we ensure every corner of our school invites connection and shared purpose."
- **Elevating Safety and Belonging**
  "Safety and belonging are the foundation of everything we build. We cultivate both through warm, welcoming spaces and relationship-centered practices that honor each individual's story."

- **Inspiring Learning Through Environment**
  "From hallways to classrooms, every element of our environment reflects our belief in possibility. We create spaces that energize, relationships that uplift, and a community that propels learners toward their highest potential."
- **Living Our Values Together**
  "We pledge to create a school culture where our values aren't just displayed, they're lived. Through shared spaces and shared purpose, we form a cohesive, connected community where every person contributes, belongs, and thrives."

The Construct a Cohesive Environment Anchor Model

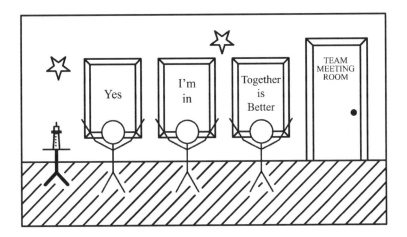

Construct a Cohesive Environment: Rooted in the Principle of Outward Connectedness

The Principle of Outward Connectedness is about creating spaces and relationships that make people feel seen, valued, and part of something greater than themselves. In schools, connectedness is not accidental—it is designed. It lives in the way classrooms are arranged, how hallways feel, how people interact, and how the culture is communicated in both visible and invisible ways. For the Construct a Cohesive Environment anchor, this principle reminds us that everything we do, say, and display contributes to the environment others experience. It is about intentionally shaping the places and interactions that connect individuals to one another and to a shared purpose.

Designing Space, Creating Cohesion

The visual model for Outward Anchor 4 features a wall with three framed pictures and a figure standing in front of them. This simple yet powerful image symbolizes how a school's **physical environment** and **relational culture** work together to reflect and reinforce its values. Just as pictures on a wall communicate meaning at a glance, every element of a school environment sends a message about what matters, who belongs, and how we treat one another.

Each picture represents a dimension of cohesiveness. Together, they remind us that a cohesive school culture is not created by chance. It is designed with care, aligned with intention, and sustained by shared commitment.

The Three Frames of the Cohesive Environment:

- **Physical Environment**
  The layout, visuals, and sensory details that shape how students, staff, and families feel when they walk through the door. Every hallway display, classroom setup, and common space should reflect the school's vision, mission, principles, and core values.
- **Relational Environment**
  The daily interactions, tone, and culture of communication that define how people connect. Positive relationships built on trust, empathy, and respect are what truly hold a school together, creating a sense of unity, belonging, and shared purpose.
- **Safety and Well-Being**
  The foundation of a thriving environment. This includes not only physical safety but also emotional safety with spaces where everyone feels free to take risks, express themselves, and know they are cared for.

Supporting Beams of a Cohesive Environment:

- **Teamwork and Collaboration**
  Cohesive schools design their spaces and their schedules to bring people together. They create systems that encourage interdisciplinary collaboration, shared leadership, and strong student-teacher partnerships.
- **Learning and Growth**
  The environment should inspire and support learning at every level. Whether it's a vibrant makerspace, a calm reflection nook, or a hallway filled with student-created work, the message should be clear: growth lives here.

This model reinforces that **Constructing a Cohesive Environment is both an art and a strategy**. When done with intention, it fosters a school culture where every space tells a story of connection and every person feels they belong in the picture.

The Guiding Question for Constructing a Cohesive Environment

What does our school environment, both physical and relational, communicate about who we are and what we believe?

Transitioning to Outward School Anchor 5: Establish Everlasting Traditions

As we move into the fifth Outward Anchor—**Establish Everlasting Traditions**—we shift our focus to the power of legacy and belonging. This anchor emphasizes the importance of creating meaningful, lasting traditions that celebrate a school's identity, honor its values, and connect its past to its future.

Everlasting traditions serve as unifying milestones, rituals and routines that remind every student, staff member, and family member that they are part of something larger than themselves. **These traditions breathe life into your school's vision and mission**, turning abstract ideals into memorable, shared experiences.

By intentionally establishing and sustaining traditions, your school can:

- Celebrate what makes your community unique
- Strengthen intergenerational connection
- Foster pride, unity, and a sense of "this is who we are"

This anchor will build upon the Cohesive Environment you've constructed and the communication practices you've cultivated, helping to embed your values in time-honored ways that endure. As you begin, reflect on the stories and rituals already living in your school and imagine what traditions could be born from the culture you're actively shaping.

Let's now explore how to intentionally craft traditions that unify, uplift, and inspire—year after year.

Outward School Anchor 5
ESTABLISH EVERLASTING TRADITIONS

The Principle of Life History

Traditions are the guideposts driven deep into our subconscious minds.
—Ellen Goodman

Establish Everlasting Traditions: Embracing the Principle of Life History

A thriving school culture isn't built only in the present; it's rooted in the past and designed to last. The **Principle of Life History** reminds us that meaningful rituals and shared experiences are what connect people to each other and to something greater than themselves. This is the essence of **Outward Anchor 5: Establish Everlasting Traditions**: intentionally creating fun, caring, and community-building experiences that everyone looks forward to and that define what it means to be part of your school.

Traditions are defining moments that carry meaning, reinforce values, and pass your school's spirit from one generation to the next. When thoughtfully crafted, these traditions become part of your school's story. They're the memories students cherish, the experiences staff reflect on with pride, and the legacies that inspire future leaders to carry the culture forward.

The Importance of Everlasting Traditions for School Culture

Everlasting traditions strengthen identity and belonging by marking time with meaning. They build bonds among students, staff, and families, creating a rhythm of togetherness that shapes school culture and character.

In strong school cultures, traditions:

- Build trust and unity across the entire school community
- Connect people to the mission and values of the school
- Generate a sense of pride and legacy
- Provide moments of celebration, reflection, and renewal
- Foster intergenerational connection and emotional safety

These traditions help define **"who we are"** and **"what we stand for"** through **repeated, joy-filled actions** that create a deep sense of connection and shared purpose.

Building a Culture of Traditions

Traditions can take many forms, such as celebrations, ceremonies, rituals, and recurring events, but the most meaningful ones are built with intention. Whether it's a school-wide service day, a Friday morning "shout-out" circle, a teacher appreciation walk, or a senior walk-through of their elementary roots, each tradition should be more than routine; it should be a reflection of who you are as a school.

The most enduring traditions:

- Reflect your school's core values and leadership principles
- Spark joy and create lasting emotional memories
- Reinforce connectedness and belonging
- Are designed to endure, but flexible enough to evolve over time

Whether big or small, simple or spirited, meaningful traditions become part of your school's identity. People may forget the exact words spoken at a meeting or the details of a lesson, **but they remember how a tradition made them feel.** That feeling is what carries your culture forward, year after year.

Leadership Snapshot: The Walk That Carries a Legacy

At Seaview Elementary, the end of the year used to arrive with little more than final report cards and waves goodbye. But five years ago, the principal posed a simple, powerful question at a staff meeting:

"What will our students remember—not just about what they learned, but about how they felt being here?"

That question sparked a conversation that led to something unforgettable:

The Legacy Clap-Out.

On the last day of school, every hallway becomes a runway of recognition. Students and staff line up shoulder to shoulder, clapping and cheering as the graduating fifth graders take their final walk through the building. Teachers hold signs that read, "You'll always be a Seaview Star." Younger students hold handmade posters with messages like, "I want to be like you someday."

The hallway echoes with joy, pride, and purpose.

What began as a single event has become a rite of passage, anchoring identity, pride, and connection. Parents tear up. Staff feel recharged. And most importantly, the students leave knowing they mattered.

Now, even kindergartners ask in September,

"When do I get to do the clap-out?"

That's the magic of an everlasting tradition.
It starts with intention. It lives through emotion.
And it lasts in memory, carrying the culture forward with every step.

Establish Everlasting Traditions Mindset Question

Which type of thinking does your school use – Default or Intentional?

- **Default Thinking:**

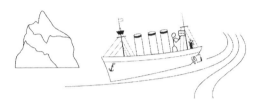

"We have a few traditions, but we don't really focus on them. We celebrate when we can."

This mindset is reactive, viewing traditions as optional extras rather than meaningful components of school identity. Traditions may occur inconsistently, without clear purpose or alignment to the school's values. Over time, this can lead to disengagement and a loss of shared connection and purpose.

- **Intentional Thinking:**

"We prioritize creating and sustaining meaningful traditions that reflect our principles, values, and mission."

This proactive mindset treats traditions as powerful tools to build belonging, connection, and pride. Traditions are not just scheduled; they are designed to last, grounded in the school's foundational identity, and celebrated by the whole community.

Why This Matters

Reflecting on these mindsets helps school leaders recognize the power of tradition as a strategic force for connection and identity. Intentional traditions don't just mark time; they create meaning. When thoughtfully designed and consistently celebrated, traditions reinforce what your school stands for and ensure that your culture is felt, shared, and remembered across generations.

Strategic Thinking Questions for Outward School Anchor 5: Establish Everlasting Traditions

1. *Which of our current school traditions best reflect our values, principles, and mission, and how can we intentionally build upon them?*

2. *How can we design traditions that foster a deep sense of belonging, joy, and unity across students, staff, and families?*

3. *What new traditions could we introduce that align with our school's identity and inspire pride, connection, and lasting memories?*

4. *How can we ensure that our traditions are meaningful for all members of our school community?*

5. *What role can each member of our school community play in establishing and maintaining these traditions?*

6. *How can we measure the impact of our traditions on school culture and community engagement?*

7. *How will we continuously refine our traditions so they remain relevant, rooted in purpose, and responsive to the evolving needs of our community?*

_____
_____
_____
_____
_____
_____

Early Drafts of Your Everlasting Traditions Statement

Traditions are the spirit of school culture, moments that connect the past, energize the present, and inspire the future. As you reflect on your school's current traditions, it's time to begin crafting a statement that will guide the intentional design and celebration of new and existing traditions.

This initial draft should serve as both a tribute and a blueprint:

- **A tribute** to the traditions that already bring joy, connection, and meaning to your school community.
- **A blueprint** for establishing enduring rituals that align with your school's mission, principles, values, and vision.

Use the following prompts as a springboard for your draft:

- What do we want every student, staff member, and family to remember, celebrate, or look forward to each year?
- What values do we want to reinforce through shared experiences?
- How can our traditions be welcoming, energizing, and purpose-driven?

As you continue building out the Outward Anchors, revisit your traditions statement to ensure it evolves with your school's growing identity. Like any great tradition, your statement should be timeless in purpose and flexible in practice.

Initial Thoughts for Your Everlasting Traditions Statement:

Everlasting Traditions Statement Examples

1. Creating Lasting Memories:
"We commit to establishing traditions that create lasting memories and foster a deep sense of belonging. Our celebrations, events, and shared rituals reflect our guiding principles and bring our community together in meaningful, joyful ways."

2. Fostering Community and Connection:
"Our school is dedicated to fostering community and connection through cherished traditions. By celebrating our shared history and values, we create a strong sense of unity and pride."

3. Honoring Our Legacy:
"We honor our school's legacy by cultivating traditions that bridge generations. These experiences celebrate where we've come from and inspire future leaders to carry forward our core values, principles, and mission."

4. Promoting Connection and Engagement:
"Our traditions are designed to promote connection, celebration, and shared ownership. We ensure that every member of our school community, including students, staff, and families, feels seen, valued, and invited to take part in experiences that define who we are."

5. Building a Positive School Culture:
"We are committed to building a positive school culture through enduring traditions. By creating fun, loving, and team-building traditions, we strengthen our community and enhance the overall school experience."

The Establish Everlasting Traditions Anchor Model

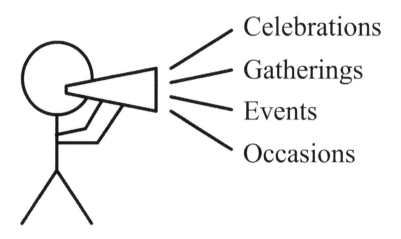

Establish Everlasting Traditions: Rooted in the Principle of Life History

The Principle of Life History reminds us that meaning is built over time through the moments we mark, the people we honor, and the stories we carry forward. In schools, traditions are how we preserve what matters most. They link generations, reinforce values, and create a sense of identity that lasts beyond any one school year. For the Establish Everlasting Traditions anchor, Life History means intentionally creating rituals and shared experiences that echo through time. These traditions are more than events. They are cultural threads that weave together the past, present, and future of your school community.

Celebrating Together to Build a Thriving School Culture

The Everlasting Traditions visual model is a simple but powerful image: a stick figure holding a megaphone, announcing four bold words: **Celebrations**, **Gatherings**, **Events**, and **Occasions**.

These aren't just announcements. They're signals of culture in motion.

They represent **the four tradition-building practices** that echo across your school community and amplify joy, connection, and shared purpose.

Here's what they mean in action:

- **Celebrations**
  Recognize and honor accomplishments, both big and small. Whether it's academic success, acts of kindness, or milestones reached, celebrations create moments of shared pride and emotional uplift.
- **Gatherings**
  Create opportunities for people to come together. From morning meetings and assemblies to staff breakfasts and community nights, gatherings foster connection and belonging.
- **Events**
  Host experiences that align with your school's mission. Think spirit weeks, service projects, or student showcases. These purposeful events turn values into action and memories.
- **Occasions**
  Establish meaningful rituals that mark time and build identity, such as welcome walks, legacy ceremonies, or end-of-year reflections. Occasions give rhythm and legacy to school life.

Why This Model Matters

This megaphone image is more than symbolic; it reminds us that traditions should be **heard**, **felt**, and **shared**.

When a school consistently voices these four practices, it creates more than a calendar of fun. It builds:

- **Community** – By bringing people together with purpose and joy
- **Continuity** – By linking the past, present, and future in meaningful ways
- **Identity** – By defining "who we are" through what we honor
- **Belonging** – By giving every person a place and a role in the celebration

> *"A tradition is a shared heartbeat—it reminds us that we belong to something greater than ourselves."*
> —Dr. Joe Famularo

The Guiding Question for Everlasting Traditions

Which meaningful traditions can we amplify to celebrate who we are, connect our community, and carry our culture forward together?

Transitioning to the Outward Anchor 6: Model a Mindset of Propelling PH2E

The final Outward Anchor—**Model a Mindset of Propelling PH2E**—invites us to bring everything together with purpose and passion. It emphasizes the power of modeling a mindset that fuels **Peacefulness, Happiness, Healthiness, and Excellence (PH2E)**, not just as outcomes, but as a way of being in our schools every day.

This anchor reinforces that culture is not only built by what we do, but amplified by how we think, speak, and show up. When school leaders and educators model a mindset grounded in optimism, purpose, and continuous growth, they inspire others to do the same.

Outward Anchor 6 strengthens all the practices we've explored, serving as the propeller that drives your school culture forward, turning aligned beliefs into collective motion. It reinforces the mindset that every individual's actions contribute to the school's upward momentum, propelling your community toward Peacefulness, Happiness, Healthiness, and Excellence (PH2E). As you move into this anchor, embrace the opportunity to model what it means to live and lead with intention, and to energize others through your example.

Outward School Anchor 6
MODEL A MINDSET OF PROPELLING *PH2E*

The Principle of Life Gifts

Happiness is the meaning and the purpose of life, the whole aim and end of human existence.
—Aristotle

Model a Mindset of Propelling PH2E: Embracing the Principle of Life Gifts

At the center of a flourishing school culture is a belief that achievement is most powerful when it is rooted in well-being. **The Principle of Life Gifts** invites us to recognize and elevate the essential life dimensions of **Peacefulness, Happiness, Healthiness, and Excellence (PH2E)** as foundational elements of a thriving school culture. While these are universally recognized as Life Gifts, they are also, in many ways, the ultimate School Gifts—conditions we cultivate, experience, and pass on through our daily leadership and learning.

This is the essence of **Outward Anchor 6:** *Model a Mindset of Propelling PH2E*— the final Outward Anchor. When school leaders, teachers, and students consistently model this mindset, they inspire those around them to lead with clarity, live with intention, and pursue excellence in a way that uplifts the entire school community.

PH2E elevates achievement by grounding it in purpose, well-being, and personal growth, making success more meaningful, sustainable, and lasting.

Cultivate a Culture of PH2E and Continuous Improvement

PH2E begins with a mindset, a belief that we can always grow, both individually and together. It's a commitment to **continuous improvement** in four essential areas of life: **Peacefulness, Happiness, Healthiness, and Excellence**. This mindset isn't a program or a checklist. It's a way of living and leading that keeps the school community moving forward.

In schools that model this mindset, improvement is not driven by pressure; it's fueled by purpose. Every challenge becomes a chance to reflect. Every success becomes a reason to build further. And every member of the community, from students to staff, sees themselves as part of something meaningful.

When PH2E is modeled daily, it raises performance and elevates the culture.

The PH2E Life Propeller

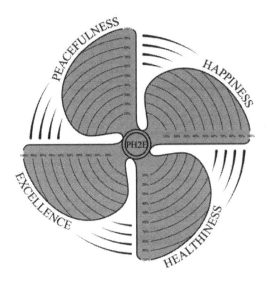

The **PH2E Life Propeller** contains the four essential life and school gifts—**Peacefulness, Happiness, Healthiness, and Excellence**. Just like a ship's propeller must be balanced, full, and well-maintained to navigate through both calm and stormy seas, your PH2E propeller also needs care and strength. When well-maintained, it propels you and your school community forward with clarity, energy, and purpose.

When one blade is weak or neglected, the entire propeller vibrates, causing strain, imbalance, and inefficiency. But when all four are nurtured, your leadership and your life move smoothly and powerfully in the right direction.

Peacefulness

Cultivate calm and clarity for yourself and your school. When peacefulness is present, you're better equipped to make thoughtful decisions, lead with steadiness, and create environments that feel safe and grounded.

Happiness

Infuse life with joy, energy, and excitement. Happiness grows through gratitude, meaningful moments, and celebrating both individual and collective successes. It's the spark that lights up a thriving school culture.

Healthiness

Strengthen your energy and resilience through movement, nourishment, and rest. Healthiness is ensured by caring for the body and mind through regular physical activity, healthy eating, and adequate sleep so you can show up fully for yourself and others.

Excellence

Fuel your mind through a mindset of continuous learning. Excellence is achieved by embracing intellectual curiosity, developing new skills, and striving for your personal best. In a PH2E-aligned culture, excellence isn't about perfection; it's about purposeful growth, every single day.

Maintaining Your PH2E Life Propeller: A Daily Leadership Routine

Like any well-built ship, even the strongest propeller needs regular care to stay sharp, balanced, and effective. Propelling PH2E isn't achieved through grand gestures; it's built through small, intentional actions repeated over time. Think of it as a daily check-in with the four blades of your life propeller:

- **Peacefulness:**
  Pause. Breathe. Reconnect with your Life Vision and Daily Mission. Build moments of stillness into your day, whether through reflection, meditation, journaling, or quiet walks. Calm fuels clarity.
- **Happiness:**
  Let joy lead. Start or end each day by naming one thing you're grateful for. Celebrate the little wins. Laugh with your team. Happiness creates momentum, it lifts morale and energizes the people around you.
- **Healthiness:**
  Your energy is your impact. Move daily, nourish intentionally, and get the rest your mind and body need. A healthy leader is a present leader, able to show up fully for others and make sound decisions under pressure.
- **Excellence:**
  Stretch your thinking. Make space for learning, whether it's reading a chapter, listening to a podcast, or asking powerful questions in meetings. Excellence grows when curiosity leads, and improvement is constant.

When you tend to each blade—**Peacefulness (calm), Happiness (joy), Healthiness (energy), and Excellence (growth)**—your leadership becomes not just sustainable, but contagious. PH2E isn't something you complete—it's something you embody. It's a rhythm that propels your school forward

Looking Ahead: Activate Your PH2E Life Propeller

In **Chapter 9**, you'll be introduced to the **PH2E Life Propeller Assessment**, a practical and powerful tool designed to help you and your school team reflect on your balance across the four Life Gifts: **Peacefulness, Happiness, Healthiness, and Excellence**.

This free assessment, available at **PH2E.com**, offers more than just a snapshot. It invites every adult in your school community to embrace a mindset of continuous improvement. It's a call to pause, evaluate your propeller, and ask: *Am I moving forward with clarity, joy, energy, and growth?*

By engaging with the PH2E Assessment:

- You gain personal insight into the areas that may need tuning or strengthening.
- Your team begins a shared journey toward **intentional well-being and excellence**.
- Your school culture embraces **reflection, growth, and alignment** as a way of being.

Imagine a school where every staff member is grounded in what propels them and encourages others to do the same. That's how a culture of PH2E is not just modeled, but multiplied.

As you continue this chapter, keep your own Life Propeller in mind and consider how this tool can help you lead others to navigate with purpose, balance, and power.

Are you ready to check your propeller and help your team do the same?

Model a Mindset of Propelling PH2E Mindset Question

Which type of thinking does your school use – Default or Intentional?

- **Default Thinking:**

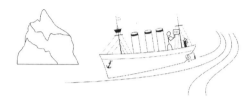

"We address well-being when issues arise. Peace, health, happiness, and excellence are secondary concerns."

This mindset is reactive. It treats well-being as an afterthought, addressing concerns only when they become visible problems. Over time, this approach can lead to burnout, disengagement, and diminished school culture.

- **Intentional Thinking:**

"We intentionally prioritize the daily cultivation of Peacefulness, Happiness, Healthiness, and Excellence (PH2E). These life and school gifts are the foundation of our success and our culture."

This mindset embraces continuous improvement, not only in achievement, but in the human experience of learning and leading. It ensures that well-being and excellence are embedded into daily decisions, behaviors, and relationships.

Why This Matters

Reflecting on these mindsets is essential for understanding how the PH2E framework can shape your school's long-term success. A mindset of propelling PH2E ensures your community remains aligned with its highest aspirations, where individuals thrive, culture flourishes, and excellence is sustained.

"When you model a mindset of PH2E, you lead with intention, balance, and heart."
—Dr. Joe Famularo

**Strategic Thinking Questions for
Outward School Anchor 6:
Model a Mindset of Propelling PH2E**

1. *What intentional practices are in place to support Peacefulness, Happiness, Healthiness, and Excellence (PH2E) across our school community?*

2. *Where are the gaps or obstacles that prevent us from making PH2E part of our everyday mindset and routine, instead of only focusing on it when problems arise?*

3. *How can we create a culture where the continuous improvement of PH2E is a shared responsibility among all school members?*

4. *What concrete actions can we take—individually and collectively—to elevate the well-being and excellence of our school culture through PH2E?*

_____
_____
_____
_____
_____
_____

5. *How can we measure the impact of our efforts to propel PH2E on the overall well-being and success of our school community?*

_____
_____
_____
_____
_____
_____

6. *What role can each member of our school community play in maintaining and enhancing the PH2E Life Propeller?*

_____
_____
_____
_____
_____
_____

7. *How can we integrate the principles of propelling PH2E into our daily routines and long-term strategic plans?*

_____
_____
_____
_____
_____
_____
_____

Early Drafts of Your Propelling PH2E Statement

As you reflect on the principles of **Peacefulness, Happiness, Healthiness, and Excellence (PH2E)**, now is the time to begin shaping a statement that captures how your school will intentionally live out these essential life and school gifts. This statement should express your commitment to cultivating a culture of **continuous improvement**—one that elevates well-being, supports thriving relationships, and advances both personal and collective excellence.

Use this as an opportunity to clarify your aspirations:

- How will PH2E show up in your daily routines, team meetings, classroom interactions, and leadership decisions?
- How will it shape how people feel, grow, and belong in your school?

This is not just a slogan—it's a mindset. Your initial draft is a strategic steppingstone: a vision-in-motion that will guide how you embed PH2E into every corner of school life and leadership.

When written with care, your PH2E Statement becomes more than a commitment. **It becomes the current that carries your schools ship forward—steady, intentional, and aligned with your highest aspirations.**

Initial Thoughts for your Propelling PH2E Statement:

Propelling PH2E Statement Examples

Below are examples of how schools can craft statements to reflect their commitment to Peacefulness, Happiness, Healthiness, and Excellence (PH2E). These examples model how to integrate a mindset of continuous improvement and whole-person well-being into your school's daily life and long-term direction:

1. Cultivating Peacefulness and Well-Being:
"We commit to cultivating a peaceful and supportive environment where every member of our school community can thrive. Through intentional practices, we promote mental well-being, calm, and inner clarity."

2. Fostering Happiness and Gratitude:
"Our school is dedicated to fostering happiness and gratitude. We create a joyful and uplifting atmosphere where achievements are celebrated, and every member feels valued and appreciated."

3. Promoting Health and Wellness:
"We prioritize health and wellness by encouraging healthy habits and providing resources for physical and mental well-being. Our school community is committed to living balanced and healthy lives."

4. Striving for Excellence in All Endeavors:
"We strive for excellence in everything we do, continuously seeking growth, innovation, and self-improvement. Our commitment to lifelong learning ensures we reach our fullest potential."

5. Embracing a Balanced Life:
"We embrace a balanced life by tending to our PH2E Life Propeller. Through reflection, gratitude, healthy living, and continuous learning, we propel ourselves—and one another—toward fulfillment and success."

6. Promoting Inner Peace and Well-Being:
"Today, we commit to promoting inner peace and well-being. By reflecting on our School Vision and Daily Mission, we cultivate a sense of calm, focus, and shared purpose."

7. Fostering Happiness and Positive Relationships:
"Our mission today is to foster happiness and meaningful relationships. Through gratitude and celebration, we create a connected and joyful environment where everyone feels seen and supported."

8. Encouraging Health and Wellness:
"Today, we focus on encouraging health and wellness. By modeling and promoting habits that nourish the body and mind, we empower our community to thrive together."

9. Striving for Excellence in Learning and Growth:
"Our daily mission is to strive for excellence in learning and growth. Through continuous improvement and skill development, we achieve our highest potential and inspire others to do the same."

10. Embracing a Holistic Approach to Well-Being:
"Today, we pledge to embrace a holistic approach to well-being. By maintaining a strong and balanced PH2E Life Propeller, we keep Peacefulness, Happiness, Healthiness, and Excellence at the heart of our daily lives."

The Model a Mindset of Propelling PH2E Anchor Model

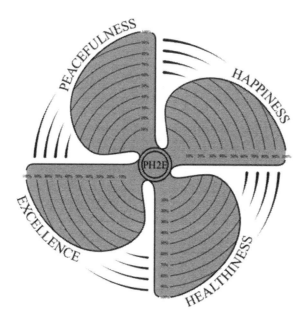

Model a Mindset of Propelling PH2E: Rooted in the Principle of Life Gifts

The Principle of Life Gifts reminds us that leadership is not only about what we achieve but also about what we cultivate. In schools, the most meaningful outcomes are often the ones we feel—calm in the halls, joy in relationships, energy in learning, and pride in excellence. These are not just ideals. They are gifts. Peacefulness, Happiness, Healthiness, and Excellence are the gifts of life we all long for. Who wouldn't want these for themselves, their students, or their school community? They are the things we carry with us, the experiences we remember, and the conditions that help people flourish. For the Model a Mindset of Propelling PH2E anchor, this principle emphasizes the importance of nurturing these life gifts as daily priorities. They are not destinations, but ongoing practices that must be modeled, protected, and continually strengthened. When all four are in motion and in balance, they generate a culture of well-being that uplifts every member of the school community.

The School's Propeller: Fueling a Culture of PH2E

This visual model symbolizes the balanced forward motion and continuous improvement needed to actively cultivate these life gifts of PH2E every day in a school environment.

- **Peacefulness:** Cultivating a calm and supportive atmosphere that promotes mental and emotional well-being.
- **Happiness:** Encouraging joy, gratitude, and positive interactions among students, teachers, staff, and parents.
- **Healthiness:** Prioritizing physical health through regular exercise, nutritious food, and adequate rest.
- **Excellence:** Striving for high standards in academic performance, personal growth, and professional development.

The Propelling PH2E model represents the concept of Upward Living, where each of the four life gifts is continuously enhanced through intentional actions and a growth mindset. **The goal is to keep the propeller balanced and ensure that each blade is equally strong, leading to a thriving school culture.**

Implementing the PH2E Model in Schools

1. **Assessment and Reflection:**
   - Encourage school members to assess their current levels of Peacefulness, Happiness, Healthiness, and Excellence.
   - Reflect on areas that need improvement and create action plans to address these areas.

2. **Balanced Growth:**
   - Focus on achieving balance across all four life gifts.
   - Develop strategies to enhance each life gift, ensuring that no area is neglected.

3. **Continuous Improvement:**
   - Embrace a mindset of continuous improvement, always seeking ways to enhance the school environment.
   - Regularly review and adjust action plans to ensure ongoing progress.

4. **Collaborative Efforts:**
   - Foster a collaborative culture where everyone contributes to propelling PH2E.
   - Share successes and challenges, learning from each other's experiences.

5. **Positive School Culture:**
    o Use the PH2E model to create a dynamic, and positive school culture.
    o Celebrate achievements, support one another, and strive for excellence in all aspects of school life.

By adopting the Propelling PH2E model, schools can create an environment where Peacefulness, Happiness, Healthiness, and Excellence are continuously cultivated, leading to a vibrant and supportive community. This means ensuring these life gifts—these school culture essentials—are actively nurtured in every classroom, hallway, and team meeting. This approach not only enhances individual well-being but also strengthens the overall school culture, making it a place where everyone can thrive and reach their full potential.

The Guiding Question for Model a Mindset of Propelling PH2E

Is our school community continuously improving by modeling Peacefulness, Happiness, Healthiness, and Excellence—or is our Life Propeller unbalanced, holding us back from thriving together?

Chapter 7

Developing Your Outward School Map (OSM)

Navigating Actions and Relationships

After exploring the 6 Outward School Anchors—**Inspire IOU Trust, Practice Positive Communication, Create Common Language, Construct a Cohesive Environment, Establish Everlasting Traditions,** and **Model a Mindset of Propelling PH2E**—you are now ready to **navigate the outward dimension** of your IOU Strategic School Map.

This chapter focuses on translating the beliefs and intentions established in your Inward School Map into outward actions and relational practices that bring your school culture to life. The **Outward School Map (OSM)** becomes your guide for cultivating trust, strengthening collaboration, and embedding your values into every aspect of your community interactions.

By **navigating relationships and actions with clarity and purpose**, you ensure alignment between what your school stands for and how it operates day to day. The OSM transforms outward culture-building from a series of isolated efforts into a **cohesive and intentional system**—one that empowers your staff, engages families, and inspires students to lead and learn with meaning.

6 Steps to Build and Launch Your Outward School Map

As you build your Outward School Map, each anchor will include a Motto to inspire, a Statement to clarify philosophy, and a set of Strategies to translate belief into action. This structure will help ensure consistency, energy, and alignment across your school community.

Step 1: Reflect on Your Journey
Take a moment to reflect on the journey through the Outward Anchors. Consider the insights and understanding you have gained about your school's relationships, communication, connectedness, traditions, and mindset. Which practices are already embedded in your school's culture? Which areas present opportunities for growth and intentional improvement?

Reflect on how your internal school culture, as defined by your ISM, has shaped the relationships and actions in your school community. This reflection will inform the development of your OSM, ensuring it aligns with the school's core values and aspirations.

Step 2: Integrate the Outward Anchors
Now it's time to gather and organize the Essential Anchors that make up your Outward School Map—each including a Motto, a Statement, and Strategies.

Each of these Outward Anchors should reflect the guiding principles from your ISM, ensuring that your internal culture is consistently represented in every action, relationship, and interaction.

- Inspire IOU Trust Statement
- Positive Communication Statement
- Common Language Statement
- Cohesive Environment Statement
- Everlasting Traditions Statement
- Model a Mindset of Propelling PH2E Statement

Each of these elements should reflect the collective insights of your team and clearly connect back to your school's vision, mission, principles and core values.

Step 3: Display Key Elements

Just as your Inward Anchors are prominently shared to reinforce school identity, the essential elements of your Outward School Map may also be shared strategically across your school community. However, it is entirely up to you to decide when, and if, you choose to display them. If you do, consider sharing them in ways that align with your school's unique culture, such as visual displays, digital platforms, or embedded communications. This ensures they remain visible, accessible, and consistently reinforced throughout the school environment. The key components include:

- **Inspire IOU Trust Statement**: A clear articulation of the trust-building commitments and practices that define your school's relationships.
- **Positive Communication Statement**: Guidelines that promote and maintain constructive communication among all stakeholders.
- **Common Language Statement**: Shared vocabulary and phrases that increase clarity, promote unity, and reinforce values.
- **Cohesive Environment Statement**: Initiatives designed to create a sense of belonging and relational safety across all school settings.
- **Everlasting Traditions Statement**: Meaningful traditions that honor your school's identity and create continuity across time.
- **Model a Mindset of Propelling PH2E Statement**: Strategies that inspire a mindset of Peacefulness, Happiness, Healthiness, and Excellence.

Step 4: Share the Inspire IOU Trust Statement

This statement captures your school's philosophy around relationships and trust. While it may be used primarily as an internal leadership tool, it can also be shared with staff, families, and students to reinforce consistency and alignment. It becomes a visible commitment to cultivating a trustworthy, transparent, and uplifting school culture.

Step 5: Implement and Observe

Even if every Outward Anchor is still in progress, begin implementing your OSM using the drafts and strategies you've developed. As with your ISM, the goal isn't perfection—it's purposeful progress. Share it with your school community and begin observing how it strengthens trust, communication, and connection. Use it to spark reflection, inform decisions, and bring greater intentionality to your outward actions.

Step 6: Evaluate and Refine Your Outward School Map (OSM)
Reflecting on progress and adjusting the strategies as needed is crucial to maintaining alignment between the school's vision and daily practices. This step encourages leaders to gather feedback from staff, students, and families, evaluate the effectiveness of the OSM, and refine strategies to ensure sustained growth, trust, and connection across the school community.

The Importance of Creating Mottos for Your Outward Anchors

As we emphasized earlier when developing the Inward Anchors, **mottos play a vital role in bringing clarity, energy, and unity to your school's culture.**

Rather than asking you to flip back to previous chapters, we revisit this tool here—with a fresh focus: applying mottos intentionally across all 6 Outward Anchors of your Outward School Map (OSM).

Each Outward Anchor—Inspire IOU Trust, Practice Positive Communication, Create Common Language, Construct a Cohesive Environment, Establish Everlasting Traditions, and Model a Mindset of Propelling PH2E—deserves its own motto. **These mottos serve as quick, powerful expressions that bring your school's commitments to life,** helping turn your outward principles into everyday experiences for students, staff, and families.

A motto is a meaningful, memorable statement that reinforces your dedication to building trust, fostering relationships, promoting well-being, and living your school's values with intention. Crafted well, mottos ensure your outward priorities are not only understood—but embraced and lived.

Note: Some mottos may be developed with wide stakeholder input (students, staff, families), while others—depending on the topic—may be crafted primarily by the leadership team. Use your judgment. The goal is clarity, ownership, and alignment, not complexity.

Why You Should Create a Motto for Each Outward Anchor:

1. **Clarity and Focus**
   A motto distills your broader vision into a clear, focused phrase. It simplifies complex ideas into a message that everyone—students, staff, and families—can quickly understand and internalize.

2. **Identity and Unity**
   A well-crafted motto builds a shared sense of identity and belonging. It becomes a unifying sail that catches the wind and propels all members of your school community toward a common purpose.
3. **Inspiration and Motivation**
   Mottos serve as daily reminders of what matters most. They inspire energy, pride, and purposeful action aligned with your school's core values.
4. **Communication and Visibility**
   Mottos enhance your school's communication efforts. When integrated into assemblies, signage, newsletters, and digital platforms, they make your school's culture tangible, visible, and recognizable.
5. **Guidance for Decision-Making**
   Mottos act as compasses. They offer a quick-reference guide for decisions, actions, and behaviors—ensuring that choices remain aligned with your school's outward commitments and principles.

Steps to Create a Motto for Each Anchor

1. **Reflect on Each Outward Commitment**
   Review each Outward Anchor—trust, communication, language, environment, traditions, and PH2E mindset. Identify the key themes, values, and principles you want consistently reinforced.
2. **Keep It Short and Memorable**
   Aim for a phrase that's short, energizing, and easy to recall. A few carefully chosen words can inspire action more powerfully than a long sentence.
3. **Incorporate Your School's Core Principles**
   Anchor each motto in the specific beliefs and commitments your school community values most. Ensure it resonates and feels authentic.
4. **Involve the Community (When Appropriate)**
   When possible and practical, invite students, teachers, and staff to help create mottos. But remember—some anchors may only require leadership-level development.
5. **Test and Refine**
   Try them out! Share draft mottos in different settings—classrooms, meetings, informal conversations. Gather feedback, refine, and finalize mottos that feel true to your school's spirit and direction.

By creating distinct mottos for each of your Outward Anchors, you equip your school community with rallying points—shared words that inspire consistency, belonging, and action. **These mottos become guiding lights, reminding everyone**

of the principles that hold your culture together and propelling your school forward every day.

Using the Outward School Map (OSM) Template

Once you've reflected on your Outward Anchors and gathered your school's commitments, the next step is to organize them into a clear and actionable structure. The Outward School Map (OSM) Template which follows provides a framework for translating your trust-building practices, communication strategies, shared language, environment plans, traditions, and PH2E mindset into a cohesive outward leadership map.

Use the following OSM template to document, refine, and communicate your outward school culture initiatives as part of your Strategic School Map (SSM).

Outward School Map (OSM) Template

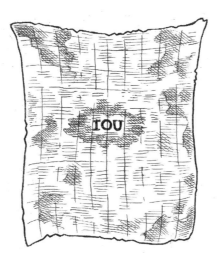

 **Outward School Map (OSM) Statements:**

The following template captures the essential Outward anchors of your Strategic School Map (SSM). Each anchor includes a Motto, a guiding Statement that reflects your school's outward philosophy, and key Strategies that align daily actions with your core principles. Use this structure to define, refine, and communicate your outward commitments with clarity and consistency.

1. Inspire IOU Trust

- **Motto:** [Insert Motto Here]
- **Statement:** [Insert Clear Statement on Trust Philosophy and Practices]
- **Strategies:**
  [Insert Strategy for Building Trust Here]
  [Insert Strategy for Fostering Reciprocal Inspiration Here]

2. Practice Positive Communication

- **Motto:** [Insert Motto Here]
- **Statement:** [Insert Clear Statement on Communication Philosophy and Practices]

- **Strategies:**
  [Insert Strategy for Enhancing Communication Skills Here]
  [Insert Strategy for Promoting Active Listening and Constructive Feedback Here]

3. Create Common Language

- **Motto:** [Insert Motto Here]
- **Statement:** [Insert Clear Statement on Common Language Philosophy and Practices]
- **Strategies:** [Insert Strategy for Developing Shared Vocabulary Here]
- **Key Phrases / Shared Vocabulary:**
  [Insert Common Language Terms or Phrases Here]

4. Construct a Cohesive Environment

- **Motto:** [Insert Motto Here]
- **Statement:** [Insert Clear Statement on Cohesive Environment Philosophy and Practices]
- **Strategies:**
  [Insert Strategy for Fostering Welcoming and Supportive Atmosphere Here],
  [Insert Strategy for Promoting Community-Building Activities Here]

5. Establish Everlasting Traditions

- **Motto:** [Insert Motto Here]
- **Statement:** [Insert Clear Statement on Traditions Philosophy and Practices]
- **Strategies:** [Insert Strategy for Creating and Celebrating School Traditions Here]
- **List of Signature Traditions:** [Insert Your School Traditions Here]

6. Model a Mindset of Propelling PH2E

- **Motto:** [Insert Motto Here]
- **Statement:** [Insert Clear Statement on PH2E Mindset Philosophy and Practices]
- **Strategies:**
  [Insert Strategy for Promoting Peacefulness, Happiness, Healthiness, and Excellence Here]
  [Insert Strategy for Encouraging Well-being and Excellence Here]
- **Daily / Weekly PH2E Practices (Optional):**
  [Insert Sample PH2E Practices Here]

Chapter 7: Developing Your Outward School Map (OSM) 329

Example 1

Outward School Map (OSM)

1. Inspire IOU Trust

- **Motto:** "Trust Builds Success"
- **Statement:** "We commit to fostering trust and integrity in all relationships, creating a supportive and collaborative school environment."
- **Strategies:**
  o Implement regular trust-building activities across classrooms and staff teams.
  o Foster reciprocal inspiration through leadership recognition programs that highlight character, responsibility, and teamwork.

2. Practice Positive Communication

- **Motto:** "Speak with Respect"
- **Statement:** "We promote positive and constructive communication, ensuring that every voice is heard and valued."
- **Strategies:**
  o Develop communication workshops focusing on active listening, clarity, and kindness.
  o Train staff and students in giving constructive feedback and using High Tide Safe Talk strategies.

3. Create Common Language

- **Motto:** "Speak the Culture, Live the Culture"
- **Statement:** "We intentionally use shared language that reflects our school's vision, values, and leadership principles to build unity and clarity."
- **Strategies:**
    - Develop a shared vocabulary and introduce it through visuals, lessons, and assemblies.
- **Key Phrases / Shared Vocabulary:**
    1. **Respectful:** Ensure all communication is respectful and supportive.
    2. **Clear Talk:** Communicate in a clear and straightforward manner.
    3. **Positive Talk:** Use positive language to encourage and motivate.
    4. **Own It:** Take responsibility for actions and words.
    5. **Begin with the End in Mind:** Focus on goals and solutions.

4. Construct a Cohesive Environment

- **Motto:** "Belong. Connect. Thrive."
- **Statement:** "We design our environment—both physical and relational—to foster belonging, trust, and shared purpose across the entire school community."
- **Strategies:**
    - Organize welcoming activities (e.g., New Student Welcome Days, Meet the Teacher events).
    - Establish mentorship programs to connect new students and staff with school culture ambassadors.
    - Engage in community service projects that unite students, families, and staff around shared causes.

5. Establish Everlasting Traditions

- **Motto:** "Celebrating Who We Are, Together"
- **Statement:** "We build meaningful traditions that connect our past, present, and future—strengthening pride, unity, and belonging for every member of our school."
- **Strategies:**
    - Create annual celebrations recognizing academic, character, and service achievements.
    - Organize school spirit days to foster enthusiasm and school pride.
    - Encourage graduating classes to complete legacy projects that reflect school values.

- **List of Signature Traditions:**
  1. Annual School Celebration Week
  2. Founder's Day Assembly
  3. Legacy Garden Project by Graduating Classes

6. Model a Mindset of Propelling PH2E

- **Motto:** "Propel with Purpose"
- **Statement:** "We commit to modeling and cultivating a mindset of Peacefulness, Happiness, Healthiness, and Excellence (PH2E) through daily actions and intentional leadership."
- **Strategies:**
  - Host Growth Mindset Workshops that connect personal development with PH2E goals.
  - Recognize and celebrate personal and team growth through quarterly PH2E awards.
- **Daily / Weekly PH2E Practices (Optional):**
  - Daily Morning Mindset Quotes (focused on one PH2E principle each week).
  - Weekly PH2E Journaling Reflections for students and staff.
  - Staff Wellness Challenges that integrate health, happiness, and excellence habits.

Closing Note:
By intentionally developing and sharing these outward elements through conversation, communication, or visible reinforcement, you foster a clear, shared understanding of your school's commitment. This includes building trust, promoting positive communication, cultivating belonging, celebrating traditions, and modeling well-being and excellence across your entire community.

Example 2

Outward School Map (OSM)

1. Inspire IOU Trust

- **Motto:** "Trust Starts with Us"
- **Statement:** "We strive to build a foundation of trust through honesty, reliability, and respect, creating meaningful relationships that support a safe and thriving school environment."
- **Strategies:**
  o Facilitate trust-building initiatives such as peer mentoring programs and leadership team-building exercises.
  o Implement "Character Spotlights," highlighting acts of trustworthiness and reliability across the school community.

2. Practice Positive Communication

- **Motto:** "Communicate to Connect"
- **Statement:** "We are committed to clear, kind, and thoughtful communication that values every person's voice and strengthens our sense of community."
- **Strategies:**
  o Introduce active listening workshops for students and staff to enhance empathetic communication.
  o Create Positive Communication Prompts for morning announcements and staff meetings to reinforce respectful dialogue.

3. Create Common Language

- **Motto:** "Words Shape Our World"
- **Statement:** "We intentionally cultivate a shared language rooted in empathy, understanding, and encouragement to build unity and belonging across our school community."
- **Strategies:**
    - Develop a schoolwide Common Language Guide and post key phrases throughout classrooms and hallways.
- **Key Phrases / Shared Vocabulary:**
    1. **Kindness First:** Begin every conversation with empathy and care.
    2. **Listen Fully:** Focus on understanding before responding.
    3. **Lift Each Other:** Use words that support, encourage, and build others up.

4. Construct a Cohesive Environment

- **Motto:** "Connected Spaces, Connected People"
- **Statement:** "We intentionally design our physical and relational environments to foster belonging, collaboration, and pride, creating spaces where everyone feels seen, supported, and valued."
- **Strategies:**
    - Promote "Shared Spaces, Shared Responsibility" initiatives encouraging student and staff ownership of school areas.
    - Establish "Connection Corners" in common areas to inspire spontaneous conversations and relationship-building.
    - Host monthly "Team Days" that pair students and staff across grades and departments for collaborative activities.

5. Establish Everlasting Traditions

- **Motto:** "Our Story, Our Strength"
- **Statement:** "We create and sustain traditions that celebrate our shared journey, building pride, connection, and a sense of belonging for generations of students and families."
- **Strategies:**
    - Celebrate School Founders' Day annually to honor the origins and evolution of the school community.
    - Host an annual Leadership Week showcasing student and staff leadership through assemblies, recognitions, and service projects.
    - Maintain a "Star Wall of Legacy" where contributions aligned to the school's principles and values are commemorated.

- **List of Signature Traditions:**
  1. School Founders' Day Celebration
  2. Annual Leadership Week
  3. "Star" Wall of Legacy Installation and Recognition

6. Model a Mindset of Propelling PH2E

- **Motto:** "Lead Like a Star: PH2E Every Day"
- **Statement:** "We actively model and nurture Peacefulness, Happiness, Healthiness, and Excellence (PH2E) as essential life and school gifts that propel individuals and our school community toward thriving and fulfillment."
- **Strategies:**
  - Begin each day with Morning Mindset Moments: brief reflections or quotes connecting to PH2E principles.
  - Encourage students and staff to maintain PH2E Journals to track personal growth across Peacefulness, Happiness, Healthiness, and Excellence.
- **Daily / Weekly PH2E Practices (Optional):**
  - Highlight one PH2E dimension each week through activities, discussions, and bulletin boards.
  - Host quarterly PH2E Celebrations recognizing individuals and teams who demonstrate exceptional growth or contribution.

Closing Note:
By introducing and sharing these Outward Anchors with clarity and purpose, schools build a living culture that reflects trust, communication, common language, cohesion, traditions, and continuous well-being. When reinforced regularly and embraced school-wide, these anchors move from intentions to daily realities—creating a vibrant and enduring school culture.

Encouragement for the Path Forward

Your **Outward School Map (OSM)** is a **living, breathing framework that will grow and evolve alongside your school.** Revisit it regularly. Reflect on what's working, refine what needs strengthening, and realign as your school community progresses. The more intentionally you nurture these Outward Anchors, the more deeply they will shape a dynamic and positive school culture.

As you move forward, let your OSM serve as a guiding light, illuminating the path toward a thriving, Upward culture grounded in trust, connection, and shared purpose. Embrace the principles of *Outward Living*, and allow them to influence your daily interactions, decisions, and initiatives.

This is not the end—it's the beginning: the beginning of the IOU process for cultivating an IOU School Culture, where **intention replaces default**, where **relationships are strengthened through shared principles**, and where Peacefulness, Happiness, Healthiness, and Excellence (PH2E) are not just aspirations—**but outcomes.**

Transition to Chapter 8: Synergizing Your Inward and Outward School Maps into a Comprehensive Strategic School Map: Full Steam Ahead

As we conclude our deep dive into the Inward School Map (ISM) and the Outward School Map (OSM), it's important to recognize that this is not the end of the journey—but a powerful turning point. Your ISM captures the heart of your school's internal identity: the principles, beliefs, and commitments that guide who you are. Your OSM brings those beliefs to life through intentional actions, relationships, and shared experiences that shape how you show up in the world.

The true power of the IOU approach lies in bringing these two maps together— *synergizing* the internal with the external. When aligned, your ISM and OSM form a cohesive **Strategic School Map (SSM)**, a compass that unites vision with action, purpose with practice. This alignment is what transforms a school from good to exceptional—from drifting to dynamically intentional.

In Chapter 8, we bring everything together—**full steam ahead**. This chapter will guide you step by step in integrating your Inward and Outward Maps into one comprehensive, principle-centered plan. You'll design a Strategic School Map that drives your school forward, aligning every element of culture, leadership, and daily practice with your greater goal: cultivating an **Upward Dynamic Positive IOU School Culture.**

Get ready to chart this next course. You've built the foundation—now it's time to set sail with clarity, alignment, and purpose. By uniting your inward reflections with your outward commitments, your entire school community will be equipped and empowered to lead, live, and grow—together.

Chapter 8

Synergizing Your Inward & Outward School Maps into a Comprehensive Strategic School Map

Full Steam Ahead

Visualize this thing that you want, see it, feel it, believe in it.
Make your mental blueprint and begin to build.
—Robert Collier

The Power of Synergy

In this chapter, we turn our focus to uniting the key elements of your Inward School Map (ISM) and Outward School Map (OSM) to create one unified, comprehensive **Strategic School Map (SSM)**. This synergy is the heart of **Inside-Out school culture design**—where inward clarity meets outward action.

The ISM captures your school's internal foundation: its **guiding beliefs, vision, mission, and principles.** The OSM extends this foundation into your school's **relationships, traditions, and daily interactions**. When these two maps are aligned and integrated, they create a living strategy—one that brings coherence, clarity, and momentum to every part of your school culture.

Synergy means that the whole is greater than the sum of its parts. This principle applies powerfully in school leadership. When your Inward Anchors and Outward Actions are connected, their impact multiplies. A Strategic School Map built through synergy ensures that your internal principles are authentically reflected in external behaviors, creating a culture that is intentional, consistent, and inspiring. It's how the philosophy of *"Inspire to Aspire"* moves from words to lived experience.

The Strategic School Map (SSM): Your Daily Guide for Leadership

Before we dive deeper into the process of uniting the ISM and OSM into a cohesive **Strategic School Map (SSM)**, let's take a moment to recognize the power this map will have in your everyday leadership.

The **SSM** is a **living guide** that will be at your side every day as you lead your school. It is designed to help you align every decision, conversation, and action with your school's deepest beliefs and values. It will support you in making intentional decisions, ensuring consistency, and guiding your staff and students toward shared goals.

Think of the **SSM** as the tool that will **empower you daily**, whether in staff meetings, leadership team planning, classroom management, parent interactions, board discussions, retreats, goal-setting sessions, strategic planning initiatives, or policy development. It's not just a document; it's a compass that continuously steers your school culture toward clarity, purpose, and alignment.

Understanding Synergy: More Than the Sum of Its Parts

Synergy is alignment in action. It's the idea that when distinct elements come together intentionally, they create a greater impact than they ever could on their own. In the context of your Strategic School Map (SSM), synergy occurs when the inner foundation of your school (ISM) connects seamlessly with its outward practices and relationships (OSM).

When these two maps are thoughtfully integrated, the result is a cohesive school map that **aligns belief with behavior, identity with action.** The Strategic School Map ensures that your school's internal principles are consistently reflected in every external interaction. It brings coherence to classrooms, hallways, leadership meetings, and community engagement—so your school's anchor principles aren't just statements; they're experienced.

This kind of alignment fosters a connected, **principle-centered school environment** where every decision and action, big or small, supports a shared vision. When synergy is achieved, the principle of **Inspire to Aspire** reveals its deeper meaning. It becomes a lived commitment to helping every member of the school community grow from the inside out. It is not just a motto but a mindset that fuels purpose, uplifts potential, and unites people through a common pursuit of Peacefulness, Happiness, Healthiness, and Excellence (PH2E).

Symbolism of the Captain, Map, and IOU School Living Wheel

At the beginning of this chapter, you'll find a visual that captures the heart of strategic alignment: **a captain holding a map with IOU Island, steering the ship's wheel.** This image serves as a powerful metaphor for the work ahead, uniting direction, identity, and leadership into one intentional journey.

Each element in the illustration symbolizes a pillar of your **Strategic School Map (SSM):**

- **The Captain** represents leadership: steady, intentional, and focused. Just as a captain must navigate changing seas, school leaders must guide their communities through challenges and opportunities, always steering toward the destination with clarity and confidence.
- **The Map with IOU Island** represents your SSM. IOU Island is the goal: your vision of an Upward Dynamic Positive School Culture marked by Peacefulness, Happiness, Healthiness, and Excellence (PH2E®). The map reflects the comprehensive plan you've built through the ISM and OSM, serving as your guide.
- **The IOU School Living Wheel** is the integration point. It symbolizes both direction and movement. Its six inward-facing handles represent the Inward Anchors: your school's beliefs, principles, and identity. The six outward-pointing arrows reflect the Outward Anchors: your external actions, traditions, and communication practices. Together, they form a complete system for navigating school culture with purpose.

This visual is a living symbol of intentional leadership. It reflects your role as the captain, your responsibility to navigate with intention and clarity, and your power to align inward beliefs with outward actions. When used consistently in staff meetings, leadership development, and schoolwide planning, it helps your team visualize their collective role in shaping a school culture grounded in trust, guided by principle, and propelled by a shared commitment to continuous growth.

Integrating the
IOU SCHOOL LIVING WHEEL

Originally introduced in Chapter 3, the **IOU School Living Wheel** now comes fully into view, revealed with greater clarity, deeper meaning, and renewed significance, as the central symbol of your **Strategic School Map (SSM)**. With the foundation of all 12 anchors in place, you can now see how this visual represents the full integration of your school's inward identity and outward actions. This wheel captures the **alignment between who you are as a school and how that identity is lived out through your daily actions**, relationships, and decisions. It brings together everything you've built, your beliefs, behaviors, and shared purpose, into one cohesive framework for leading with intention.

This wheel is a **living representation of your culture in motion**. At its center lies your school's **SelfCulture**, anchoring all beliefs and actions in **timeless principles**. The six **inward-facing handles** represent your **Inward School Anchors**, defining your **identity, vision, and purpose**. The six **outward-pointing arrows** radiate from the same center, symbolizing your **Outward School Anchors**, how your school expresses that identity through its **environment, communication, traditions, and relationships**.

In essence, the IOU School Living Wheel reminds us that a **thriving school culture is designed with intention**. When **inward principles and outward practices** are in alignment, the result is a **dynamic, principle-centered culture** that is **authentic, sustainable, and empowering** for all stakeholders.

As we move into the process of integrating your **Inward and Outward School Maps** into one cohesive **Strategic School Map (SSM)**, let the **IOU School Living Wheel** serve as a **visual symbol of that alignment**—a daily reminder that **leadership is about holding the wheel, staying the course, and propelling your culture forward with clarity and care**. With this wheel in motion and your direction now clear, your school is ready to move **full steam ahead**—uniting belief with behavior and vision with velocity.

> *"The IOU School Living Wheel turns on timeless principles—anchoring identity, guiding action, and advancing a leadership-driven culture."*
> —Dr. Joe Famularo

Steps to Creating Your Comprehensive SSM

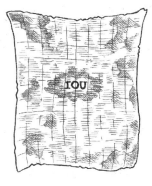

Developing your **Strategic School Map (SSM)** is a powerful process that brings clarity, cohesion, and purpose to your school culture. It begins by reviewing and aligning the foundational components of your **Inward School Map (ISM)** with the relationship-centered elements of your **Outward School Map (OSM)**. The goal is to create a living map that reflects true **Inward-Outward alignment** across your entire school community.

1. Review and Align Inward Anchors

Start by revisiting the six components of your ISM. These anchors define your school's identity and internal compass:

- **School SelfCulture Statement:** This represents the foundation of your school culture, capturing the values, beliefs, and principles that shape how your community thinks, speaks, and acts.
- **School Vision Statement:** A forward-looking declaration of the school's long-term goals and aspirations.
- **Daily School Mission Statement:** A concise statement outlining the school's daily purpose and activities to achieve the vision.
- **School Leadership Principles:** The principles guiding leadership practices within the school.
- **School Core Values**: Fundamental beliefs and values that drive the school's culture and behavior towards others.
- **School Goals:** Specific, measurable objectives that the school aims to achieve.

Ensure that each element connects to the others, creating a unified, strategic direction for your school.

As you review each of the **Inward Anchors**, ask yourself:

- How do these elements reinforce each other?
- Are they aligned in spirit as well as in language?
- Do they reflect the shared beliefs and aspirations of your school community?

The goal is not just consistency in wording, but a **unified message** that is reflected in every part of your school culture. When the ISM is aligned, it serves as a **guiding compass**, helping to ensure that all decisions and actions are grounded in your school's identity and principles.

2. Review and Align Outward Anchors

Now, turn your focus to revisiting the six components of your **OSM**. These **Outward Anchors** reflect how your school's internal beliefs, vision, and principles are **actively demonstrated** through interactions and relationships across the school community.

- **Inspire IOU Trust Statement:** Building a foundation of trust through integrity and reliability.
- **Practice Positive Communication Statement:** Promoting open, honest, and constructive dialogue.
- **Create Common Language Statement:** Developing a shared vocabulary to enhance understanding and collaboration.
- **Construct a Cohesive Environment Statement:** Creating a welcoming and supportive atmosphere.
- **Establish Everlasting Traditions Statement:** Developing meaningful traditions that foster a sense of belonging.
  Model a Mindset of Propelling PH2E Statement: Demonstrating behaviors that promote peace, happiness, healthiness, and excellence.

As you align these **Outward Anchors** with your **Inward Principles**, it ensures that your school culture becomes visible, vibrant, and actively cultivated through daily actions.

When your **Inward Anchors** align with your **Outward Anchors**, your school culture becomes a living, breathing reflection of its foundational principles. This alignment creates a **dynamic ecosystem** where every aspect of your school is unified and purpose-driven. The next step is to integrate these anchors into a cohesive **Strategic School Map (SSM)** that will guide your school community toward a shared vision and actionable goals.

Completing Your Strategic School Map (SSM) Template

Bringing your Strategic School Map to life is a **collaborative act of culture-building**. This map connects your school's internal values and external actions, capturing your vision, mission, principles, core values, goals, and relationship-building strategies, into one cohesive and actionable framework. The SSM is a **living guide** that will steer your decisions, shape daily practices, and keep your culture aligned with your mission. It's not just a document; it's a **living reflection** of your school's purpose.

Using the SSM Template to create your Strategic School Map provides both a visual and strategic foundation for uniting your ISM and OSM. Customize it to reflect the unique identity and priorities of your school. Whether developed through team collaboration, schoolwide engagement, or input from community stakeholders, the process fosters clarity, alignment, and shared ownership. The more intentional and participatory the process, the more your map will resonate with everyone involved.

When you thoughtfully develop and use your SSM, you ensure:

- A **clear alignment** between your internal beliefs and external actions.
- A **unified direction** for your team, with **purpose-driven leadership** at every level.
- A **purposeful culture**—anchored in principles that everyone is invested in, from leadership to students, staff, and families.

Customizing the Framework to Reflect Your Community

This process is not about enforcing a single model. Instead, it offers a **flexible foundation**, designed to be shaped by your school's **context, voice,** and **values**.

Every school has its own **character**. The **IOU Strategic School Map** honors that uniqueness. It encourages **co-creation** of a framework that mirrors your students' needs, your staff's strengths, and your community's aspirations.

When you design your SSM with **local context in mind**:

- Your **culture becomes authentic**—not borrowed, but built.
- Your **commitments become lived**—visible in action, not just words.
- Your **map becomes more than a tool**—it reflects **who you are** and **where you're headed**.

This is what makes **Inside-Out alignment** so powerful. It **roots culture in identity** and fuels progress with intention.

Introducing the Strategic School Map (SSM) Template

To support you in implementing your Strategic School Map, the following pages provide a **fillable, practical template**. This template captures the essence of both your Inward and Outward School Maps (ISM and OSM) and offers a cohesive space to document your school's vision, mission, principles, core values, goals, and outward strategies.

Whether used by leadership teams, staff, or during collaborative planning sessions, this tool ensures your strategic direction is clear, intentional, and cohesively aligned. Remember, the SSM is a living document that will grow and evolve alongside your school's culture. **Start where you are, and continue refining it over time.**

This template is provided here for immediate use, and you'll also find it included in **Appendix B** for ongoing reference and planning. **Following the template, you'll find real-life examples** that show how schools have captured their unique identity while successfully aligning their Inward and Outward Anchors through their Strategic School Map.

The Strategic School Map (SSM) Template

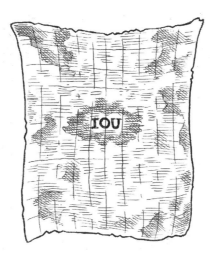

 **Inward School Map (ISM) Statements:**

Note: The 4 Foundational Inward Anchors
These 4 Foundational Inward School Anchors (School Anchors: 2, 3, 4, 5) should be prominently displayed along with the school's/district's branding elements to reinforce and communicate the school's foundational principles to all members of the community.

1. School Vision Statement & Motto:

- [Insert School Motto Here]
- [Insert School Vision Statement Here]

2. Daily School Mission Statement & Motto:

- [Insert School Motto Here]
- [Insert Daily School Mission Statement Here]

3. School Leadership Principles:

- [Insert Leadership Principle 1 Here]
- [Insert Leadership Principle 2 Here]
- [Insert Leadership Principle 3 Here]
- [Insert Leadership Principle 4 Here]
- [Insert Leadership Principle 5 Here]

4. School Core Values:

- Core Value 1: [Insert Definition Here]
- Core Value 2: [Insert Definition Here]
- Core Value 3: [Insert Definition Here]
- Core Value 4: [Insert Definition Here]
- Core Value 5: [Insert Definition Here]

Incorporating Branding Elements:

- Logo: [Insert School Logo]
- Mascot [Insert School Mascot]
- School Colors: [Insert School Colors Here]
- Visuals: [Insert Visual Descriptions Here]

School SelfCulture Statement:
This statement provides an overarching narrative of the school's culture for internal use; however, it may also be shared with the broader community.

- [Insert School SelfCulture Motto & Statement Here]

School Goals:
Goals should be discussed in meetings and shared with school leaders, staff, and parents, as appropriate. Each goal should be specific to the individual or group responsible for its implementation.

- [Insert School Goal 1 Here]
- [Insert School Goal 2 Here]
- [Insert School Goal 3 Here]
- [Insert School Goal 4 Here]

Note:

You may insert the comprehensive details of your goals here or attach them to your Inward School Map (ISM). Use the **REBEL Goals™ Framework** to ensure each goal includes clear direction, actionable steps, measurable progress, ongoing evaluation, and sustained support.

Outward School Map (OSM) Statements:

1. Inspire IOU Trust

- **Motto:** [Insert Motto Here]
- **Statement:** [Insert Clear Statement on Trust Philosophy and Practices]
- **Strategies:**
  - [Insert Strategy for Building Trust Here]
  - [Insert Strategy for Fostering Reciprocal Inspiration Here]

2. Practice Positive Communication

- **Motto:** [Insert Motto Here]
- **Statement:** [Insert Clear Statement on Communication Philosophy and Practices]
- **Strategies:**
  - [Insert Strategy for Enhancing Communication Skills Here]
  - [Insert Strategy for Promoting Active Listening and Constructive Feedback Here]

3. Create Common Language

- **Motto:** [Insert Motto Here]
- **Statement:** [Insert Clear Statement on Common Language Philosophy and Practices]
- **Strategies:**
  - [Insert Strategy for Developing Shared Vocabulary Here]
- **Key Phrases / Shared Vocabulary:**
  - [Insert Common Language Terms or Phrases Here]

4. Construct a Cohesive Environment

- **Motto:** [Insert Motto Here]
- **Statement:** [Insert Clear Statement on Cohesive Environment Philosophy and Practices]

- **Strategies:**
  - [Insert Strategy for Fostering Welcoming and Supportive Atmosphere Here]
  - [Insert Strategy for Promoting Community-Building Activities Here]

5. Establish Everlasting Traditions

- **Motto:** [Insert Motto Here]
- **Statement:** [Insert Clear Statement on Traditions Philosophy and Practices]
- **Strategies:**
  - [Insert Strategy for Creating and Celebrating School Traditions Here]
- **List of Signature Traditions:**
  - [Insert Your School Traditions Here]

6. Model a Mindset of Propelling PH2E

- **Motto:** [Insert Motto Here]
- **Statement:** [Insert Clear Statement on PH2E Mindset Philosophy and Practices]
- **Strategies:**
  - [Insert Strategy for Promoting Peacefulness, Happiness, Healthiness, and Excellence Here]
  - [Insert Strategy for Encouraging Well-being and Excellence Here]
- **Daily / Weekly PH2E Practices (Optional):**
  - [Insert Sample PH2E Practices Here]

Implementing Your SSM: Start Now, Refine Later

It's important to begin implementing your SSM even if all of the elements are not fully developed. By starting now, you can observe the immediate impact and make continuous improvements. Here's how:

1. **Complete Each Section:** Fill in the relevant details for each of the foundational Inward Anchors and outward strategic school map statements.
2. **Incorporate Branding:** Ensure the logo, mascot, school colors, and relevant visuals are added to reinforce your school's visual identity.
3. **Share and Implement:** Post the School Vision Statement, Daily School Mission Statement, School Leadership Principles, and School Core Values throughout the school. Share the comprehensive SSM with staff and stakeholders to align efforts.
4. **Observe and Refine:** Regularly revisit and refine the SSM based on feedback and observations to ensure it remains aligned with your school's journey and evolving needs.
5. **Engage the Community:** Involve students, teachers, and staff in discussions about the SSM to foster a sense of ownership and collective effort towards achieving your school's vision and mission.

Remember, your SSM is a living document that will evolve over time. Implement what you have now and make refinements as you gather more insights and feedback. This iterative process will help you continuously improve and foster a dynamic and positive school culture. Don't wait for perfection. What matters most is setting your direction and gaining momentum. With clarity as your compass, you're ready to go **full steam ahead.**

Like a steamship building pressure in its engine room, your Strategic School Map generates power through alignment, each Inward and Outward Anchor contributing to the energy that drives your school forward. Once that energy is focused and released, movement happens. Momentum builds. The course becomes clear.

Now is the time to harness that steam and move with intention, confidence, and purpose.

Example 1

(SSM)
Strategic School Map

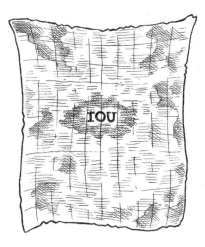

Inward School Map (ISM) Statements

The Foundational Inward Anchors
This section should be prominently displayed throughout the school to reinforce and communicate the school's foundational principles and values to all members of the community.

School Vision Statement & Motto

"Inspire to Aspire"
"Our vision is to foster a nurturing and inclusive learning environment where every student is encouraged to discover their unique potential and positively impact the world around them."

Daily School Mission Statement & Motto

"Empowering Potential, Fostering Excellence"
"Our mission is to provide a safe, nurturing, and dynamic learning environment where academic excellence, personal growth, and social responsibility are fostered every day by all members of our school community."

School Leadership Principles

1. **Lead** with purpose and authenticity, ensuring actions align with core values and vision.
2. **Foster** collaborative partnerships by encouraging teamwork and shared decision-making.
3. **Empower** staff and students by providing the tools and support needed for personal and professional growth.
4. **Embrace** continuous learning, modeling growth and improvement in every aspect of leadership.
5. **Champion** well-being and development by prioritizing the emotional, social, and academic growth of every individual.

School Core Values

1. **Respect:** Valuing others› perspectives, listening actively, and showing appreciation for everyone›s contributions.
2. **Teamwork:** Collaborating with others, sharing responsibilities, and supporting one another to achieve common goals.
3. **Trust:** Building dependable relationships through openness, honesty, and reliability in all interactions.
4. **Compassionate:** Showing empathy, kindness, and care for others in both words and actions.
5. **Integrity:** Acting with honesty, responsibility, and transparency, holding ourselves accountable for our actions.

Incorporating Branding Elements

- Logo: A **Compass wrapped around a torch**, symbolizing visionary leadership and direction.
- Mascot: The **Eagle**, representing inspired potential, strength, and soaring excellence.
- School Colors: **Blue and Gold**
- Visuals: Use illustrations of the eagle in action, soaring, focused, or guiding, to appear throughout school messaging, decor, and events. Include the torch and compass iconography subtly on signage, stationery, and leadership materials.

School SelfCulture Statement

"Our school culture is defined by our commitment to fairness, empowerment, and continuous improvement. We strive to create an environment where every member feels valued, respected, and motivated to achieve their best. Our School Core Values, respect, excellence, integrity, collaboration, innovation, and access, guide our actions and decisions, fostering a community of learners who are inspired to aspire."

School Goals

1. Academic Excellence

- Increase student academic performance by 10% across all grade levels by the end of the academic year.
- Implement a comprehensive professional development program for staff focused on differentiating teaching practices.

2. Student Engagement & School Climate

- Foster a positive school climate by reducing disciplinary incidents by 20%.
- Increase student engagement in extracurricular activities by promoting opportunities and support for diverse student interests.

3. Community Engagement

- Enhance family and community engagement through regular workshops, events, and communication channels.
- Strengthen partnerships with local organizations to provide additional support and resources for students and families.

4. Staff Development & Collaboration

- Provide ongoing training to staff to promote innovative teaching strategies and improve instructional quality.
- Establish collaborative teams for teachers to share best practices and support continuous improvement in classroom instruction.

5. School Environment & Culture

- Redesign key common spaces to reflect the school's Core Values and foster a strong sense of belonging and pride.
- Launch a school-wide recognition program to celebrate students and staff who embody the "Inspire Greatness" mindset in their actions.

Note:
You may insert the comprehensive details of your goals here or attach them to your Inward School Map (ISM). Use the **REBEL Goals™ Framework** to ensure each goal includes clear direction, actionable steps, measurable progress, ongoing evaluation, and sustained support.

Outward School Map (OSM) Statements

1. Inspire IOU Trust

- **Motto**: "Trust Builds Success"
- **Statement**: "We commit to fostering trust and integrity in all relationships, creating a supportive and collaborative school environment."
- **Strategies**:
    o Implement trust-building activities and workshops for staff and students.
    o Foster reciprocal inspiration through character-building programs and leadership challenges.

2. Practice Positive Communication

- **Motto**: "Speak with Respect"
- **Statement**: "We promote positive and constructive communication, ensuring that every voice is heard, valued, and strengthened through kindness and clarity."
- **Strategies**:
    o Develop a comprehensive communication skills curriculum for students and staff.
    o Promote active listening and constructive feedback through regular training sessions and leadership practices.

3. Create Common Language

- **Motto**: "Speak the Culture, Live the Culture"
- **Statement**: "We intentionally use shared language rooted in our principles to build unity, reinforce belonging, and make our mission visible and actionable."
- **Strategies**:
    o Develop a shared vocabulary for the school community to enhance understanding and collaboration.
    o Ensure consistent use of common language in all school communications and classrooms.

- **Key Phrases / Shared Vocabulary**:
  - **Respectful**: Ensure all communication is respectful and supportive.
  - **Clear Talk**: Communicate in a clear and straightforward manner.
  - **Positive Talk**: Use positive language to encourage and motivate.
  - **Own It**: Take responsibility for actions and words.
  - **Begin with the End in Mind**: Focus on goals and solutions.

4. Construct a Cohesive Environment

- **Motto**: "Belong. Connect. Thrive."
- **Statement**: "We intentionally design our environments, physical, emotional, and relational, to foster belonging, connection, and a shared sense of purpose across our entire school community."
- **Strategies**:
  - Foster a welcoming and supportive atmosphere through team-building activities and practices.
  - Promote community-building events that strengthen relationships among students, staff, and parents.

5. Establish Everlasting Traditions

- **Motto**: "Celebrating Who We Are, Together"
- **Statement**: "We build meaningful traditions that connect our past, present, and future, strengthening pride, unity, and belonging for every member of our school."
- **Strategies**:
  - Create and celebrate school traditions that honor the school's history and values.
  - Foster a sense of belonging and continuity through regular events and celebrations.
- **List of Signature Traditions**:
  - Annual School Celebration Week
  - Founder's Day Assembly
  - Legacy Garden Project by Graduating Classes

6. Model a Mindset of Propelling PH2E

- **Motto**: "Propel with Purpose"
- **Statement**: "We commit to modeling and cultivating a mindset of Peacefulness, Happiness, Healthiness, and Excellence (PH2E) through daily habits, leadership actions, and personal growth."

- **Strategies**:
  - Promote well-being and excellence through mindfulness programs and health initiatives.
  - Encourage a culture of continuous improvement and personal growth for students and staff.
- **Daily / Weekly PH2E Practices (Optional)**:
  - Daily Morning Mindset Reflections tied to PH2E elements.
  - Weekly Journaling Prompts focused on Peacefulness, Happiness, Healthiness, and Excellence.
  - Staff and Student Wellness Challenges celebrating progress and growth.

Example 2

(SSM)
Strategic School Map

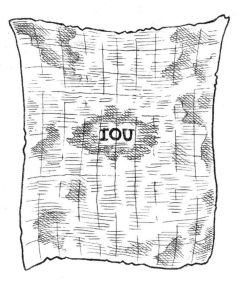

Inward School Map (ISM) Statements

School Vision Statement & Motto

"Together We Thrive"
"Our vision is to build a dynamic and cooperative educational community where every student thrives through creativity, collaboration, and the pursuit of excellence, preparing them to contribute meaningfully to the global community."

Daily School Mission Statement & Motto

"Learn, Lead, Succeed"
"Our mission is to provide a supportive and dynamic educational setting that nurtures academic achievement, personal growth, and leadership skills every day."

School Leadership Principles

1. **Lead** with transparency and integrity, building trust and setting a strong ethical example.
2. **Create** a culture of shared leadership by encouraging participation and collaboration in decision-making.
3. **Inspire** growth through empowerment, fostering an environment where every individual is motivated to reach their full potential.
4. **Commit** to lifelong learning by continuously seeking new knowledge and improving leadership practices.
5. **Prioritize** holistic development, supporting the emotional, physical, and intellectual well-being of staff and students.

School Core Values

1. **Respect:** Treating others with dignity, listening to understand, and fostering a positive, inclusive environment.
2. **Dependable:** Being someone others can rely on, following through on commitments and responsibilities.
3. **Service to Others:** Helping others selflessly, offering support, and working together to improve the community.
4. **Supportive:** Approaching challenges with a constructive attitude, encouraging others, and offering help when needed.
5. **Honesty:** Demonstrating truthfulness in all interactions, being open and transparent in communication.

Incorporating Branding Elements

- **Logo:** A flourishing tree with digital leaves and a human silhouette at the center, symbolizing collective growth, innovation, and the upward journey of every learner.
- **Mascot:** *Tide the Turtle* – a wise green sea turtle, representing resilience, steady progress, and the power of continuous improvement.
- **School Colors:** Green and White
- **Visuals:** Display the tree logo prominently in school spaces, hallways, banners, and communications, to reflect shared values and school identity. Feature *Tide the Turtle* in murals, leadership lessons, and assemblies to reinforce themes of character, collaboration, and long-term growth. Include leafy and wave elements in design motifs to echo the school's message of thriving together through unity and intention.

School SelfCulture Statement

"Our school culture is defined by our commitment to collaboration, innovation, and excellence. We strive to create an environment where every member feels valued, respected, and motivated to achieve their best. "Our School Core Values, respect, excellence, integrity, collaboration, innovation, and access, guide our actions and decisions, fostering a community of learners united in their pursuit of success."

School Goals

1. Academic Excellence

- Increase the percentage of students performing at or above grade level in core subjects by implementing targeted intervention and enrichment groups.
- Expand advanced coursework and academic competitions to provide additional challenges for high-achieving learners.
- Integrate cross-disciplinary projects that foster critical thinking, creativity, and real-world problem-solving.

2. Student Empowerment

- Launch a student leadership program that includes peer mentoring, service learning, and opportunities for students to actively contribute to school decisions.
- Increase student-led events and exhibitions by 30%, allowing students to showcase their learning and talents across all grade levels.

3. Community & Global Engagement

- Create opportunities for global citizenship through virtual exchanges, language programs, and international partnerships.
- Host monthly "Community Connection" events that engage families, alumni, and local organizations in supporting student success.

4. Staff Excellence

- Develop a leadership pathway for aspiring teachers and administrators to cultivate future school leaders.
- Implement quarterly instructional rounds and collaborative coaching cycles to promote the sharing of best practices and improve instruction.

5. School Culture & Environment

- Redesign key common spaces to reflect the School's Core Values and foster a strong sense of belonging and pride.
- Launch a school-wide recognition program to celebrate students and staff who embody the "Inspire Greatness" mindset in their actions.

Note:
You may insert the comprehensive details of your goals here or attach them to your Inward School Map (ISM). Use the **REBEL Goals™ Framework** to ensure each goal includes clear direction, actionable steps, measurable progress, ongoing evaluation, and sustained support.

Outward School Map (OSM) Statements

1. Inspire IOU Trust

- **Motto**: "Trust Starts With Us"
- **Statement**: "We believe that trust is built through consistency, honesty, and care. When we honor our word and act with integrity, we create a school environment where students and adults feel safe, supported, and empowered to lead."
- **Strategies**:
  - Launch a "Trust Tracker" that allows students and staff to recognize peers for actions that demonstrate reliability and honesty.
  - Facilitate leadership circles where teams reflect on how trust is built, challenged, and restored.
  - Integrate trust-building checkpoints into collaborative class projects, allowing students to self-assess how they contribute to team success.

2. Practice Positive Communication

- **Motto**: "Speak with Heart. Listen with Purpose."
- **Statement**: "We foster a culture of communication rooted in empathy, clarity, and respect. Every voice matters, and we are committed to ensuring that all members of our school feel seen, heard, and understood. Through intentional conversations and a spirit of kindness, we strengthen relationships and grow together."
- **Strategies**:
  - Begin meetings and classroom lessons with "Pause and Connect" prompts that promote mindful and respectful conversation.
  - Host student-led "Dialogue Days" that focus on topics such as empathy, belonging, and school culture.
  - Offer workshops for families that focus on strengthening communication habits between home and school through shared language and strategies.

3. Create Common Language

- **Motto**: "One Voice. One Vision."
- **Statement**: "We intentionally speak the language of our principles to build unity, strengthen identity, and guide daily decisions. A shared vocabulary creates alignment and reinforces a sense of belonging across the entire school community."
- **Strategies**:
    - Create a "Language of Leadership" wall featuring key phrases, principles, and student-created definitions.
    - Lead cross-grade assemblies that introduce and model shared language connected to the school's values.
- **Sample Shared Language Phrases**:
    - "Choose Unity" – Promote cooperation over competition.
    - "Lead from Within" – Focus on personal integrity and character.
    - "Lift the Room" – Contribute positively to the emotional climate.
    - "Anchor in Values" – Make decisions rooted in what matters most.

4. Construct a Cohesive Environment

- **Motto**: "Design Belonging. Live Connection."
- **Statement**: "We purposefully shape our school spaces and relationships to reflect unity, emotional safety, and shared identity. Every student and adult should feel welcome, valued, and connected to something greater than themselves."
- **Strategies**:
    - Redesign underused spaces as "Connection Corners" where students can collaborate, reflect, or restore.
    - Conduct "Culture Walks" where classrooms and common areas display visual expressions of the school's core principles and leadership commitments.

5. Establish Everlasting Traditions

- **Motto**: "Rooted in Legacy, Growing Together"
- **Statement**: "We celebrate who we are through meaningful traditions that honor the past, connect the present, and inspire the future. These shared experiences strengthen school pride and unity for generations to come."
- **Strategies**:
    - Create a "Voices of the School" tradition where graduating students and alumni share reflections or letters to the next class.

- o Host a "Unity Tree Ceremony" where students contribute messages of growth and gratitude to mark their learning journey.
- **Sample Traditions**:
  - o "Torch of Leadership" Relay for major student transitions.
  - o Annual Schoolwide Day of Service focused on legacy-building.
  - o "Family Table Week" celebrating intergenerational storytelling and shared meals.

6. Model a Mindset of Propelling PH2E

- **Motto**: "Lead a Life That Lifts"
- **Statement**: "We model and promote a mindset focused on Peacefulness, Happiness, Healthiness, and Excellence (PH2E). When these elements are practiced daily, they shape the way we lead, learn, and live together."
- **Strategies**:
  - o Launch "PH2E Pathways" where students and staff set personal goals tied to one of the four elements.
  - o Facilitate monthly "Life Balance Circles" where individuals reflect on wellness and celebrate personal growth.
- **Ongoing PH2E Practices**:
  - o "Midweek Mindful Minutes" led by students to center the community.
  - o "PH2E Spotlights" during assemblies highlighting actions that reflect key values.
  - o "Excellence Exit Slips" where students briefly share how they practiced PH2E that day.

Example 3

(SSM)
Strategic School Map

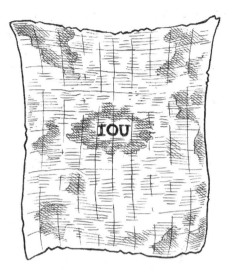

Inward School Map (ISM) Statements

School Vision Statement & Motto

"A Community of Learners"
"Our vision is to cultivate a collaborative and welcoming educational community where every student is inspired to learn, grow, and contribute positively to society."

Daily School Mission Statement & Motto

"Lead and Learn"
"Our mission is to foster an environment of leadership and learning every day, empowering students to achieve academic excellence and personal growth."

School Leadership Principles

1. **Lead** with clarity and vision, setting clear goals and direction for the entire school community.
2. **Encourage** collaboration and inclusivity by creating spaces for all voices to be heard and valued.
3. **Support** and develop every individual by providing personalized guidance, resources, and opportunities for growth.
4. **Foster** a growth mindset, embracing challenges as opportunities for learning and improvement.
5. **Prioritize** emotional and academic wellness, ensuring that both well-being and achievement are central to the school experience.

School Core Values

1. **Respect:** Showing kindness, appreciation, and understanding for others' ideas and contributions.
2. **Supportive:** Demonstrating strong support for our school community and fostering lasting, positive relationships.
3. **Perseverance:** Showing determination and persistence in the face of challenges, supporting others to keep going.
4. **Engaging:** Actively participating in meaningful conversations, valuing contributions, and ensuring everyone is involved in the community.
5. **Motivated:** Encouraging self-driven progress and inspiring others to achieve their full potential with enthusiasm and dedication.

Incorporating Branding Elements

- **Logo:** An open book transforming into a rising sun, symbolizing knowledge, growth, and the promise of new beginnings through learning and leadership.
- **Mascot:** *The Cardinal* – a bold red bird representing energy, courage, and a vibrant community spirit that uplifts and connects.
- **School Colors:** Red and White
- **Visuals:** Feature the rising sun book emblem on school signage, publications, and digital platforms to reinforce the values of learning and leadership. Illustrate *The Cardinal* throughout the school, on banners, student recognition materials, and leadership programs, to energize school pride and celebrate the collective journey of growth, voice, and community.

School SelfCulture Statement

"Our school culture is grounded in mutual respect, continuous improvement, and a commitment to fostering a welcoming and supportive community where every member is valued and empowered to achieve their best."

School Goals

1. Academic Excellence:

- Increase student proficiency in core subjects by 10% over the next academic year.
- Implement project-based learning to enhance critical thinking skills.
- Achieve a 95% graduation rate within the next three years.

2. Personal Growth:

- Develop and implement a student mentorship program to support personal and academic growth.
- Increase student participation in extracurricular activities by 20%.

3. Community Engagement:

- Strengthen partnerships with local businesses and organizations to provide more opportunities for student internships and community service.
- Host quarterly community forums to engage parents and stakeholders in school activities and decision-making processes.

4. Staff Development:

- Provide ongoing professional development opportunities focused on innovative teaching strategies and student engagement.
- Increase staff satisfaction and retention rates by 15% over the next two years.

5. School Environment:

- Enhance school facilities to create a more welcoming and conducive learning environment.
- Implement a school-wide sustainability initiative to reduce the school's carbon footprint.
- Increase student proficiency in reading and math by 15% by the end of the academic year.

Note:

You may insert the comprehensive details of your goals here or attach them to your Inward School Map (ISM). Use the **REBEL Goals™ Framework** to ensure each goal includes clear direction, actionable steps, measurable progress, ongoing evaluation, and sustained support.

Outward School Map (OSM) Statements

1. Inspire IOU Trust

- **Motto**: "Trust Grows Together"
- **Statement**: "We cultivate a community of mutual trust through honesty, responsibility, and collaboration, nurturing meaningful relationships that empower every member to thrive."
- **Strategies**:
  o Facilitate regular trust-building circles and leadership team-building initiatives.
  o Implement a "Community Honor Code" rooted in respect, reliability, and ethical leadership.

2. Practice Positive Communication

- **Motto**: "Connect with Care"
- **Statement**: "We commit to fostering clear, thoughtful, and respectful communication that builds bridges of understanding and strengthens our shared learning journey."
- **Strategies**:
  o Develop a Positive Communication Curriculum incorporating active listening, empathy, and solution-seeking language across all grade levels.
  o Launch 'Connection Corners': dedicated spaces and prompts for positive dialogue among students and staff.

3. Create Common Language

- **Motto**: "Speak to Inspire, Speak to Unite"
- **Statement**: "We intentionally develop and use shared language that reflects our School's Core Values of respect, innovation, and collaboration, ensuring unity in how we think, speak, and act."
- **Strategies**:
  o Create a Common Language Guide emphasizing schoolwide norms and phrases rooted in growth, resilience, and teamwork.

- **Key Phrases / Shared Vocabulary**:
  - "Grow Together"
  - "Lead with Integrity"
  - "Lift as You Climb"
  - "Innovation in Action"
  - "Everyone Belongs"

4. Construct a Cohesive Environment

- **Motto**: "Belong. Collaborate. Flourish."
- **Statement**: "We design welcoming physical spaces and nurturing relational environments that respect diversity, foster connection, and promote continuous growth for all."
- **Strategies**:
  - Launch "Unity Spaces" across the school, areas designed for teamwork, conversation, and collaboration.
  - Create quarterly "Flourish Days" that bring together students, families, and staff for service learning and celebration of collective progress.

5. Establish Everlasting Traditions

- **Motto**: "Our Traditions, Our Growth Story"
- **Statement**: "We celebrate our collective journey through meaningful traditions that honor our history, ignite community pride, and inspire future innovation."
- **Strategies**:
  - Host an annual "Together We Thrive Festival" celebrating milestones of academic, personal, and community growth.
  - Dedicate Leadership Legacy Projects where graduating students design initiatives aligned with School Core Values.
- **List of Signature Traditions**:
  - Together We Thrive Festival (Spring)
  - Founders' Reflection Day (Fall)
  - Leadership Legacy Gallery Installation

6. Model a Mindset of Propelling PH2E

- **Motto**: "Grow Steady, Shine Bright"
- **Statement**: "We embody a daily commitment to Peacefulness, Happiness, Healthiness, and Excellence (PH2E), modeling resilience, joy, and intentional growth as a way of life for our entire community."

- **Strategies**:
  - Start each day with a 'Mindful Morning Message' spotlighting one PH2E principle.
  - Celebrate monthly PH2E Growth Milestones at assemblies, recognizing students and staff.
- **Daily / Weekly PH2E Practices (Optional)**:
  - Weekly Gratitude Walls (Happiness)
  - Fitness Fridays (Healthiness)
  - Calm Corners and Mindful Breathing Breaks (Peacefulness)
  - Leadership Showcases (Excellence)

Example 4

(SSM)
Strategic School Map

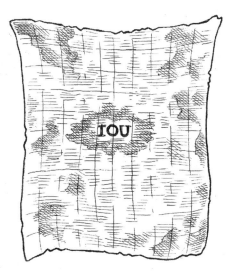

Inward School Map (ISM) Statements

School Vision Statement & Motto

"Inspire Greatness"
"Our vision is to establish an inspiring and forward-thinking learning environment where each student is empowered to excel academically, grow personally, and contribute to a better world."

Daily School Mission Statement & Motto

"Every Day, Every Student, Every Success"
"Our mission is to provide a safe, supportive, and engaging learning environment where every day, every student is encouraged to achieve their personal best, excel academically, and contribute positively to our community."

School Leadership Principles

1. **Lead** with excellence and purpose, inspiring others through actions that reflect commitment and high standards.
2. **Promote** collective leadership by empowering others to take ownership of their role in the school community.
3. **Support** empowerment through opportunity, ensuring every individual has the resources and encouragement to succeed.
4. **Commit** to continuous growth and innovation, seeking out new approaches and solutions for ongoing improvement.
5. **Foster** a culture of well-being and belonging, ensuring every member feels valued, supported, and integral to the school's success.

School Core Values

1. **Trust:** Building strong, reliable relationships by being consistent, honest, and dependable in all interactions.
2. **Supportive:** Maintaining a constructive attitude, inspiring others with encouragement, and creating an environment where everyone feels valued.
3. **Teamwork:** Collaborating effectively with others, contributing to shared goals, and celebrating collective success.
4. **Courageous:** Facing challenges with bravery, standing up for what is right, and supporting others in difficult situations.
5. **Dedication:** Committing to our responsibilities, demonstrating unwavering focus, and striving to achieve excellence together.

Incorporating Branding Elements

- **Logo:** A stylized mountain peak with a rising star at its summit, symbolizing the pursuit of personal excellence, growth, and aspiration—capturing the spirit of "Inspire Greatness."
- **Mascot:** *The Stallion* – representing strength, determination, and forward momentum. The stallion symbolizes students and staff charging ahead with purpose, resilience, and unity in pursuit of excellence.
- **School Colors:** Red and White
- **Visuals:** Feature the mountain-and-star emblem in entryways, leadership documents, and student recognition displays to reinforce achievement and aspiration. Incorporate imagery of the stallion in action, such as galloping, leading, or poised to leap, to energize school events, spirit wear, and classroom branding, symbolizing drive, confidence, and collective progress.

School SelfCulture Statement

"Our school culture is centered on inspiring greatness in every student, every day. We foster an environment rooted in respect, integrity, and collaboration, where innovation is encouraged, excellence is pursued, and everyone is supported to grow and succeed. Through shared responsibility and a commitment to continuous improvement, we strive to create a community where all learners feel empowered to lead, learn, and make a meaningful impact."

School Goals

1. Academic Excellence

- Increase the percentage of students demonstrating growth on benchmark assessments by 12%, using adaptive tools and formative assessments.
- Improve schoolwide writing proficiency by 15% through consistent, cross-curricular writing routines and rubrics.
- Launch "Anchor Labs" in core subjects, targeting 90% student participation in at least one lab per trimester for enrichment or intervention.
- Increase student enrollment in hands-on STEM electives by 25%, expanding opportunities in robotics, coding, and design.
- Implement schoolwide "Show What You Know" presentations, with a goal of 100% participation and rubric-based reflection.

2. Student Empowerment

- Launch a schoolwide leadership program that includes peer mentoring, service learning, and voice-in-decision initiatives.
- Increase participation in student-led events, panels, and exhibitions by 30%, with students showcasing leadership and learning.
- Introduce a "Voice and Choice" survey, targeting a 90% student response rate, and use feedback to guide school programming.
- Establish grade-level "Leadership Journals," aiming for 75% consistent use across upper-grade students by year's end.
- Create a "Student Innovation Fund," with the goal of supporting at least 10 student-led projects each school year.

3. Community & Global Engagement

- Host a minimum of 10 "Community Connection" events per year, inviting families, alumni, and community partners to support learning.

- Launch a virtual global exchange initiative, aiming for 25% student participation in cross-cultural digital learning experiences.
- Increase involvement in civic and service-learning projects by 20%, connecting academic work with community improvement.
- Collaborate with local organizations to co-host student leadership challenges, targeting at least 5 public showcases per year.
- Embed a "Global Lens" curriculum across grade levels, with a goal of 100% student exposure to global competencies by year's end.

4. Staff Excellence

- Create a "Teacher Leadership Academy," aiming for 20% staff participation in formal leadership development within two years.
- Implement instructional rounds and peer coaching cycles, with a goal of 80% staff participation each semester.
- Increase engagement in professional learning surveys by 25%, using results to tailor staff development plans.
- Include staff-led breakout sessions during in-service days, with 30% of sessions facilitated by internal team members.
- Monitor and improve staff wellness indicators, aiming to increase positive responses by 10% in annual school climate surveys.

5. School Culture & Environment

- Redesign key school spaces, including hallways and gathering areas, to reflect core values and visual reminders of school pride, with a goal of completing 3 upgrades per semester.
- Launch a monthly "Culture of Belonging" theme, ensuring 100% classroom participation in related discussions and activities.
- Establish a schoolwide "Recognition Ripple" system to highlight core values in action, aiming for 60 recognitions per month across students and staff.
- Increase student-reported sense of belonging by 15%, measured through annual climate surveys and follow-up reflection sessions.
- Host quarterly "Culture Showcase Events," targeting a 20% increase in family and community attendance compared to the previous year.

Note:
You may insert the comprehensive details of your goals here or attach them to your Inward School Map (ISM). Use the **REBEL Goals™ Framework** to ensure each goal includes clear direction, actionable steps, measurable progress, ongoing evaluation, and sustained support.

Outward School Map (OSM) Statements

1. Inspire IOU Trust

- **Motto**: "Trust the Climb"
- **Statement**: "We intentionally build trust through transparency, reliability, and recognition, empowering every student and staff member to take bold steps toward their personal best."
- **Strategies**:
  - Establish a "Climb Together" peer recognition program celebrating acts of integrity, effort, and leadership.
  - Host quarterly Trust Circles where students and staff reflect on challenges, growth, and mutual accountability.

2. Practice Positive Communication

- **Motto**: "Speak Greatness Into Being"
- **Statement**: "We cultivate a culture of upliftment by communicating with clarity, respect, and encouragement, fueling confidence, connection, and collective success."
- **Strategies**:
  - Implement "Positive Voice Workshops" focusing on feedback that celebrates effort, fosters resilience, and inspires growth.
  - Launch a "Voice of Greatness" spotlight series where students and staff share success stories and lessons learned.

3. Create Common Language

- **Motto**: "Words That Elevate, Words That Empower"
- **Statement**: "We intentionally use shared phrases and affirmations that reinforce our Core Values, setting a high bar for how we think, speak, and act as a learning community."
- **Strategies**:
  - Develop a "Language of Greatness" toolkit featuring core affirmations and principles aligned with aspiration, perseverance, and responsibility.

- **Key Phrases / Shared Vocabulary**:
  - "Inspire Greatness"
  - "Own Your Climb"
  - "Every Step Matters"
  - "Strength Through Unity"
  - "Lead with Integrity"

4. Construct a Cohesive Environment

- **Motto**: "Together, We Rise"
- **Statement**: "We create spaces and structures that foster belonging, collaboration, and ambition, ensuring every student and staff member feels seen, supported, and inspired to excel."
- **Strategies**:
  - Redesign common spaces with motivational visuals and student voice artifacts that reflect the pursuit of greatness.
  - Launch "Unity Days" focused on strengthening cross-grade, staff-student, and community connections through collaborative experiences.

5. Establish Everlasting Traditions

- **Motto**: "Celebrate the Climb, Honor the Journey"
- **Statement**: "We establish and honor traditions that showcase perseverance, leadership, and collective growth, embedding pride and legacy into the fabric of our school."
- **Strategies**:
  - Launch the annual "Summit Celebration" recognizing milestones of academic excellence, leadership, and community service.
  - Create a "Legacy Wall" to celebrate graduating students' and staff members' contributions toward inspiring greatness.
- **List of Signature Traditions**:
  - Summit Celebration Week
  - Legacy Wall Dedication Ceremony
  - Annual Stallion Spirit and Leadership Day

6. Model a Mindset of Propelling PH2E

- **Motto**: "Fuel Greatness, Propel Growth"
- **Statement**: "We lead by example, modeling Peacefulness, Happiness, Healthiness, and Excellence (PH2E) as daily disciplines that empower each individual to thrive and contribute at their highest potential."

- **Strategies**:
  - Integrate a "Greatness Journal" initiative where students and staff reflect weekly on PH2E moments and personal victories.
  - Host a monthly "Propeller Spotlight" assembly celebrating individuals who exemplify steady progress in PH2E dimensions.
- **Daily / Weekly PH2E Practices (Optional)**:
  - Daily Calm Moments before the first lesson (Peacefulness)
  - "Greatness Gratitude" Friday shoutouts (Happiness)
  - Wellness Wednesday fitness or mindfulness breaks (Healthiness)
  - Excellence Awards posted monthly across grade levels (Excellence)

Important Reminders and Encouragement

Implement as You Go

We know—we've said this before. In fact, we've said it several times throughout this leadership manual. But it's worth repeating here, at the finish line: **you don't need to wait until every anchor is fully developed to begin implementation**.

As educators, we often want everything perfectly in place before we launch something new. It's part of our DNA: plan it, polish it, then present it. But this isn't a book report, it's a culture. And culture is built through process, not perfection.

Your Strategic School Map (SSM) is a living, evolving tool. If you've built the Inward and Outward Anchors, even in draft form, **you're ready to start**. Use what you've created. Share it. Speak from it. Let it guide your decisions, conversations, and daily routines. The act of implementing, **even in small, imperfect steps**, creates the very alignment you're aiming for.

By starting now, you'll build momentum, foster clarity, and empower your community to grow with you. Every step you take helps shape your school's direction, and every iteration brings you closer to a culture of purpose, connection, and IOU-aligned leadership.

Naming Your Strategic School Map (SSM)

Your Strategic School Map serves as the comprehensive framework for your school's culture, direction, and aspirations. While this guide refers to it as the *Strategic School Map*, you're encouraged to create a name that reflects your school or district's identity, spirit, and community pride.

A personalized name makes the SSM more relatable and inspiring. It reinforces your unique voice and helps everyone feel connected to the journey. Here are a few naming ideas to spark inspiration:

1. Use Your School or District Name

- *"Copper Valley's Educational Blueprint"*
- *"Bellport's Guiding Map"*
- *"Falcon's Flight Strategic Plan"*

2. Incorporate Your Mascot

- *"Eagle's Vision Plan"*
- *"Tiger's Path to Excellence"*
- *"Lion's Legacy Strategic Plan"*

3. Reflect Your Mission or Core Values

- *"Pathway to Success"*
- *"Journey to Excellence"*
- *"Empowerment Through Learning Plan"*

4. Get Creative with Local Symbols or Identity

- *"Harborview's Lighthouse Plan"*
- *"Mountain Peak's Strategic Path"*
- *"Sunset Ridge Horizon Map"*

Encourage input from your community. Involve students, staff, and families in choosing the name; it's a powerful way to build ownership and pride. When everyone helps name the map, they're more likely to feel invested in living it.

Above all, **have fun with it.** Your name becomes a symbol of what you stand for, your shared commitment to excellence, growth, and unity. Make it meaningful. Make it yours.

Transition to Part III: Reaching Your IOU Destination

By synergizing your Inward School Map (ISM) and Outward School Map (OSM), you've created a comprehensive Strategic School Map (SSM)—a unified framework that aligns foundational principles with purposeful actions, shaping a vibrant and values-driven school culture. With this foundation in place, you're now poised to explore the ultimate outcome of the IOU journey: **Upward Living**—the **U** in IOU.

Part III invites you to envision and receive the results of your alignment work. Upward Living isn't something you do; it's what you receive when your culture is grounded in clarity, consistently lived, and lifted by purpose. It reflects a flourishing school community where **Peacefulness, Happiness, Healthiness, and Excellence (PH2E®)** are not abstract ideals, but daily realities.

In **Chapter 9**, *The Lighthouse Guide: The Path to Upward Living*, you'll discover how the lighthouse becomes your symbolic guide. It casts light over your Strategic School Map, helping your school stay true to its course, even through challenges and change. You'll explore the five elements that fuel Upward Living, define your Upward Desired Outcomes, and evaluate the current trajectory of your culture: upward, wayward, or downward.

To support this growth, you'll engage with two powerful tools:

- The **PH2E Life Propeller Self-Assessment**, which empowers individuals to reflect on their well-being and balance across four dimensions
- The **IOU School Culture Assessment**, which helps your leadership team evaluate your school's culture alignment and guide continuous improvement.

Together, these tools ensure your Strategic School Map remains a living, breathing guide. It's not just a plan, but a practice. As you enter this part of the journey, you'll learn how to keep your culture energized, focused, and future-ready.

This is the path to becoming an **Upward Dynamic Positive Culture**. Every member of your school community is empowered to thrive and fulfill their greatest potential.

Part III

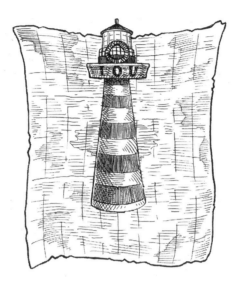

Reaching Your IOU Destination

As you embark on this essential part of your IOU journey, the lighthouse emerges as a guiding symbol, representing the culmination of your strategic efforts. It stands tall on the shores of educational aspiration, casting light over the path toward success, growth, and **Upward Living**.

This beacon doesn't just point the way. It represents the destination itself: a school culture grounded in **Peacefulness, Happiness, Healthiness, and Excellence (PH2E®)**. It illuminates the journey a school takes when inward principles and outward practices align, creating an **Upward Dynamic Positive Culture** where every member of the community is empowered to thrive.

Chapter Overview

Chapter 9 explores the **"U"** in IOU—**Upward Living**. It marks the peak of the journey, where **Inward Living (I)** and **Outward Living (O)** converge to generate powerful and lasting results.

Upward Living isn't achieved by chance; it is the **natural byproduct of intentional alignment**: clarity of inward principles, consistency in outward actions, and a sustained commitment to reflection and growth. The result is a culture that embodies PH2E.

You are invited to define your **Upward Desired Outcomes**. Reflect deeply: What does genuine success look like in your school? How do you envision excellence, not just in performance, but in culture, relationships, and well-being? Through guided reflection, you'll shape a shared vision for thriving together.

Five Foundational Elements of "U" Upward Living:

The "U" in Upward Living can be broken down into five foundational elements that act as daily guiding principles for sustaining a dynamic, thriving culture:

- **Upliftment** – Raising others through encouragement and support
- **Unity** – Building a strong, connected community
- **Understanding** – Leading with empathy and clarity
- **Ubiquity** – Ensuring the School's Core Values are present in every interaction
- **Unleashing Talent** – Creating opportunities for every individual to shine

These principles work collectively, fostering a school environment where success and positive culture flourish organically.

Assessing and Propelling PH2E: The Life Propeller Model

Creating a thriving school culture begins with individual reflection and collective growth. The **PH2E Self-Assessment Tool**, available at PH2E.com, helps individuals and school communities evaluate their current levels of:

- Peacefulness
- Happiness
- Healthiness
- Excellence

Using the **Life Propeller** visual model, each person assesses personal strengths and identifies growth areas. Each propeller blade represents one aspect of PH2E. A balanced propeller signifies resilience and forward momentum; imbalance highlights areas needing attention and realignment.

Using the PH2E Self-Assessment Effectively:

- **Private Reflection** – Complete the assessment individually, fostering personal awareness.
- **Collective Conversations** – Share general insights as a team, discussing collective strengths and challenges.
- **Collaboration and Support** – Develop strategies for mutual support and continuous growth.
- **Regular Reassessment** – Monitor progress, adapt strategies, and maintain momentum.

IOU School Culture Assessment

The **IOU School Culture Assessment** (Appendix D) is an essential tool, strategically designed to evaluate your school's alignment with the IOU Framework at any stage of your journey. Use it to:

- Identify current strengths and growth areas across your Inward and Outward School Anchors.
- Establish a leadership team baseline, revisiting annually to track progress and alignment.
- Facilitate ongoing dialogue and reflective practices among staff.
- Guide long-term implementation and refinement of your Strategic School Map with clarity and purpose.

When individuals on your leadership team use this assessment independently and collaboratively share results, meaningful conversations emerge, perspectives deepen, and team alignment strengthens.

The IOU School Culture Assessment ensures your Strategic School Map remains dynamic and responsive, continuously steering your school toward the sustained realization of PH2E.

This strategic combination of reflective tools, the **PH2E Self-Assessment** for individual growth and the **IOU School Culture Assessment** for collective alignment, strengthens your foundation, ensuring that **Upward Living** isn't just a goal but a daily reality.

Chapter 9

The Lighthouse Guide

Nobody can make you feel inferior without your consent.
—Eleanor Roosevelt

The Path to Upward Living

As we navigate this essential chapter, we explore the culminating element of your IOU journey—the "U" in IOU, representing **Upward Living**. This stage is where your diligent work with the **Inward (I)** and **Outward (O)** principles converges to create an empowered, thriving school culture.

Upward Living isn't simply attained; it emerges naturally from the alignment of intentional inward clarity and consistent outward action. The result is a vibrant culture defined by **Peacefulness, Happiness, Healthiness, and Excellence (PH2E®)**. It symbolizes the peak of purposeful leadership and intentional school culture development.

This chapter encourages you to envision your school's **Upward Map (UP-Map)**. Reflect deeply on your desired outcomes:

- What does thriving look and feel like in your school community?
- How do relationships, daily practices, and overall culture reflect authentic excellence?

With your **Strategic School Map (SSM)** as your compass, and the lighthouse as your guiding beacon, this chapter guides you toward achieving lasting alignment and schoolwide impact.

The Lighthouse as Your Symbolic Guide

The lighthouse serves as your enduring symbol of direction, hope, and unwavering clarity. Standing resilient amidst life's challenges, it signifies the guiding power of your Strategic School Map, ensuring every action aligns with your mission, vision, and deepest aspirations.

Situated atop your personalized IOU Island, crafted from your school's foundational vision, mission, principles, and core values, the lighthouse illuminates your journey, casting clarity over every decision.

Remember: you're not drifting; you're navigating with intentionality, purpose, and shared vision. Let the lighthouse symbolize your inspirational commitment, encouraging your entire school community to **Inspire to Aspire**, transforming dreams into daily realities.

Understanding Upward Living

The Meaning of 'U' in IOU
The "U" in IOU symbolizes **Upward Living**, the powerful, positive outcomes achieved through the deliberate alignment of inward principles and outward actions. Upward Living isn't a direct result of commands or control; rather, it's the natural byproduct you receive when your school's inner commitments authentically align with outward practices.

At this stage of your journey, **Upward Living** reflects a culture abundant in PH2E. These outcomes become lived experiences when your school consistently embodies its principles and values through genuine daily interactions and intentional leadership.

The Five Key Elements of "U" Upward Living
Upward Living is a vibrant culture shaped by five foundational elements. These elements provide structure to your Strategic School Map, transforming it from a static plan into a lived daily reality:

- **Upliftment**
  Promote encouragement, gratitude, and optimism in every interaction, fueling morale and motivation across your school community.
- **Unity**
  Build deep, meaningful connections through collaboration, mutual respect, and a shared sense of purpose among students, staff, and families.
- **Understanding**
  Lead with empathy, clarity, and active listening, fostering emotional safety and trust throughout your school.
- **Ubiquity**
  Ensure your foundational principles and values are consistently visible and authentically practiced in every space, classroom, and interaction—creating a cohesive and unified school culture.
- **Unleashing Talent**
  Recognize, nurture, and empower individual strengths, providing opportunities for personal growth and collective excellence.

Together, these five elements transform your Strategic School Map from a static plan into a living culture, one where greatness is not demanded, but drawn out from within.

The U Principle: Receiving Your Desired Outcomes

Upward Living—the "U" in IOU—is not something you do; it's something you receive. It's the natural result of living and leading with alignment between your Inward School Map (ISM) and Outward School Map (OSM). When inward principles are clearly defined and outward actions are lived with intention, schools begin to experience a culture shaped by **Peacefulness, Happiness, Healthiness, and Excellence (PH2E®)**.

This is the power of the U Principle: when alignment is sustained, outcomes transform. Cultures shift. Spirits rise. Communities thrive.

Upward Living reflects the **desired outcomes** of your strategic efforts, not just in academic performance, but in how people feel, grow, and connect within your school. It's the flourishing state of a school culture where everyone is empowered, seen, and supported.

Unlike the planning and actions involved in building the "I" and "O," the "U" is a byproduct. It cannot be directly manufactured, but it will **naturally emerge** when a school consistently lives its beliefs with clarity and integrity.

In essence: You don't chase the "U."
You create the conditions for it.

Control Over I and O

While **Upward Living (U)** is the result, the true work of leadership lives in the "I" and the "O." These are the areas fully within your control—and where your daily focus must remain.

- **Inward Development (I – ISM):**
  This is your school's foundation. It includes clarifying your vision, mission, leadership principles, and core values. It's about defining who you are as a school and grounding every decision in that identity.
- **Outward Actions (O – OSM):**
  This is your school's expression. It includes how you build trust, communicate, shape the environment, and engage with your community. It's where your beliefs are made visible—where what you say is what others experience.

By consistently cultivating both your inward clarity and outward consistency, you **set the stage** for Upward Living to take root and thrive. These daily actions are how you build culture—not by chance, but by choice.

Focus on the "I" and the "O," and the "U" will follow.

Potential Outcomes: The IOU Continuum — Upward, Wayward, or Downward

The "U" in IOU—**Upward Living**—is not guaranteed. It is the byproduct of a school's intentionality, alignment, and consistency. How you engage with your Inward and Outward Maps determines the trajectory your school will follow—whether it leads to sustained progress, stagnation, or decline. This dynamic is captured in what we call the **IOU Continuum**.

There are three possible cultural trajectories:

- **Upward (U):**
  When your ISM and OSM are lived with clarity and alignment, your school experiences **PH2E**—as a natural outcome. This is the hallmark of a thriving, principle-driven culture where both individuals and the collective community flourish.
- **Wayward (W):**
  When implementation becomes inconsistent, surface-level, or reactive, your school starts to drift. The result is mediocrity, confusion, or stagnation. There may still be activity and effort, but without clear direction or coherence, progress stalls.
- **Downward (D):**
  When foundational principles are ignored or misaligned, negativity can take root. Trust erodes. Communication falters. The culture begins to decline, often triggered by reactive leadership, unchecked habits, or the loss of mission focus.

Your school's trajectory is never fixed; it is shaped daily by the quality and consistency of your Inward and Outward actions. The good news? You can always course-correct. With renewed clarity and intentional effort, alignment can be restored, and the journey redirected toward a healthier, more purpose-driven destination.

Clarity of purpose and consistency of action are the two levers that determine your school's direction on the IOU Continuum.

> *"If you want better results, build a better foundation—*
> *starting from within."*
> —Dr. Joe Famularo

Changing Results: Know Your "I," Own Your "O," and Receive the "U"

The results you are experiencing right now, whether they reflect upward growth, wayward drifting, or downward decline, are directly tied to two things: the strength of your "I" (Inward development) and the alignment of your "O" (Outward actions). Together, these elements form the foundation of your school's culture and outcomes.

If you want to change your results, you cannot simply chase the byproduct—the "U" (Upward Living). Real change begins by strengthening what lies beneath: who you are (I) and how you live that identity out loud (O).

You must first **Know Your I** and **Own Your O**—and only then will you **Receive the U**.

Why Focus on "I" and "O" First?

The Power of "I" (Inward Development):
This is where your true identity lives. Your school's SelfCulture, vision, mission, principles, and core values form the core of who you are. When these Inward Anchors are clearly defined, deeply understood, and consistently owned by your leadership and staff, they serve as the compass for every decision and action. Without a strong "I," the outward practices will lack coherence and credibility.

The Impact of "O" (Outward Actions):
Your outward actions are the visible expression of your inward beliefs. Trust isn't built just through good intentions—it's built through consistent outward behaviors. Communication, relationships, traditions, environments—all these external practices either validate or contradict your inward commitments. When your "O" is aligned with your "I," your culture gains clarity, credibility, and strength.

You don't grow a great culture by chasing results ("U").
You build it by **knowing your principles ("I")** and **owning your actions ("O")** with intention and integrity.

How to Change Results: The Clear Path Forward

If your current outcomes aren't where you want them to be—whether you feel stuck in neutral (Wayward), slipping backward (Downward), or simply seeking to elevate and deepen an already positive culture (Upward)—the path forward is simple, but powerful:

- **Know Your I:** Clarify your SelfCulture. Reconnect with your school's guiding beliefs, vision, and values. Strengthen the roots so the branches can grow.
- **Own Your O:** Align your outward practices with your inward identity. Make sure your communication, your traditions, your leadership actions, and your daily relationships consistently reflect who you claim to be.
- **Receive the U:** When your I and O are authentically aligned, Upward Living (PH2E - Peacefulness, Happiness, Healthiness, and Excellence) will emerge naturally as the byproduct. Upward results aren't something you force. They are something you earn through alignment.

Remember:

- No lasting change begins with the "U."
- It always begins with the "I."
- It is sustained by the "O."
- It is received in the "U."

Upward Living is not something you chase.
It is the natural outcome of living inwardly with clarity and outwardly with purpose.

The moment you **know your I** and **own your O**, is the moment your culture begins to move upward—one decision, one relationship, one action at a time.

Envisioning Your U Desired Outcomes

Now that you've explored the meaning of Upward Living and how it emerges from strong Inward and Outward practices, it's time to **define your school's vision for the "U."** What does success actually look like—not just in data, but in energy, relationships, and culture?

This is your opportunity to **dream boldly** and clarify what you hope to receive when your IOU alignment is lived fully.

Use the following prompts to shape your **Upward Living**—a vivid, principled-based picture of the results your school strives to embody:

- **Desired Outcomes:**
  What long-term results do you want for your students, staff, and school community? What legacy will your culture leave behind?
- **Ideal School Culture:**
  Picture a school where unity, understanding, ubiquity, upliftment, and unleashed talent are part of daily life. How do those principles shape behavior, climate, and connection?
- **Key Anchors in Action:**
  How will your vision, mission, leadership principles, and core values be lived—not just written? What does it look like when those anchors are so ingrained they show up automatically?
- **Imagination and Aspiration:**
  Think beyond limitations. What does a thriving, joyful, upward-moving school feel like? How would it inspire every person who walks through your doors?

When you begin with the end in mind, your vision becomes your lighthouse, illuminating each step and keeping your journey aligned with your highest aspirations.

Assessing and Propelling PH2E in Your School Community: The Life Propeller Model

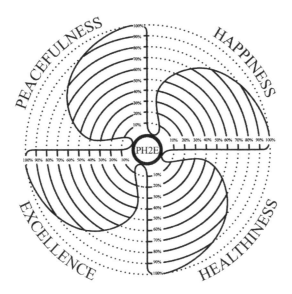

While Upward Living is a schoolwide aspiration, it starts with individuals. Each person, teacher, staff member, leader, or student, carries the responsibility to reflect, reset, and realign. That's why the **PH2E Self-Assessment** is such a powerful tool: it helps you understand how you're truly showing up in the areas of **Peacefulness, Happiness, Healthiness, and Excellence**.

The PH2E Self-Assessment, available for free at PH2E.com, is designed to help individuals and teams evaluate their well-being across these four essential dimensions. Once completed, the results are visualized through the **Life Propeller**, a simple, intuitive model showing balance or imbalance across each area:

- A **balanced propeller** means you're equipped to move forward with strength and stability.
- An **unbalanced propeller** reveals the areas where growth is needed—just like a boat can't move effectively with one damaged blade.

This tool isn't about perfection or performance, it's about awareness. When individuals gain clarity on their own well-being, they're better prepared to contribute positively to a thriving, upward-moving culture.

Upward Living begins with individual alignment.
When each person strengthens their propeller, the whole school moves forward together.

The Purpose of the PH2E Life Propeller Assessment

The **PH2E Life Propeller Assessment** acts as a mirror. It invites individuals to reflect honestly on how they're showing up in life and leadership across four essential areas:

- **Peacefulness** – Do I feel calm, centered, and grounded in the midst of challenges?
- **Happiness** – Am I experiencing joy, gratitude, and meaningful connection in my daily interactions?
- **Healthiness** – Am I caring for my physical and mental well-being in intentional, sustainable ways?
- **Excellence** – Am I actively learning, growing, and striving to make a positive impact?

This self-assessment builds self-awareness. And when individuals become more aware of their current state, they're better equipped to strengthen the areas that need attention.

The impact goes beyond the individual. When each person reflects on their balance, the entire school benefits:

- **Stronger individuals lead to stronger teams.**
- **Stronger teams create a more resilient and positive school culture.**

Personal growth fuels collective alignment.
The Life Propeller helps everyone lead from within, so they can lift others around them.

How to Use the PH2E Assessment

The PH2E Self-Assessment becomes most powerful when it's embedded into a rhythm of **reflection, conversation, and continuous growth**. Here's how to use it meaningfully within your school or leadership team:

1. **Private Reflection**
   Each individual completes the assessment on their own, rating themselves on a scale of 1 (Low) to 7 (High) in each PH2E dimension. Sample reflection prompts include:
   - Do I maintain a sense of peace during stressful moments?
   - How often do I feel genuinely joyful and express gratitude?
   - Am I prioritizing habits that enhance my physical and mental well-being?
   - Am I actively setting and pursuing goals that align with my purpose?
2. **Collective Conversations**
   While results remain personal, team members can share general insights, trends, or areas they're focusing on. These conversations, whether in leadership meetings or retreats, can spark powerful dialogue around well-being and school culture.
3. **Collaboration and Support**
   Use insights to foster a supportive environment. Teams can develop collective strategies for growth, such as mindfulness routines, wellness initiatives, gratitude practices, or goal-setting exercises that strengthen PH2E across the board.
4. **Regular Reassessment**
   Embed the PH2E Self-Assessment into your calendar: quarterly, seasonally, or annually. This promotes a culture of reflection and resilience, helping individuals monitor their progress while encouraging schoolwide accountability for well-being.

Reflection fuels growth.
Shared reflection fuels culture.

By using the PH2E Life Propeller routinely, you empower individuals to take ownership of their own balance—while supporting a collective commitment to upward living.

The PH2E Life Propeller Analogy

Imagine your life, or leadership, as a ship. Your ability to move forward with strength and direction depends on one thing: a **balanced propeller**.

The **PH2E Life Propeller** visualizes this concept. Each of its four blades represents one of the life gifts:

- **Peacefulness**
- **Happiness**
- **Healthiness**
- **Excellence**

If one blade is too short, cracked, or neglected, the entire propeller wobbles. You may still move, but you'll feel resistance, imbalance, or even burnout. In contrast, a strong and balanced propeller generates smooth, sustainable momentum.

Balance doesn't just feel better—it works better.

This metaphor is more than a visual—it's a guide. It challenges individuals and leaders to regularly ask:

- **Which blade needs attention right now?**
- **What small action can I take to strengthen it?**

The goal isn't perfection; it's propulsion. The stronger and more balanced your blades, the more confidently and effectively you can lead, learn, and live.

Strong blades propel strong schools.
When individuals thrive, school culture thrives.

Striving for Balance and Improvement

Once you've assessed your PH2E Life Propeller, take a closer look at the blade with the **lowest score**—that's the area asking for your attention.

Start small. Start specific. Start now.

Here are simple examples of actions that strengthen each blade:

- **Peacefulness** → Add 10 minutes of quiet reflection, breathing, or journaling each morning.
- **Happiness** → Begin or end your day with gratitude. Celebrate small wins and moments of connection.
- **Healthiness** → Focus on one habit, such as hydration, movement, rest, or nutrition, that boosts your physical and mental energy.
- **Excellence** → Revisit a goal that inspires you. Take one step forward. Reignite your growth.

Your first goal is **balance**, ensuring all four blades are strong enough to move you forward without resistance. Once that's in place, you can focus on **strengthening each blade** to reach its fullest potential.

When individuals engage in regular reflection and small improvements, they grow into what this framework calls an **IOU Life Leader**, someone who leads from within, supports others outwardly, and receives excellence as a natural outcome.

This isn't just about personal wellness. It's about building a school culture where balance, support, and growth are not the exception—they're the norm.

Balance fuels momentum.
Momentum powers culture.
Culture shapes lives.

Incorporating the PH2E Life Propeller into Your School

While the **PH2E Life Propeller** begins as an **individual reflection tool**, its greatest power is unleashed when it becomes part of your **schoolwide rhythm and identity**.

Encourage your staff to engage with the **PH2E Self-Assessment**—not as a **one-time activity**, but as a **consistent check-in** that **propels reflection, wellness, and alignment forward**. Like a propeller, it **generates momentum from within**—serving as a **wellness anchor**, a **conversation starter**, and a **practical tool** to keep your school moving toward **Peacefulness, Happiness, Healthiness, and Excellence (PH2E)**.

Here are ways to bring the Life Propeller to life in your school:

- **Individual Growth Plans**
  Invite staff and leaders to include PH2E focus areas in personal goals or reflections. Highlight progress, not perfection.
- **Team Conversations**
  Use the Life Propeller to guide team discussions. What patterns are surfacing? Which blades seem strong collectively—and which need attention?
- **Wellness and Professional Development Initiatives**
  Align PD, wellness days, or mindfulness moments with PH2E themes. Offer experiences that restore balance and build community.
- **Schoolwide Strategic Integration**
  Weave PH2E into morning announcements, staff meetings, student leadership programs, and even visual displays in hallways or classrooms. Make it part of the language of your culture.

This is the heart of IOU Leadership: **inward clarity, outward action, and upward results**. The PH2E Life Propeller offers a concrete way to evaluate and support that journey—one individual, one blade, one conversation at a time.

**When reflection becomes routine,
Resilience becomes reality.**

Ready to begin?
Visit **PH2E.com** and take your first step toward a more balanced, resilient, and purpose-driven school culture.

Charting Your Course: The IOU School Culture Assessment

As your Strategic School Map (SSM) guides your daily journey and the PH2E Life Propeller ensures individual balance, there comes a moment when leadership must pause to evaluate the full course.

That moment is now.

To ensure you're truly navigating with alignment, you need more than inspiration—you need insight. The **IOU School Culture Assessment** provides exactly that. It's your diagnostic compass: a tool designed to assess how well your Inward School Map (ISM) and Outward School Map (OSM) are being lived and experienced across your school community,

THE IOU SCHOOL CULTURE ASSESSMENT

Evaluating Your IOU School Culture

Whether you're just beginning to outline your **Strategic School Map (SSM)** or have already developed and implemented it, the **IOU School Culture Assessment** is a flexible and powerful tool to guide your journey. Located in **Appendix D**, this assessment can be used at any stage to evaluate alignment, inform planning, and ensure intentional growth.

Use it to:

- **Identify current strengths and areas for improvement** across your Inward and Outward School Anchors
- **Establish a baseline** for your leadership team and revisit annually to track progress
- **Foster continuous dialogue and reflection** among staff as your culture evolves
- **Guide the long-term implementation and refinement** of your SSM with purpose and clarity
- **Use it as your schoolwide compass**—a strategic guide to help leadership determine which IOU principles need focused attention first, and how to navigate toward deeper alignment and a more vibrant school culture.

This is **more than a one-time checklist**: it's a **strategic reflection tool** that promotes **shared ownership** of your school's culture. **When used by individuals on your leadership team and compared collaboratively**, the assessment **sparks meaningful conversations, uncovers different perspectives**, and **strengthens team alignment**.

By incorporating this process into your **leadership rhythm**, you ensure your **SSM remains a living, breathing guide**; anchored in principle and continuously steering your school toward **Peacefulness, Happiness, Healthiness, and Excellence**.

Transition to Part IV: Navigating Your IOU Strategic School Map (SSM)

You've built your Strategic School Map.
You've aligned your Inward and Outward practices.
And now, you've defined what Upward Living looks like for your school.

It's time to set sail.

In **Part IV**, symbolized by the **compass**, we turn from **design to direction**, from **vision to navigation**. This is where your Strategic School Map becomes more than a framework. It becomes your tool for daily guidance, course correction, and collaborative progress.

You'll learn how to **implement**, **monitor**, and **lead** with your ISM and OSM fully activated, ensuring that every member of your community moves together, with clarity, toward your highest aspirations.

The map is drawn.
The lighthouse is lit.
Let's navigate.

Part IV

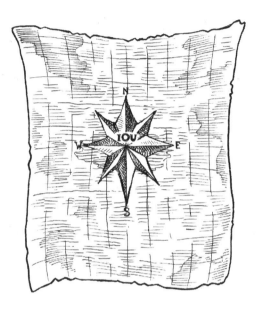

Navigating Your IOU Strategic School Map (SSM)

In the final part of our journey, we turn to the **compass** as our guiding symbol. A compass is essential for navigation, providing direction and helping travelers stay on course. In the context of our book, the compass represents the **Strategic School Map (SSM)** - a comprehensive tool combining your **Inward School Map (ISM)** and **Outward School Map (OSM)**. It helps schools implement, navigate, and sustain the principles of IOU Leadership, ensuring continuous progress toward an **Upward Dynamic Positive IOU School Culture.**

Chapter 10: Propelling Your ISM and OSM to Your Destination: Putting Your Strategic School Map into Action

In this final chapter, we focus on integrating the insights and strategies developed from your Inward and Outward Anchors into a cohesive **School Strategic Map**

(SSM), emphasizing that it is not just a document but a **living guide** to navigate your school toward its aspirational goals. The chapter highlights the importance of continuous improvement, integrating the Inward School Map (ISM) and Outward School Map (OSM) into daily school life, and promoting key principles to foster a thriving school culture. By consistently applying these maps, schools can achieve PH2E. The chapter also outlines strategies for embedding these principles into the school community, ensuring that the school remains on course to a dynamic, positive culture. A key component discussed is the **IOU School Guiding Handle**, representing your True North, which helps keep your school aligned with its core values and vision, especially in times of uncertainty or challenge. This chapter emphasizes that you don't need to wait until everything is completed and perfect to start implementing your SSM. The journey towards upward living is a continuous process of reflection, action, and adjustment.

Chapter 10

Propelling Your ISM and OSM to Your Destination

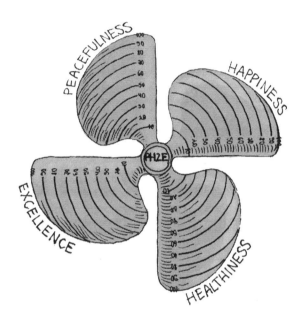

You must be the change you wish to see in the world.
—Mahatma Gandhi

Putting Your Strategic School Map into Action

Throughout the process of implementing your **Strategic School Map (SSM)**, it's essential to understand that this map isn't just a document—it's a **living, breathing guide** that will navigate your school towards its aspirational goals. Your **ISM and OSM** serve as your **navigation system and sails**, steering your school forward with clarity and momentum—through both calm waters and stormy seas.

This chapter will focus on **putting your SSM into action**, ensuring that your school community thrives in all aspects of your **Upward desired results** receiving **Peacefulness, Happiness, Healthiness, and Excellence (PH2E)**.

Embracing Continuous Improvement

Essential to the IOU School Culture is the principle of **continuous improvement.** It's a mindset that encourages everyone in the school community to **strive for excellence daily**.

As you implement your ISM and OSM, keep in mind that this journey is ongoing. Regularly revisit and refine your strategies, ensuring they remain aligned with your school's vision, principles, mission, and core values.

Key Components of Your SSM:

- **Inward School Map (ISM):** Focuses on the internal aspects such as vision, mission, principles, values, and goals.
- **Outward School Map (OSM):** Emphasizes outward actions, relationships, and communication strategies.
- **Upward Results:** Represents the desired outcomes of Peacefulness, Happiness, Healthiness, and Excellence (PH2E).

Steps to Implement Your SSM:

1. Start with What You Have:

- Begin implementing the strategies and actions you have already developed from your ISM and OSM. Don't wait for every school anchor to be completed and perfect. Take the first step with the tools and plans you have.

2. Align with Your Vision and Mission:

- Ensure that all actions and initiatives align with your school's vision and mission. This alignment keeps the school focused on its ultimate goals.

3. Engage the School Community:

- Involve students, teachers, staff, and parents in the implementation process. Their input and participation are crucial for the successful adoption of new practices and policies.

4. Monitor and Adjust:

- Continuously monitor the progress of your initiatives. Be prepared to make adjustments as needed to stay on course towards your goals.

5. Celebrate Milestones:

- Recognize and celebrate achievements along the way. Celebrating successes boosts morale and reinforces the positive changes being made.

> *By failing to prepare, you are preparing to fail.*
> —Benjamin Franklin

Daily Implementation and Promotion of Your Strategic School Map (SSM)

Consistent Implementation

To fully realize the potential of your Strategic School Map (SSM), it is crucial to prepare and integrate it into the daily life of the school. This involves strategic planning and also the consistent application of the principles and goals outlined in these maps. Think of your SSM as the compass for your school, guiding every action and decision. Just as a captain and crew rely on a compass to keep their ship on course, your school community relies on these maps to navigate toward a dynamic, positive culture where everyone thrives.

Keeping School Anchors in the Forefront

To embed the SSM deeply into your school culture, keep its School Anchors at the forefront. Incorporate these anchors into every speech, team meeting, and school event. This constant reinforcement helps to align everyone's actions with the school's vision and goals, creating a cohesive and focused environment.

1. **Use Every Opportunity**

    - **Morning Announcements:** Start each day by reinforcing the key elements of the ISM and OSM during morning announcements. Highlight specific core values, leadership principles, or school goals, and relate them to daily activities or current events within the school. Regular share the mottos for both your School Vision and Daily Mission Statements.
    - **Staff Meetings:** Incorporate discussions about the ISM and OSM into regular staff meetings. Use these sessions to review progress, share success stories, and brainstorm solutions to any challenges encountered in implementing the maps.
    - **Classroom Activities:** Encourage teachers to integrate the language and concepts of the ISM and OSM into their lesson plans. This can be done through projects, discussions, and classroom norms that reflect the school's core values and goals.

2. **Promote the Language Developed**

    - **Consistent Messaging:** Ensure that the language developed in the ISM and OSM is consistently used across all communications. This

includes newsletters, emails, social media updates, website, and official school documents. Consistency in language reinforces the principles and goals of the school.
- **Visual Displays:** Create visual displays around the school that highlight key elements of the ISM and OSM. Posters, banners, and bulletin boards can serve as constant reminders of the school's mission, vision, leadership principles, core values, and strategic goals.
- **Student Involvement:** Involve students in promoting the ISM and OSM. This can include student-led assemblies, peer mentoring programs, and student councils that focus on upholding and spreading the school's principles, core values, and goals.

3. **Foster a Culture of Reflection**

    - **Regular Reflection Sessions:** Schedule regular reflection sessions for both staff and students to discuss how the ISM and OSM are being applied in daily life. These sessions can help identify areas of success and opportunities for improvement.
    - **Feedback Mechanisms:** Implement mechanisms for gathering feedback from the entire school community. Surveys, suggestion boxes, and open forums can provide valuable insights into how well the ISM and OSM are being integrated and what adjustments may be needed.

4. **Celebrate Successes**

    - **Acknowledgment Programs:** Establish programs to acknowledge and celebrate individuals or groups who exemplify the principles and goals of the ISM and OSM. Recognitions can include awards, certificates, and public commendations during assemblies or meetings.
    - **Sharing Success Stories:** Regularly share success stories that illustrate the impact of the ISM and OSM. Highlight how specific actions and behaviors aligned with the school's principles, values, and goals have led to positive outcomes.

5. **Training and Professional Development**

    - **Ongoing Training:** Provide ongoing training and professional development opportunities focused on the ISM and OSM. This can include workshops, seminars, and collaborative planning sessions that equip staff with the skills and knowledge needed to effectively implement the maps.

- **New Staff Orientation:** Ensure that new staff members are thoroughly oriented on the ISM and OSM. This includes understanding the school's mission, vision, principles, values, and goals, as well as how to incorporate them into their daily work.

6. **Community Engagement**

    - **Parent and Community Involvement:** Engage parents and the broader community in the implementation of the ISM and OSM. This can include informational sessions, collaborative projects, and opportunities for community members to participate in school activities that reflect the school's leadership principles, core values, and school goals.
    - **Partnerships:** Develop partnerships with local organizations and businesses that align with the ISM and OSM. These partnerships can provide additional resources, support, and opportunities for students to engage with the community.

Implementing with Intention and Design

Living by design is not a quick thought; it's understanding your Inward Anchors and moving forward in a clear, well-planned, and goal-directed manner. Implementing your SSM must be done with **intention and by design** to ensure that every action taken aligns with the school's vision and mission. If you are living even slightly on autopilot, it can alter your life destination. For example, if a ship is off-course by only three degrees, it can significantly affect the destination. For the first 50 miles, you might not even realize you are off-course. You probably think it will arrive close enough to the target destination. Still, as the illustration below depicts, a three-degree deviation over 100 miles will take you to a completely different destination, five miles from where you intended to go! This analogy highlights the importance of intentional, well-designed implementation. As a leader, you must continually check the course—small early corrections prevent major detours later.

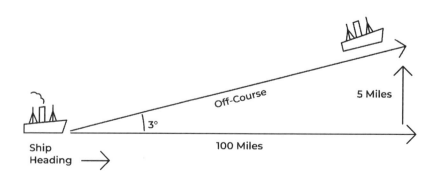

You must revisit your **School Vision, Daily School Mission, School Leadership Principles, and School Core Values** constantly to make sure you are on your desired course. Drifting a few degrees off-course without immediate correction can change the navigation line to your school's desired destination. It takes constant and persistent internal checks early in your journey with minor adjustments to get back on course. If you ignore your course and fail to adjust, it will be too late, and the byproduct will ultimately be a downward trend in school performance and culture.

The Importance of Intention in Implementation

1. **Preventing Drift**: By implementing with intention, schools can prevent drift away from their goals. Even a small deviation, if not corrected, can lead to significant off-course outcomes.
2. **Early Corrections:** Constant and persistent internal checks allow for early corrections. This ensures that minor deviations are addressed before they become major issues.
3. **Achieving Desired Outcomes:** Intentional implementation ensures that every action contributes to the desired outcomes, fostering a dynamic and positive school culture where everyone thrives.

Implementing SSM with Intention

1. **Establish Clear Objectives**

    - **Define Goals Clearly:** Ensure that each goal within the ISM and OSM is clearly defined, measurable, and aligned with the school's mission and vision.
    - **Set Milestones:** Break down larger goals into smaller, manageable milestones to monitor progress and make necessary adjustments along the way.

2. **Plan and Design Strategies**

    - **Detailed Planning:** Develop detailed action plans for achieving each goal. Include timelines, required resources, and responsible individuals or teams.
    - **Strategic Alignment:** Ensure that all strategies and actions are aligned with the overall school vision and mission. This alignment will keep the

school on course and prevent deviations that could lead to undesired outcomes.

3. **Regular Monitoring and Evaluation**

   - **Continuous Monitoring:** Implement regular monitoring and evaluation processes to track progress. Use the REBEL Goals framework to assess whether actions are moving the school towards its goals. Whatever tool you use for setting goals, incorporating the components of the REBEL Goals framework—Rudder, Engine, Buoys, Evaluate, and Lifeline—will ensure a comprehensive and effective strategy for achieving success.
   - **Feedback Loops:** Establish feedback loops to gather input from stakeholders and make data-driven decisions. Adjust strategies as needed based on this feedback.

4. **Intentional Communication**

   - **Consistent Messaging:** Communicate the goals and progress regularly to all stakeholders. Use the language developed in the ISM and OSM to ensure consistency and clarity.
   - **Engage Stakeholders:** Actively engage students, staff, parents, and the community in the implementation process. Their involvement and buy-in are crucial for the success of the strategic plans.

5. **Reflect and Adjust**

   - **Regular Reflection:** Schedule regular reflection sessions to review the implementation process. Assess what is working well and what needs improvement.
   - **Make Adjustments**: Be prepared to make necessary adjustments to keep the school on course. Small, timely corrections can prevent major deviations from the desired path.

6. **Brand the School's Identity**

   - **Create a Unified Branding Guide:** Develop a school branding guide that includes the school logo, color palette, fonts, symbols, and graphic elements.
   - **Standardize Mottos and Messaging:** Ensure mottos, taglines, and key phrases from the ISM and OSM are consistently used in signage, communications, and promotional materials.

- **Promote Visual and Schoolwide Consistency:** Use the guide across newsletters, school websites, presentations, apparel, and digital platforms to reinforce a cohesive and recognizable school identity.
- **Empower Everyone to Represent the Brand:** Provide access to branding resources for staff, students, PTA, and families to ensure everyone is aligned and can contribute to promoting the school's identity with pride and clarity.

"Direction without intention leads to drift. Great schools course-correct daily to stay aligned with their purpose."
—Dr. Joe Famularo

The IOU School Guiding Handle: Finding Your True North

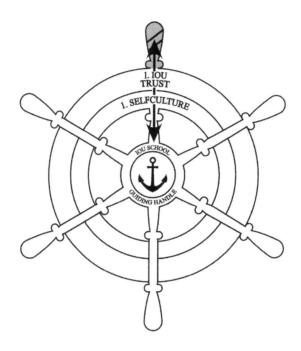

The captain's wheel is a significant symbol for navigating an **IOU School Culture**. Have you noticed the **hash marks on the top handle** for both Inward School Anchor 1 (School SelfCulture) and Outward School Anchor 1 (Inspire IOU Trust)? These hash marks have been on every captain's wheel in this book, representing the texture purposely placed on only one handle of an actual captain's wheel. This ingenious tool was and is still used by every captain as an important guide. The **texture makes the top handle** feel different from the other handles and is extremely important to a captain when steering a ship.

I refer to it as the *IOU School Guiding Handle*. This handle represents your **True North**—the timeless and universal principle that is always there to guide you. When a captain is in a storm or disoriented because of the darkness of night or other elements and needs to navigate the boat straight immediately, this is easily accomplished because of the textured handle. When the captain grabs the textured IOU School Guiding Handle and moves it to the top or north position, it moves the rudder perfectly straight in line with the hull. In the dark or a storm, the captain can simply feel for the IOU School Guiding Handle and keep focused on the journey ahead. Without that ability, the captain must guess which handle will move the rudder dead straight. In rough seas, not knowing the exact position of the rudder could result in danger or even capsizing the boat.

The most **critical and foundational** Inward and Outward School Anchors are represented by this **IOU School Guiding Handle**. In the IOU School Culture of Leadership, your two most important guiding School Anchors are aligned to your School Guiding Handle—an Inward Anchor and an Outward Anchor. They are **Inward School Anchor 1 (School SelfCulture)** and **Outward School Anchor 1 (Inspire IOU Trust)**. These two anchors are your **go-to Anchors** when you are in the dark or the midst of a storm. Whenever you are disoriented or challenged, find the textured handle and align it at the top, setting your course true once again. **Reach for your IOU School Guiding Handle** and reflect on your **School SelfCulture Statement** and **Inspire IOU Trust Statement** for stability regarding who you are, what you believe inwardly, and your closest outward supportive relationships.

There will be many times when you will be faced with a major decision, and you are pondering the right course of action to take. By finding your **IOU School Guiding Handle** and putting it on top, front, and center, it will ground and remind you of **who you are and your beliefs**. It will point you back to your School Vision, Daily School Mission, School Leadership Principles, and School Core Values, which is your School SelfCulture. This will help clear your mind and help you easily find the correct heading or direction and get you back on course.

It especially helps to weed out all the outward forces trying to influence your course of action. When you are under pressure, your IOU School Guiding Handle is about **clarity of mind**. Our mind is usually weighed down by many options, usually influenced by external pressures that are urgent but not necessarily important to us. When you think in accordance with your School SelfCulture, which you have developed throughout your educational journey, and act according to the highest form of trustworthiness to others, the decision or course of action will become clear.

Inspire IOU Trust is the foundation for all of our closest relationships within the school community. In times of difficulty, put your IOU School Guiding Handle to the top and **lean on your Inspire IOU Trust relationships**. These are the most important relationships in your school. This special relationship leads to mutual growth and the positive benefits of a supportive school environment. When you have Inspire IOU Trust, you know you have someone to help overcome any problem. In those relationships, you can be vulnerable, let your guard down, and share challenges and fears. You have someone who will provide **WholeHearted Listening** for you, giving you the freedom to be authentic and know you will not be judged.

The next time you have a difficult challenge and need support, **grab your IOU School Guiding Handle** on your personal captain's wheel and put it straight up to align your rudder. Remember **who you are with your School SelfCulture** and your important **Inspire IOU Trust relationships**. This will help your well-being and create stability for your educational ship, getting you back on course for your school's journey. Together, these guiding anchors will steer you through any storm, ensuring a prosperous and fulfilling journey for your entire school community.

Elevating Leadership Communication: How the IOU Framework Builds Trust and Alignment

Opening a presentation, report, or school board discussion with part or all of your **Strategic School Map (SSM)**, especially the **12 Essential School Anchors** and the **IOU Framework**, instantly transforms your message from reactive explanation to **vision-driven leadership**.

It's a mindset and a model that elevates your school leadership communication to the highest level of professionalism, trust-building, alignment, and clarity.

Why This Matters

Most school presentations begin with data, problems, or proposed solutions. While those are essential, they often miss the opportunity to first establish the 'why' and the 'who,' which are the foundation of trust and alignment. When you begin with your **IOU Strategic School Map**, grounded in your **Inward identity, Outward practices, and Upward aspirations**, you are not just sharing information. You are sharing **a story, a direction, and a conviction**.

This creates immediate alignment around three powerful leadership questions:

1. **Who are we as a school?**
2. **What do we stand for, believe in, and commit to daily?**
3. **Where are we headed—and how will we get there together?**

Whether presenting to staff, your board of education, parents, or external stakeholders, grounding your message in these answers sets a tone of **intentionality, transparency, and trust**.

Use the IOU Framework as the Opening of Every Presentation

No matter what you're preparing to present, whether it's a new academic program, a shift in curriculum, a safety protocol, a wellness initiative, or a budget proposal, **your Strategic School Map is the foundation**. It is the lens through which every initiative, challenge, and goal should be viewed.

Whether your communication is a written report or an oral presentation, **begin with your school maps**—your ISM, OSM, and the 12 Anchors. This shows your audience that:

- The initiative is aligned with your school's identity and long-term vision.
- There is a deeper strategy guiding your work.
- You are leading with clarity, trust, and alignment

This becomes your opening every time. By making this a leadership habit, you consistently reinforce alignment, professionalism, and a shared sense of purpose.

A Professional Edge and a Strategic Standard

Using the IOU Framework and Strategic School Map in your leadership presentations signals:

- A **clearly articulated vision** and internal foundation.
- A **principle-centered, trust building approach** to every initiative and decision.
- A leader who is both strategic and grounded.
- Confidence and coherence in everything you present—because it's rooted in identity, not urgency.

This practice builds credibility over time. Stakeholders begin to **expect** this structure—and respect it. It raises the bar for all communication within the district or school and models the very culture of excellence you're cultivating.

Practical Ways to Start With Your Strategic School Map

- Open meetings with your **vision, mission, and core values**—tie them to the topic at hand.
- Include the **ISM and OSM visuals** at the beginning of your slides, memos, or reports.

- Start presentations by naming the **anchor(s)** connected to the initiative you're proposing.
- Use the **School Living Wheel or Captain's Wheel** to show how the work fits into the whole.
- Keep language consistent across communications so that your leadership identity becomes part of the culture—and trust grows through alignment.

Your Strategic School Map is More Than a Tool—It's a Statement

It says:
"This is who we are. This is how we lead. This is the foundation behind everything we do."

It positions you as a **visionary architect** of culture, growth, and success.

In a time where school leadership is more complex than ever, this practice centers your message in what matters most, and ensures your audience feels that everything you're doing is **on course, on purpose, and aligned with something greater.**

For a quick-reference overview, see *Appendix E: IOU Framework Presentation Guide*. This one-page summary offers a ready-to-use reminder of how to start any report or presentation with clarity, consistency, and purpose.

Conclusion

Navigating an IOU School Culture

The image above, and on the cover, captures the essence of your journey.

Layered atop an aged nautical map, you'll see four timeless symbols: the **anchor**, the **captain's wheel**, the **compass**, and the **lighthouse**. This visual doesn't just represent direction; it embodies the entire IOU School Culture Framework. Each symbol tells a story:

- The **anchor** represents your Inward foundation—principled, steady, and secure.
- The **captain's wheel** reflects your 12 School Anchors—6 Inward and 6 Outward—that give direction to your leadership.
- The **compass** symbolizes your Strategic School Map (SSM)—a tool for alignment, course correction, and intentional culture-building.
- The **lighthouse** points to your Upward aspirations—your desired outcomes of Peacefulness, Happiness, Healthiness, and Excellence (PH2E®).

Together, these elements form the living system of IOU, a dynamic, principle-centered way to lead your school community with purpose, clarity, and heart.

Anchoring Culture in IOU

At the heart of the IOU Framework is a transformational truth:

We lead best when we live Inside-Out.

By grounding your school in the IOU Principle, you've chosen to build a culture that inspires others to aspire, a place where every student, staff member, and stakeholder feels seen, supported, and empowered.

IOU is not a program—it's a way of being.
It's how we treat one another.
How we align our intentions with our actions.
And how we navigate forward with conviction and care.

The 12 Essential School Anchors

The IOU Framework is made up of 12 anchors—6 Inward, 6 Outward—designed to foster alignment, unity, and culture that grows from the inside out.

Inward Anchors
These give your school identity, clarity, and foundation:

1. **School SelfCulture**
2. **School Vision**
3. **Daily School Mission**
4. **School Leadership Principles**
5. **School Core Values**
6. **School Goals**

Outward Anchors
These ensure that your internal identity is lived through relationships, communication, and culture-building:

1. **Inspire IOU Trust**
2. **Practice Positive Communication**
3. **Create Common Language**

4. **Construct a Cohesive Environment**
5. **Establish Everlasting Traditions**
6. **Model a Mindset of Propelling PH2E**

Together, they form your full-circle map, providing direction, connection, and consistency for how your school thinks, speaks, acts, and leads.

Building and Living the Strategic School Map (SSM)

Your **Strategic School Map (SSM)** is the unifying vessel that combines your **ISM (Inward School Map)** and **OSM (Outward School Map)**. It turns your beliefs into strategies, and your strategies into action.

But remember, this map is not something to complete and shelf. It's your school's **compass**, your **captain's wheel**, and your daily **course corrector**.

It must be revisited, refined, and lived intentionally to keep your school aligned on the path toward **Upward Living**.

Daily Practice and Continuous Improvement

Every anchor, every principle, every part of the SSM comes alive **not in the writing—but in the doing**.

- Speak the mission.
- Celebrate the values.
- Model the principles.
- Reflect. Refine. Realign.

Use the IOU School Culture Continuum, the Strategic School Map, visual displays, and consistent language routines introduced throughout this book to maintain momentum.

Sustainable culture is not built by accident. It is built by design.

Inspire to Aspire

The heartbeat of this journey is the mindset of **"Inspire to Aspire."**
To inspire is to **breathe life into others**.
To aspire is to **reach for what's possible—together**.

By cultivating a school culture rooted in IOU, you're creating more than just academic success. You're cultivating **human greatness**, the kind that builds confident learners, thoughtful leaders, and compassionate citizens.

Final Reflection: Navigating to IOU Island

Visualize your school approaching **IOU Island**, the symbolic destination where Inward, Outward, and Upward are fully aligned.

- The **anchor** keeps you grounded in who you are.
- The **captain's wheel** gives you the handles to lead with purpose.
- The **compass** (your SSM) ensures you stay aligned through every decision.
- The **lighthouse** represents your Upward aspirations—**Peacefulness, Happiness, Healthiness, and Excellence (PH2E®).**

And when the waters get rough? Reach for your **IOU School Guiding Handle**—anchored in SelfCulture and Trust. It keeps your school steady and on course.

Anchoring the Legacy

This is not the end of a book.
This is the beginning of a legacy.

The work you do today—the conversations you lead, the commitments you model, the culture you co-create—will ripple far beyond what you can see. It will shape classrooms, uplift communities, and inspire generations to come.

Every moment of alignment...
Every principle-centered decision...
Every voice lifted in trust and belonging...
Moves your school closer to becoming a true beacon of Upward Living.
Your Strategic School Map is more than a plan.
It's a promise—to lead with purpose, to live Inside-Out, and to ensure that every student and educator knows they matter.

Thank you for navigating this journey with us.

Your leadership matters.
Your vision matters.
And your unwavering commitment to building a better future—**from the inside out**—is the legacy that will last.

Stay the course.
Breathe life into others.
And always, always—Inspire to Aspire.

Keep the momentum going—visit iouliving.com and explore the IOU Resources tab for tools and downloads to bring this work to life with your team.

References

Bolton, R., & Bolton, D.G. (2018). *Listen up or lose out: How to avoid miscommunication, improve relationships, and get more done faster.* New York, NY, NY: AMACOM.

Brown, B. (2018). *Dare to lead: Brave work. Tough conversations. Whole hearts.* New York, NY: Random House.

Bryk, A.S., & Schneider, B. (2004). *Trust in schools: A core resource for improvement.* New York, NY: Russell Sage Foundation.

Covey, S.R. (1989). *The 7 habits of highly effective people.* New York, NY: Simon & Schuster.

Covey, S.M.R. (2008). *The SPEED of trust: The one thing that changes everything.* New York, NY: Free Press.

Covey, S. M. R., Kasperson, R., & McKinley Covey, M. (2022). *Trust and inspire: How truly great leaders unleash greatness in others.* New York, NY: Simon & Schuster.

Cramer, K.D., & Wasiak, H. (2008). *Change the way you see yourself through asset-based thinking.* Philadelphia, PA: Running Press.

Daniel, M. (2024, October 31). *Google Maps updates: Gemini arrives, Immersive View expands and more.* Google. Retrieved from https://blog.google/products/maps/gemini-google-maps-navigation-updates/

Famularo, J. S. (2021). *IOU Life Leadership: You owe it to yourself and others.* Author Academy Elite.

Feltman, C., Hammond, S.A., Hammond, R., Marshall, A. & Bendis, K. (2009). *The thin book of trust: An essential primer for building trust at work.* Bend, OR: Thin Book Publishing.

Kethledge, R.M., & Erwin, M.S. (2018). *Lead yourself first: Inspiring leadership through solitude. London,* England: Bloomsbury Publishing.

Korzybski, A., & Pula R.P. (2005). *Science and sanity: An introduction to non-Aristotelian systems and general semantics.* Forest Hills, NY: Institute of General Semantics.

Maxwell, J. (2015, February 25). *Culture vs. vision: Is it really either-or?* John Maxwell Blog. https://www.johnmaxwell.com/blog/culture-vs-vision-is-it-really-either-or/

Seligman, M.E.P. (2012). *Flourish: A visionary new understanding of happiness and well-being.* New York, NY: Free Press.

Vygotsky, L.S. (2012). *Thought and language.* Cambridge, MA: The MIT Press.

Appendix A

IOU School Culture Continuum Reflection Tool

Use this tool to assess your school's current position across four key dimensions of school culture. Begin with the reflection question in each row to guide your thinking, then consider where your school currently aligns across the continuum.

Category	Reflection Prompt	IOU – Upward Leading	IOW – Wayward Drifting	IOD – Downward Draining
School Culture Trajectory	Where is our school currently headed? What evidence supports this?	Clear, principle-driven progress	Directionless or reactive; inconsistent growth	Regressive; disengagement or dysfunction
School Culture Impact	What is the emotional tone in our school? How do people feel here?	Dynamic, inspiring, and mission-aligned	Passive or neutral; not toxic but not uplifting	Toxic, divisive, and disempowering
School Culture Performance	Are our actions aligned with our goals? What's working, what's not?	Effective strategies leading to meaningful results	Occasional progress with limited cohesion	Misaligned systems resulting in poor outcomes
School Culture Outcomes	What are students and staff truly experiencing each day?	PH2E – Peacefulness, Happiness, Healthiness, and Excellence	Impassivities – Apathy, Indifference, Unfitness, Mediocrity	School Drains – Anxiety, Unhappiness, Unhealthiness, Ineffectiveness

Appendix B

The Strategic School Map (SSM) Template

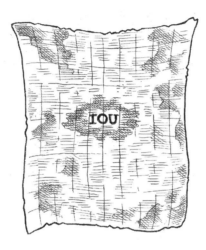

 **Inward School Map (ISM) Statements:**

The following template captures the essential Inward anchors of your Strategic School Map (SSM).

Note: The 4 Foundational Inward Anchors
These 4 Foundational Inward School Anchors (School Anchors: 2,3,4,5) should be prominently displayed along with the school's/district's branding elements to reinforce and communicate the school's foundational principles to all members of the community.

1. School Vision Statement & Motto:

- [Insert School Motto Here]
- [Insert School Vision Statement Here]

2. Daily School Mission Statement & Motto:

- [Insert School Motto Here]
- [Insert Daily School Mission Statement Here]

3. School Leadership Principles:

- [Insert Leadership Principle 1 Here]
- [Insert Leadership Principle 2 Here]
- [Insert Leadership Principle 3 Here]
- [Insert Leadership Principle 4 Here]
- [Insert Leadership Principle 5 Here]

4. School Core Values:

- Core Value 1: [Insert Definition Here]
- Core Value 2: [Insert Definition Here]
- Core Value 3: [Insert Definition Here]
- Core Value 4: [Insert Definition Here]
- Core Value 5: [Insert Definition Here]

Incorporating Branding Elements:

- Logo: [Insert School Logo]
- Mascot [Insert School Mascot]
- School Colors: [Insert School Colors Here]
- Visuals: [Insert Visual Descriptions Here]

School SelfCulture Statement:

This statement provides an overarching narrative of the school's culture and may be shared with the broader community.

- [Insert School SelfCulture Motto & Statement Here]

School Goals:

Goals should be discussed in meetings and shared with school leaders, staff, and parents, as appropriate. Each goal should be specific to the individual or group responsible for its implementation.

- [Insert School Goal 1 Here]
- [Insert School Goal 2 Here]
- [Insert School Goal 3 Here]
- [Insert School Goal 4 Here]

Note:

You may insert the comprehensive details of your goals here or attach them to your Inward School Map (ISM). Use the **REBEL Goals™ Framework** to ensure each goal includes clear direction, actionable steps, measurable progress, ongoing evaluation, and sustained support.

 **Outward School Map (OSM) Statements:**

The following template captures the essential Outward anchors of your Strategic School Map (SSM). Each anchor includes a Motto, a guiding Statement that reflects your school's outward philosophy, and key Strategies that align daily actions with your core principles. Use this structure to define, refine, and communicate your outward commitments with clarity and consistency.

1. Inspire IOU Trust

- **Motto:** [Insert Motto Here]
- **Statement:** [Insert Clear Statement on Trust Philosophy and Practices]
- **Strategies:**
  [Insert Strategy for Building Trust Here]
  [Insert Strategy for Fostering Reciprocal Inspiration Here]

2. Practice Positive Communication

- **Motto:** [Insert Motto Here]
- **Statement:** [Insert Clear Statement on Communication Philosophy and Practices]
- **Strategies:**
  [Insert Strategy for Enhancing Communication Skills Here]
  [Insert Strategy for Promoting Active Listening and Constructive Feedback Here]

3. Create Common Language

- **Motto:** [Insert Motto Here]
- **Statement:** [Insert Clear Statement on Common Language Philosophy and Practices]
- **Strategies:**
  [Insert Strategy for Developing Shared Vocabulary Here]
- **Key Phrases / Shared Vocabulary:**
  [Insert Common Language Terms or Phrases Here]

4. Construct a Cohesive Environment

- **Motto:** [Insert Motto Here]
- **Statement:** [Insert Clear Statement on Cohesive Environment Philosophy and Practices]
- **Strategies:**
  [Insert Strategy for Fostering Welcoming and Supportive Atmosphere Here], [Insert Strategy for Promoting Community-Building Activities Here]

5. Establish Everlasting Traditions

- **Motto:** [Insert Motto Here]
- **Statement:** [Insert Clear Statement on Traditions Philosophy and Practices]
- **Strategies:**
  [Insert Strategy for Creating and Celebrating School Traditions Here]
- **List of Signature Traditions:**
  [Insert Your School Traditions Here]

6. Model a Mindset of Propelling PH2E

- **Motto:** [Insert Motto Here]
- **Statement:** [Insert Clear Statement on PH2E Mindset Philosophy and Practices]
- **Strategies:**
  [Insert Strategy for Promoting Peacefulness, Happiness, Healthiness, and Excellence Here]
  [Insert Strategy for Encouraging Well-being and Excellence Here]
- **Daily / Weekly PH2E Practices (Optional):**
  [Insert Sample PH2E Practices Here]

Appendix C

REBEL Goals Framework: Strategic Goal-Setting Template

School/District Name:
Goal Title:
Date:

RUDDER – Defining the Goal

- **Goal Statement:**
  Clearly define the objective in one focused sentence.
- **Why this Goal Matters:**
  Explain how this goal aligns with your school's vision, mission, or strategic priorities.

ENGINE – Action-Oriented Strategies

Identify the key steps and initiatives needed to propel your school toward this goal.

- Action 1:
- Action 2:
- Action 3:
- Action 4:
- Action 5:

BUOYS – Measurable Progress Checkpoints

Establish clear, trackable checkpoints to monitor progress and celebrate wins.

- Buoy 1:
- Buoy 2:
- Buoy 3:
- Buoy 4:

EVALUATE – Continuous Improvement

Outline how you will review progress and adapt strategies when needed.

- Collection Methods:
- Frequency of Review:
- Adjustment Strategies:

LIFELINE – Support and Accountability

Define the people and systems responsible for sustaining momentum.

- Accountability Partners / Committees:
- Stakeholder Engagement Strategies:
- Communication Channels:

Stretch Goal Zone Check

Use the Goal Setting Circle to determine whether your overall goal and each REBEL component are appropriately challenging.

Goal Type	Indicators	Check
Comfort Goal	Too easy, low effort, minimal change	Yes No
Stretch Goal	Ambitious but achievable, pushes growth	Yes No
Delusional Goal	Unrealistic given current resources or timeframe	Yes No

Reflection Notes:
Review your current strategies. Do they match the level of challenge you intend? If not, revise your REBEL components to bring them into the Stretch Zone.

This template is designed to help schools create intentional, impactful, and inspiring goals using the REBEL framework. It serves not only as a planning tool but also as a strategic roadmap that guides your school community toward shared success.

Appendix D

IOU School Culture Assessment

Instructions:

This assessment is designed to help school leaders and staff evaluate the presence and effectiveness of the IOU School Culture within their educational environment. By completing this assessment, you will gain a clearer understanding of your **Strategic School Map (SSM)**—a roadmap for cultivating a **Dynamic Positive School Culture**.

The SSM is built upon two critical maps:

- **The Inward School Map (ISM)** – Formed by the **6 Inward School Anchors**, defining your school's foundational identity, values, and guiding principles.
- **The Outward School Map (OSM)** – Composed of the **6 Outward School Anchors**, shaping relationships, trust, and the collective school environment.

Many schools operate without a clear map, leading to a culture that drifts rather than moves forward with purpose. This assessment helps you determine whether your **school has a well-defined ISM and OSM**, or if it is time to intentionally develop these maps. As you go through each anchor, reflect on how clearly defined these elements are in your school. The results will provide insight into strengths and areas for growth, helping you **strategically navigate toward an Upward Culture.**

Each section corresponds to one of the **12 Essential School Anchors**. Please rate each statement using the following scale by marking (X) in the appropriate column.

Scoring Scale:

- 5 - Strongly Agree
- 4 - Agree
- 3 - Neutral
- 2 - Disagree
- 1 - Strongly Disagree

Inward School Map (ISM)

6 Inward School Anchors

1. SelfCulture

Questions:	1	2	3	4	5
Our school has a distinct and positive culture that reflects our collective beliefs, behaviors, and attitudes.	☐	☐	☐	☐	☐
Our school culture fosters a sense of belonging, respect, and shared purpose among all members.	☐	☐	☐	☐	☐
Staff and students are aware of and actively contribute to shaping our school's SelfCulture.	☐	☐	☐	☐	☐

Subtotal for SelfCulture: Total:___/15

2. School Vision

Questions:	1	2	3	4	5
Our school has a clear, inspiring vision that guides decision-making and daily operations.	☐	☐	☐	☐	☐
All stakeholders (students, staff, families) understand and align with the school vision.	☐	☐	☐	☐	☐
The vision is evident in our school's strategic planning and initiatives.	☐	☐	☐	☐	☐

Subtotal for School Vision: Total:___/15

3. Daily School Mission

Questions:	1	2	3	4	5
Our school has a mission statement that drives daily actions and decision-making.	☐	☐	☐	☐	☐
Staff and students understand how their roles connect to the mission.	☐	☐	☐	☐	☐
The mission is visibly integrated into school activities, meetings, and learning experiences.	☐	☐	☐	☐	☐

Subtotal for Daily School Mission: Total:___/15

4. School Leadership Principles

Questions:	1	2	3	4	5
Our school operates based on clearly defined leadership principles.	☐	☐	☐	☐	☐
Leadership at all levels (students, teachers, administrators) is encouraged and nurtured.	☐	☐	☐	☐	☐
Decision-making reflects a commitment to leadership principles.	☐	☐	☐	☐	☐

Subtotal for School Leadership Principles: Total:___/15

5. School Core Values

Questions:	1	2	3	4	5
Our School's Core Values are well-defined and drive behavior and interactions.	☐	☐	☐	☐	☐
Staff and students embody these values in daily interactions.	☐	☐	☐	☐	☐
Core values are consistently reinforced through policies, traditions, and communication.	☐	☐	☐	☐	☐

Subtotal for School Core Values: Total:___/15

6. School Goals

Questions:	1	2	3	4	5
Our school has clear, measurable goals aligned with its vision and mission.	☐	☐	☐	☐	☐
Progress toward these goals is regularly assessed and communicated.	☐	☐	☐	☐	☐
The school community is engaged in goal-setting and continuous improvement efforts.	☐	☐	☐	☐	☐

Subtotal for School Goals: Total:___/15

Appendix D: IOU School Culture Assessment 443

Outward School Map (OSM)

6 Outward School Anchors

1. Inspire IOU Trust

Questions:	1	2	3	4	5
Trust is a foundational element in relationships among staff, students, and families.	☐	☐	☐	☐	☐
School leadership models integrity, transparency, and reliability.	☐	☐	☐	☐	☐
There is a shared sense of accountability and responsibility in fostering trust.	☐	☐	☐	☐	☐

Subtotal for Inspire IOU Trust: Total:___/15

2. Practice Positive Communication

Questions:	1	2	3	4	5
Open, honest, and respectful communication is encouraged and practiced.	☐	☐	☐	☐	☐
Active listening and empathetic communication are prioritized.	☐	☐	☐	☐	☐
There are structures in place to ensure all voices in the school community are heard and valued.	☐	☐	☐	☐	☐

Subtotal for Practice Positive Communication: Total:___/15

3. Create Common Language

Questions:	1	2	3	4	5
Our school has developed a shared language around leadership, learning, and culture.	☐	☐	☐	☐	☐
Common language is used to reinforce our vision, mission, leadership principles, and core values.	☐	☐	☐	☐	☐
Students and staff naturally incorporate this language in daily conversations and reflections.	☐	☐	☐	☐	☐

Subtotal for Create Common Language: Total:___/15

4. Construct a Cohesive Environment

Questions:	1	2	3	4	5
Our school's physical and relational environment supports collaboration, trust, and learning.	☐	☐	☐	☐	☐
Spaces and resources reflect our mission, principles, and values.	☐	☐	☐	☐	☐
There is a strong sense of safety, belonging, and engagement in our school environment.	☐	☐	☐	☐	☐

Subtotal for Construct a Cohesive Environment: Total:___/15

5. Establish Everlasting Traditions

Questions:	1	2	3	4	5
Our school has meaningful traditions that foster pride, belonging, and connection.	☐	☐	☐	☐	☐
These traditions reflect and reinforce our Core Values and vision.	☐	☐	☐	☐	☐
New traditions are intentionally created to celebrate progress and success.	☐	☐	☐	☐	☐

Subtotal for Establish Everlasting Traditions: Total:___/15

6. Model a Mindset of Propelling PH2E

Questions:	1	2	3	4	5
Our school actively encourages the pursuit of Peacefulness, Happiness, Healthiness, and Excellence (PH2E®).	☐	☐	☐	☐	☐
Staff and students are provided with opportunities to grow personally and professionally.	☐	☐	☐	☐	☐
The concept of PH2E is integrated into school-wide initiatives and daily practices.	☐	☐	☐	☐	☐

Subtotal for Model a Mindset of Propelling PH2E: Total: ___/15

Total Score for all 12 IOU School Anchors _____

Scoring & Interpretation Guide

- **150-180:** Highly aligned with IOU School Culture—strong foundations in place. Maintain momentum and continue reinforcing best practices using the **12 IOU Essential School Anchors**.

- **120-149:** Moderate alignment—some areas for growth and refinement. Identify specific anchors needing enhancement and take targeted action, while continuing to reinforce best practices using the **12 IOU Essential School Anchors**.

- **90-119:** Developing alignment—intentional focus needed on strengthening anchors. Prioritize professional development and collaborative efforts to bridge gaps, while using the **12 IOU Essential School Anchors** as a guiding framework.

- **Below 90:** Limited alignment—requires strategic action to integrate IOU principles. Immediate attention is needed to develop a plan for strengthening school culture, ensuring inside-out alignment with the **12 IOU Essential School Anchors**.

Reflection & Action Planning

1. Which anchors scored the highest? What contributes to their success?
2. Which anchors scored the lowest? What challenges exist?
3. What specific actions can be taken to strengthen the weaker areas?
4. How can school leadership and staff work together to reinforce the IOU School Culture?
5. What professional development, strategies, or resources are needed to ensure continuous improvement?
6. How can the school celebrate and recognize progress in fostering an IOU-aligned culture?

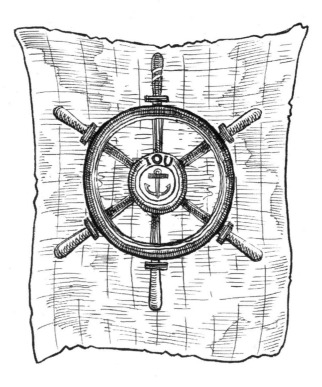

Copyright PH2E Ventures, LTD
Dr. Joe Famularo
iouliving.com

Appendix E

This appendix offers practical guidance for leaders seeking to present their Strategic School Map with greater clarity and impact.

IOU Framework Presentation Guide

As a school leader, presenting with clarity, professionalism, and intention is vital—especially when sharing plans with **staff, boards of education, district teams**, or **stakeholder groups**. One of the most powerful ways to elevate the effectiveness of your communication is to begin with your Strategic **School Map (SSM)**, the **IOU Framework**, and the **12 Essential School Anchors**. These essential anchors establish shared purpose and foundational direction, instantly conveying that your work is part of a well-developed, mission-driven plan.

> **Why start every presentation, report, or proposal with your IOU Strategic School Map?**
>
> - It immediately frames your message within the school's overarching vision, mission, and foundational beliefs.
> - It positions your initiatives or updates as part of a long-term, strategic journey—not as isolated decisions.
> - It communicates clarity, intentionality, and professionalism to your audience.
> - It helps stakeholders understand how each new idea supports existing priorities, values, and goals.

Recommendation for Leaders: Open every leadership presentation, whether to staff, boards of education, or community members, by showcasing the IOU School Culture Framework. Whether you use the entire Strategic School Map or select anchors most relevant to the presentation, this approach sets a tone of confidence, alignment, and purpose.

About the Author

Dr. Joe Famularo is an award-winning educational leader, #1 bestselling author, national speaker, and dedicated leadership coach committed to transforming school culture through intentional leadership. With over 30 years of experience in education—including 19 years as a superintendent—he has been at the forefront of innovation, leadership development, and school transformation. His work has earned him numerous recognitions, including being named the **2024 New York State Superintendent of the Year** and leading a nationally recognized **Lighthouse School District**.

Dr. Famularo is the author of the #1 bestselling book *IOU Life Leadership*, which is rooted in timeless, universal principles for positive, intentional living and leadership. His passion continues in *Navigating an IOU School Culture*, where he introduces the **Inside-Out** approach to cultivating thriving school environments. Through the **12 Essential School Anchors**, he equips school leaders with practical strategies to foster trust, shared language, and a deeply embedded culture of excellence and empowerment.

He also teaches aspiring leaders as a professor in graduate educational leadership programs and serves on several college educational advisory boards. Known for his authentic style and practical wisdom, Dr. Famularo is a sought-after mentor for superintendents, principals, and leadership teams across the country.

In addition to his leadership books, Dr. Famularo is the author of a growing collection of children's books based on the IOU Framework. These include an IOU Kid Anchor overview book and a series of engaging titles that introduce young learners to the Inward School Anchors, introducing the foundational principles of leadership and character in developmentally engaging ways.

Beyond his work as an author and educator, Dr. Famularo is an accomplished musician, often integrating music into his keynote presentations to move and inspire audiences. He has held numerous leadership positions in state and regional educational organizations, advocating for student-centered policy, school culture, and intentional leadership.

Dr. Famularo resides on Long Island, New York, with his wife. Together, they have raised three children and three dogs, fostering a strong family bond and a love for learning.

To learn more about Dr. Joe Famularo's work, leadership philosophy, and speaking engagements, visit **www.IOULiving.com**.

Acknowledgments

Writing *Navigating an IOU School Culture* has been a journey of reflection, collaboration, and deep gratitude. This book, like the work we do each day, is the result of many hearts, hands, and voices coming together with purpose.

First and foremost, I want to thank the incredible staff I have the privilege of working alongside every day—our dedicated teachers, non-instructional team members, administrators, and Board of Education. Your passion, commitment, and belief in every student shape the culture of our schools in profound ways. To our parents and families, thank you for being true partners in leadership and learning. Your trust, support, and shared commitment to our vision make all the difference in helping our students thrive. And to our students—the Bellmore Stars—you are the reason we lead. Your light, your voice, and your potential inspire every page of this book.

To my colleagues across Long Island, New York State, and around the country: your leadership, friendship, and shared pursuit of educational excellence continue to energize and challenge me. I've learned so much from our conversations, collaborations, and shared experiences.

A special thank you to PH2E Publishing and our book designers for bringing this vision to life with such care and creativity. I'm especially thankful to the small but talented editing team who helped sharpen the message and offered thoughtful feedback throughout the process. To all those who graciously read early drafts, provided feedback, or offered endorsements—your words brought affirmation, insight, and encouragement.

Finally, to my family—thank you for your unwavering love, support, and understanding throughout the many early mornings, late nights, and quiet hours spent writing. You are my life compass.

With respect, gratitude, and belief in what's possible,
Dr. Joe Famularo

Learn about the *12 Essential Life Anchors*™
to help keep your Life Ship on Course!

#1 Bestseller

The #1 bestselling book *IOU Life Leadership* is available at *iouliving.com* and where all books are sold.

The IOU LIFE ANCHORS for YOUNG LEARNERS BOOKS

By Dr. Joe Famularo

IOU Kid Anchors: Teaching Essential Life Lessons

⚓	IOU Life Anchors Book Series Title	IOU Inside "Kid Anchors"	IOU 6 Essential Inward Life Anchors™
IOU Overview	My IOU Life Ship	Get ready for the Journey!	IOU Life Leadership
Kid Anchor 1	IOU My Story	Who I Am	SelfCulture™
Kid Anchor 2	A Dreamer's Paradise	My Life Passion and Dreams	Life Vision
Kid Anchor 3	I'm Ready, Are You?	My To Do List for Today	Daily Mission
Kid Anchor 4	Mr. Buoy Rules!	The Principles that Guide and Lead Me	Life Principles
Kid Anchor 5	IOU Respect & Kindness	How I Treat Others	Life Values
Kid Anchor 6	Mike's Marvelous Map to the Lighthouse	My Big Goals	Life Goals

IOU Life Anchors for Young Learners Books
are available at *iouliving.com* and where all books are sold.

Made in the USA
Middletown, DE
10 September 2025